HOLLYWOOD SECRETS AND SCANDALS

the truth behind stars' closed doors

By SUE CAMERON

Published in the USA by:
BearManor Media
P O Box 71426
Albany, Georgia 31708
www.bearmanormedia.com

ISBN: 978-1-62933-306-9
BearManor Media, Albany, Georgia
Printed in the United States of America
Book design by Robbie Adkins, www.adkinsconsult.com
Back cover photo by Dawn Moore

Table of Contents

Dedication

To Tichi Wilkerson, the publisher of The Hollywood Reporter,
who always kept her word to me

To Kim Novak, Debbie Reynolds, and Joan Rivers
MY SUPREMES

To my "Guardian Angels"—Sandy Pressman, Irena Medavoy, and
Jackie DeShannon
and
To Michele Ross, who guided me into "adulthood"

Sue Cameron

PROLOGUE

My first job after graduating from University of Southern California with a bachelor's in journalism was to go to work for the rock radio station KFWB in Los Angeles. They wanted to start a rock music underground newspaper called the *Hitline,* a weekly eight-pager, and they hired me to write it and be the interviewer/photographer, lay-out designer, and production manager. I did everything but deliver it all by myself.

KFWB Hitline.

This threw me from sweet private, well-mannered USC, where I wore knee socks, penny loafers, a plaid skirt, and a powder-blue Oxford cloth shirt (thinking that drinking just one beer was a sin—so I never did it), into the insane, drug-filled world of rock and roll.

I was initially surrounded by The Mamas and Papas, The Beatles, The Doors, Jimi Hendrix, Phil Spector, Jackie De Shannon, Sonny and Cher, The Ronettes, Elvis, The Rolling Stones, The Supremes, James Brown, Ike and Tina, The Four Tops, The Jackson Five—you name it. I met EVERYONE and saw EVERY show or concert that happened from 1965-on.

In the 70s, I switched to interviewing movie and TV actors, so my circle expanded even more.

Many of these people became friends.

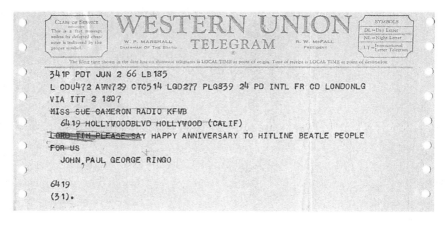

My Beatles telegram.

In particular, I'd like to single out Jackie De Shannon, who I met when "What the World Needs Now Is Love" became the No 1 record in the country. She was dressed in a navy-blue coat, knee socks, and had a Jackie Kennedy handbag (when she wasn't in cowboy boots and a rough-side leather fringed jacket.) Jackie took one look at our mutual knee socks and said, "You're going to be killed in this business. I'd better protect you. You're going to see things you never knew existed, 'Miss USC'."

She was so right.

Dino, Desi, Billy, and Sue from the KFWB Hitline.

I worked almost 24 hours a day, seven days a week for 40 years. It was no accident that I was allowed into people's lives, because I had worked hard at earning respect by being honest, fair, and trustworthy. That's why I was let into people's lives behind closed doors. They considered me a reporter, but a friend first. We were, and are, always on equal footing. I am not *Zelig*, a stranger who liked to push himself into photos of celebrities. I'm not the "kid" from *Almost Famous*, a groupie who chased after rock groups to get near stardom.

Jackie DeShannon celebrates my becoming the entertainment editor of TEEN *Magazine at a party at a music biz hang-out, Martoni's.*

I ended up playing drums with Bobby Darin and Frank Zappa. I sang with Cass, Jackie, and Dusty Springfield. I danced with James Brown. I went wig shopping with Diana Ross. I had long talks with Cher about fear. Met Frank Sinatra at Nancy's "Boots" party. Danced with Gene Kelly at Liza Minnelli's wedding to Jack Hayley, Jr. Tapped with Debbie Reynolds. Just to name a few. It is what was behind those great events that is THE story. I was never an outsider, as most reporters were. I was invited to participate.

I literally saw the concert and/or interviewed every artist who had a hit record from 1965 and on. Starting in 1970, my world opened up to adding TV and movie actors.

These connections only increased when I became the daily TV columnist for *The Hollywood Reporter*, then one of only two Hollywood trade papers. Everyone wanted to have a feature interview by me in the *Reporter*, and I had access to anyone I wanted. I also had my own weekly talk show on KABC Radio, where my friends would stop by and talk, and I was a regular for many years on various talk shows as their Hollywood insider. Today it seems like there are hundreds of former "Miss Texas" talking heads on TV on multiple entertainment news shows. Those girls today aren't reporters. They are "newsreaders" who have no off-camera connections with stars' lives.

So many people took me under their wings, like Cass Elliot, Debbie Reynolds, Marlo Thomas, Kim Novak, and Joan Rivers.

I, in turn, also looked out for their highest good. I ended up being "adopted" by the families of Lucie Arnaz, Marlo Thomas, Valerie Harper, Connie Stevens, the aforementioned Jackie De Shannon, The Nelsons, Debbie Reynolds, and Joan Rivers. They included me on many holidays and vacations—and sought my counsel while I also sought theirs. I knew their children, their parents, attended everything from christenings and Sweet 16 parties, to funerals of their loved ones.

Our mutual love and respect has continued through decades, and will always be there.

This is a book about friendship and love, and is completely written from my perspective. I have spent years behind closed doors with famous people, and been privy to the most dramatic, challenging, happy, and sad parts of their lives. When I tell you a story and I quote these people, I can do it because I was IN THE ROOM.

I know of no other reporter/columnist who has ever had my access.

I initially never even thought of publishing this book. It was the first time I had written something and not gotten paid up front. I just wanted to put the stories on pages for posterity. It poured out of me over a two-month period. I sent a few chapters to friends, who all said to me, "You're going to publish it, aren't you?"

"No," I answered.

"Yes, you are. All the truths you reveal must be heard. You are the voice for all these people, and it must go down in history. It's too important."

OK. And, God bless all my beautiful friends in this book. It's been an honor. This book was written totally out of love.

Note: I am well aware that many of you will look in the table of contents and turn to the celebrity who interests you the most, rather than read it in order. That's fine by me! I just want you to know that, because I knew there would be a good chance this book would be read out of order, you will find some deliberate repetition about where I was working at different times. That is only to help you in the timeline.

Chapter One

CASS ELLIOT—THE TRUTH, THE HAM SANDWICH, AND ME

July 26th, 1974
Los Angeles

"Hey," said Cass. "I want you to see the run-through of my show before I leave for the London Palladium. We're doing it at three today in a studio space in North Hollywood. Can you come?"

"Of course! I'll be there this afternoon," I replied, sitting in my office at *The Hollywood Reporter*. I just adored Cass. She was extremely intelligent, funny, and had a sophisticated wit.

I was scared when I first saw the Mamas and Papas at a rehearsal for the TV show *Shivaree* in the late 70s. It was my regular beat to cover all the rehearsals and tapings of the rock shows like *Shivaree*, *Shebang*, and *Shindig* every week and interview the stars.

My first job out of college was at KFWB Radio, the number one rock station in Los Angeles. I started the first underground music newspaper. I picked KFWB because it was my favorite radio station. It was located on Hollywood Blvd, near Cahuenga, in what was a solid front office building with one door on the front, which was kind of hidden and led directly to stairs to the second floor. I had no appointment, but it never occurred to me that I needed one. They needed me, I thought, as I marched up to the front desk, clutching my columns from the *USC Daily Trojan* called "Parties and Pinnings." I was a college graduate with a journalism degree. I asked to see the general manager of the station immediately.

With no surprise and absolute certainty that this would happen, I actually was led into the office of Bill Wheatley, the general manager. He looked like an insurance salesman. I looked like a fourteen-year-old girl who escaped from a convent.

We hit it off immediately.

I basically told him how I was the best and the brightest (way before Halberstam) and he should hire me.

"I could use someone in the traffic department," he said.

"What's a traffic department? I asked, thinking he wanted me to go onto Hollywood Blvd and direct cars.

He showed me to a dingy room with a few people in it looking at pieces of paper with lots of writing and numbers on them. I had no idea what I was seeing.

"This is the traffic department. They schedule all the commercials and make sure they get on the air at the right time," he explained.

"That sounds awful," I answered to what might have been my first employer.

He led me back to his office and told me he had another idea. He had been thinking for a while that KFWB should start a weekly newspaper about all the rock artists with interviews and photos. Would I be interested in doing that?

"Of course," I answered quickly. "I've been putting out newspapers since grammar school."

"OK. Your salary will be $100 a week. We have a camera in a closet somewhere that you can use. All the stars come here in person to promote their records. All you have to do is trap them when they're up here and get the story and pictures. Of course you have to lay out all the pages on a dummy, drive it to the print house, and proof the pages, and have a new issue every week," he said.

"Do I have to deliver them too?" I asked. I never learned to edit my thoughts.

My first job as a reporter, even one who was barely out of her teens, wasn't a learning curve. I had been studying performers for years. Only actors and musicians with real talent impressed me, and those were few and far between. I was afraid of hippies. We were from different worlds. I can actually remember when *TEEN* magazine (by then I had left KFWB and was now entertainment editor of *TEEN*) sent me to do a story on the hippie movement in the Haight-Ashbury district in San Francisco. I was terrified. I thought I'd get some sort of disease by even breathing their air. I wish I were kidding, but I'm not. My idea of covering Haight-Ashbury was to check into the five-star Fairmont Hotel on Nob Hill and hire a limo to drive me through the district. For the first time, I confess that I wrote that story without ever getting out of the limo to interview anyone. I did have to go to Bill Graham's Fillmore, though, and, once again, I avoided touching anything. It was very dark inside. As I walked, my feet kept sticking to the floor and I had no idea what substance was making that happen. The air was putrid and smelled of smoke. Some screaming group was onstage surrounded by screens showing multi-colored moving forms. They were called the Jefferson Airplane. People were all over the floor just staring. Did I know they were on drugs? No. Did I know why they were staring? No.

Therefore, the Mamas and Papas scared me—and they weren't even a "hard rock group!"

I had gone to high school with Michelle Phillips. Her name was Michelle Gilliam back then, and she was the typical California blonde. Boys were all over her. I remember her getting suspended for different misdeeds, and eventually she never came back at all. There was a rumor she was thrown out for being "too cheap." Now I was about to see her again.

John was dour and Denny smiled a lot and wore funny clothes. That's what I thought. When I looked at Cass that day, I saw a girl having a fabulous time. She just loved her life and loved being on stage and being successful.

I did a really quick interview; Michelle didn't recognize me and I said nothing. John and Denny were vacant personalities on that day, and Cass was great. We liked each other immediately and exchanged phone numbers.

"Hey," said the voice on the phone. "It's Cass. I have to go to a wedding this Saturday and I was hoping you'd go with me. John, Michelle, and Denny are going too, and I'd love to have you with me."

"Great. Just tell me where I'm going."

Cass Elliot.

"I'm picking you up and we're all meeting at John and Michelle's house on Bel Air Road. It's early, so I'll pick you up at eleven."

I wasn't happy about having to see Michelle again. I think I was embarrassed that I was part of the "brainy kids" she ignored in high school. I didn't want her to think I was uncool. I prayed that she wouldn't recognize me. That thinking was a ridiculous waste of my energy. Everyone in rock knew I wasn't cool because I didn't do drugs and I dressed like a lawyer. But, what my saving grace always was, was that I "got" the music. Once they knew that, I was "in" no matter what.

We got to John and Michelle's, and as soon as I walked into this beautiful, classic Bel Air mansion, I was shocked by the filth. The inside looked like it hadn't been cleaned in years. Half-eaten, decaying food was left everywhere. Clothes were just dropped wherever; papers and junk all over. I didn't want to touch anything or sit anywhere. Fortunately, everyone was ready to leave.

Just as Cass and I were ready to go, a lanky brown-haired, country-bumpkin type guy emerged from the kitchen.

"This is Jimmy," Cass said. "He's going to ride with us."

"Hi, Jimmy," I said. "I'm Sue."

"Pleased to meet you," he said.

Hmm. Sweet guy.

We drove for almost two hours to Palos Verdes, California, a beautiful city right on the ocean. Wayfarer's Chapel is all glass and sits on a bluff overlooking the ocean. It was very famous as a wedding location, and I had never seen it. I have no idea who got married. There was no reception. Cass, Jimmy, and I drove back to John and Michelle's. We all got out and went back into the house. By this time I wanted to go home. It had been a long day and I had no idea what kind of partying was about to begin. I very reluctantly entered the house.

To my surprise, about five new people were already in the living room when we got back. I have no idea how they got in or who they were, but they all looked like musicians.

I was making small talk with someone when I saw Jimmy sit down at the piano. He started to play and everyone got quiet. Country-bumpkin Jimmy played and sang a new song he had just written called "MacArthur Park." Our jaws dropped. This kid was named Jimmy Webb. He had just gotten into town. He had no record contract. No one knew who he was. He then sang "By the Time I Get to Phoenix" and "Up, Up and Away." None of us had heard these songs before, obviously, but we all knew that we were witnessing something extraordinary.

I've never lost contact with Sweet Jimmy, and his beautiful soul has never changed.

A few years later, I was the TV editor of *The Hollywood Reporter*, and daily columnist. *The Reporter* was one of only two trade papers covering Hollywood. Their power was enormous, and so was mine. I had moved into covering all of TV (as well as music and theatre and nightclub acts). Cass had broken away from the group and was a star on her own.

Cass' personal manager, a person a star hires to guide all aspects of a career, was Allan Carr. Allan was an overweight gay guy who wore caftans. He also managed Ann-Margret and a number of terrific people. Allan was a real character. He came to Hollywood as a pudgy kid, desperate to make it in some form, and he did. He was ridiculed by many, but he was smart. He did a good job for his clients, and I liked him. Everybody loved going to Allan's parties—including me. I was way over my hippie fear. I was dealing with actors and performers who had as much respect for me as I had for them. I no longer was hanging around studios or sets to grab interviews. Press agents were calling me to set up appointments for private lunches with their clients. We were all on equal footing.

Allan lived in a big Tudor house on Benedict Canyon in Beverly Hills. It was decorated beautifully, and it was famous for a complete disco nightclub set up in the basement. It was also famous for Allan's array of young boy toys in various states of dress, or undress, as the parties went on into the night.

I was talking to Ann-Margret, who had recently married Roger Smith. Ann is a real angel—so kind and beloved by all. Cass came over and picked up Ann's hand to check out her very large ring.

"Oh my God, I could skate on that!" said Cass.

From that moment on, Cass and I were soul sisters. We lived a few blocks apart in Laurel Canyon and were at each other's houses all the time. "Your pool or mine?" was a frequent question.

We also played tennis every week at the Hollywood Indoor Tennis Club. For a while, Columbia Pictures (and other studios) were craving other income streams. Columbia decided to literally convert empty soundstages into tennis courts. I'm not kidding. They thought tying it to Hollywood and offering a few stars free memberships would guarantee success. It did not, but we sure had fun for a couple of years playing there.

I remember that Michelle Phillips was nominated for a Golden Globe at that time, and Cass was positive she was going to win. I told her Michelle didn't stand a chance.

"Wanna make a bet?" asked Cass. "I'll buy you a tennis racquet if she loses."

"Deal," I answered.

Of course I won— and I still have the tennis racquet. What I wasn't prepared for

The tennis racquet Cass had to buy me to pay off our bet.

was Cass's comment as she gave me the racquet.

"Michele and I had an affair you know. We got sick of sleeping with men."

On that July day in 1974, as I drove to the Valley to see Cass' very first nightclub act, I was so happy for her. She had signed a contract with CBS for solo TV specials, and two had already aired to much acclaim. She'd had some solo hit records. Everything was going well. She'd gotten her dream. What I didn't know, was that she was abusing drugs. I never could tell when anyone was on anything, and no one ever did drugs in front of me. They knew I was adamant against them. And, by the way, I knew that a person I won't name was hired to go with her to London as a "minder." I had an idea that it was someone to keep her off drugs. I disliked him on site and knew he couldn't be trusted.

I walked into the large rehearsal hall and greeted her conductor, Marvin Laird, who was also Dusty Springfield's conductor. We knew each other well. Cass had back-up dancers and singers there, and they launched into the first number, Martha and the

Vandellas' "Dancin' in the Streets." I sat there as an audience of one and saw the whole show that she was going to do at the London Palladium set for July 28th.

After the rehearsal was over, Cass asked me to go with her to the opening of a new restaurant in Beverly Hills called Mr. Chow. She had to leave for London the next morning and wanted to celebrate at dinner. I went home and changed, and she picked me up at 6:30 p.m. in her purple Cadillac convertible. The top was white leather and the license plates said ISIS. The goddess people. It was 1974!

"You don't have a purse," I said.

"Don't worry, I have all we need," she said, opening the door and sticking out her white Capezio flat ballerina shoe. She reached into the shoe and pulled out a credit card. I still use that trick today. Thanks, Cass.

She decided to take the long way to Beverly Hills along Mulholland Drive, the famous mountaintop street with 360-degree views. The July heat was comfortable, the convertible top was down, and as we drove along, "Monday, Monday" came on the radio. She sang along, literally with the breeze, and it was one of the most perfect moments in time.

At dinner in a corner booth, which is still there, unchanged since 1974, and I touch it every time I go in, she asked me to go to London with her.

"C'mon! Your friend Debbie Reynolds is closing and then staying for my opening. You can see both of us and we'll have a ball."

It was really tempting, but I couldn't just pick up and leave without notice. I had to turn in a column every day by 10 a.m. and, when I left for a vacation, I had to write the right number of columns in advance to run in my absence. The notice was too short.

We pulled up to her house after dinner and she turned to me and said, "I really like you. I'd really like to sleep with you."

I was not expecting that and was shocked, but I stayed cool. I explained that that wouldn't work for me and thanked her for the offer. Yes, that's what I said. I'm always polite.

She was totally fine and switched the subject. "I don't like the people I've hired to stay in my house while I'm gone. I don't trust them. I'm also concerned about leaving my daughter in their care, so keep an eye on her. I'm going to go in the house and get things I care about and give them to you for safekeeping."

In a few minutes, she came back to the car, loaded down with things like her grandmother's comforter, some pictures, jewelry, original sheet music, and other things. I took all of them and put them in my car.

"Have a great time, " I said. "I promise I'll see the next show you do."

We hugged in the moonlight and she went into the house.

July 29th, 1974

I started the day in a regretful mood because I was really sorry I couldn't see Debbie and Cass. I left *The Hollywood Reporter* around noon in order to make a lunch date at The Beverly Hills Hotel Polo Lounge. To this day, I have no recollection of the person I interviewed because of what happened next.

I returned to the office around 2:30 p.m., and an assistant who sat at the group city desk in the center of the room (columnists had private cubicles) yelled out, "Hey, you're a friend of Cass Elliot's. Does she spell her name with one t or two?"

"One," I yelled back. "Why?"

"Because she just died."

The room slowly turned black and I couldn't feel my body. We had just said goodbye forty-eight hours earlier. Her things were still in my car. My hands felt like they were falling off. I wasn't breathing.

I regained my senses long enough to say, "Don't anyone write that story, do you hear me?" I shouted at the top of my lungs. I was maniacal. The only thing I had control over that second was to make sure the story was right. I had to do it for my friend first, and then take care of myself later.

All the reporters were looking at me.

"Leave me alone until I turn this in!"

Cass had given me the phone number of the flat in London. Ironically, 9 Curzon St. was where Howard Portugais, one of Dusty Springfield's managers, stayed when he was in London, so I knew the flat. I dialed the number.

"Hello," said Allan Carr.

"Allan!" was all I could get out before all the crying I withheld at first started to come out. He was crying, too. "What happened? What happened?" I asked.

"Listen to me," said Allan urgently. "There's something you have to write right now and send out the story immediately. You're the only reporter I'm talking to so we can control the story. You are to write that she choked on a ham sandwich and had a heart attack."

"What????"

"I said, you are to write exactly what I tell you. THIS is the story we want to get out. She choked on a ham sandwich after attending a party at Mick Jagger's house. I can't talk any more. I'm bringing her home as soon as I can and then we'll talk face to face. Hang up and turn that story in now!"

So there you have it. Allan Carr and I covered up the real story. You can blame us for the ham sandwich.

Also in that flat, by the way, was conductor Marvin Laird, who confirmed what Allan later told me when we met back in Los Angeles.

"Allegedly," Mick Jagger had given Cass cocaine and heroin at his party and her heart couldn't take it. There was strain on her heart because of her weight, so technically, she died of a heart attack.

BUT WAIT.

As soon as the story was written and had gone on all the wire services, I drove to Cass' house. No one was there, and the door was open. Can you imagine how eerie and strange that was?

It was a traditional, yet country, two-story house with a pool on Woodrow Wilson Dr. A few years later, Dan Ackroyd and his wife Donna Dixon bought it and lived there for a long time.

The living room was just as it looked forty-eight hours ago, but the beloved owner had vanished into air. Cass' essence was everywhere, as if she were going to walk into the room from the kitchen any second. The sheet music from "New World Comin'" was on the piano. Her director's chair from the CBS TV specials was in the living room. It was purple wood with a canvas backing in dark purple with the word Cass on it in pink. I knew it would be only a matter of minutes before fans and "friends" would try to come in a raid the house. That's what always happens. So I took that director's chair, and it has been sitting in my house since 1974. The sheet music is framed and hangs in my den. She had a cheese-burger candle on the coffee table along with a magnetized puzzle. They are in my den. I know Cass would have wanted that.

I went upstairs, worried now about drugs. I finally had heard the rumors of her drug use, even though I still had never seen it. I figured the police would be coming, and I wanted to check the medicine cabinet and her bedroom. There was nothing.

It was years later, around 2010, that I met a former model named Leon Bing. She was a famous model for Rudi Gernreich. Leon and I met at a party, and for some reason ended up talking about Cass. I found out then that she had been in Cass' house only minutes before me and cleaned out all the drugs. Imagine, thirty-three years later, two people at a party meeting to discover they shared that fateful day and never knew it.

As I drove the few blocks to my house, I started to shake. My body was falling apart. I'd held it together for the ham sandwich and the drug removal, but I couldn't keep it together any more. I got into my bed and didn't leave for over a week. Cass was older than I was, but I was convinced that since she died at thirty-two, I could, too, and I was terrified when that year came for me. It was not rational, but nothing about Cass was rational. She was a comet who splashed and burned, and the world was deprived of what I know would have been a great concert and acting career.

I was deprived of a dear friend.

But most important of all, was that little Owen, Cass' daughter, lost her mother and ended up with Cass' jealous sister, in another rock and roll home. Fortunately, Cass' mother, a fabulous woman, really helped Owen through.

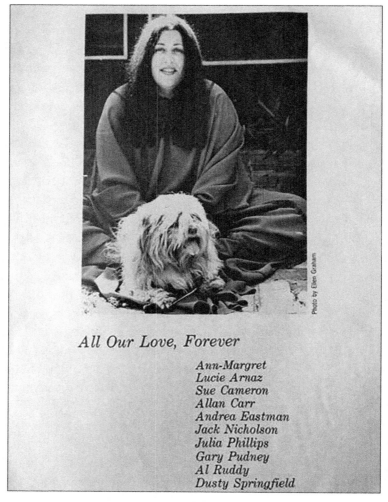

All Our Love, Forever

Ann-Margret
Lucie Arnaz
Sue Cameron
Allan Carr
Andrea Eastman
Jack Nicholson
Julia Phillips
Gary Pudney
Al Ruddy
Dusty Springfield

The Hollywood Reporter *ad we bought to honor Cass.*

Owen was whisked away to the east coast, but when she was around seventeen she came back to Los Angeles. I got a hold of her number and called her. She knew who I was because she'd read all the press on her mother and knew we were friends. She also knew I was the ham sandwich lady!

"I'd like to see you, Owen. We have so much to talk about," I said. We made a date. It was 1992. I had held on to all the things that Cass had given me in 1974, waiting for Owen to grow up. When I saw her, and then heard her speak and felt her energy, it was like

Cass was alive again. They are so much alike. We have taken over the friendship I had with her mother.

I can remember so clearly saying, "And this is your great grandmother's comforter that your mother wanted you to have, and this is a picture of so and so, here are your mother's baby shoes on and on. I was crying. It was an honor to keep that commitment.

Note: When children grow up in chaotic, rock and roll homes, they can either turn to that themselves, or they can make the choice to go the opposite way. Owen Elliot is a PTA carpool mom of two wonderful children. She and her (only husband) and their children live in the San Fernando Valley. And, yes, Owen has Cass' singing voice. How proud Cass would be of her sane, bright, funny daughter.

Another note: Cass will reappear in the Manson Murders chapter. Why? You won't believe it!

Chapter Two

THE JIMS—JIMI HENDRIX, JIM MORRISON, JAMES BROWN, WITH A LITTLE ZAPPA THROWN IN FOR FLAVOR

I was loose in rock and roll land, interviewing one rocker after another. I would meet them at the recording studio, or I might do an interview before or after their show at a nightclub or big arena. Sometimes, I would meet them in their hotel room. What an unbelievably dangerous thing to do, as I look back on it. I was fearless, innocent in thought and experience. It never occurred to me that something might happen.

The only time it crossed my mind was when I was alone with Otis Redding in his hotel room, not suite, at the Continental Hyatt Hotel on the Sunset Strip. Its nickname was the Continental Riot House, since so many rockers and parties there ended up with police arriving.

Otis met me alone in the lobby and I thought nothing of it when he suggested we do the interview in his room. Why didn't he suggest doing it in the hotel lounge? I never thought that at the time.

He was dressed in rust from head to toe, including his shiny rust shoes. He had on a rust sweater and I remember thinking what an awful color that was.

When we got to his room, there was no place to sit except the bed. That was when I remember him looking at me funny. It was only a second, but I felt it. He sat near the pillows and I sat at the foot of the bed and did a normal interview. Nothing happened. Thank God he was a gentleman. I would have been doomed. Whew!

I did have a "rock and roll guardian angel" by the name of Jackie De Shannon. When we met in 1965, her recording of "What the World Needs Now " was No. 1. She'd also had hits on "Needles and

Pins" (which she wrote with Sonny Bono and Jack Nitzsche and they didn't give her credit) and "When You Walk In the Room," plus she was the opening act for the Beatles on their very first tour after making it. Later on, Jackie wrote, "Put a Little Love in Your Heart" (and she's still making a fortune since it seems to be used for every TV commercial), and she won a Grammy for writing "Bette Davis Eyes."

Jackie arrived in L.A. from her home in Kentucky and got successful very fast. She had learned the ropes, and when she met me she saw how innocent I was and she decided I was going to be her project. When I talk about going to the Whisky a Go Go or the Trip to see acts, Jackie was always with me. I also went to every single one of her recording sessions and met her back-up singers, the Blossoms (lead singer Darlene Love), who worked with Elvis and Phil Spector. It was Jackie, by the way, who was asked to be a regular on Shindig, and suggested they hire The Blossoms as back-up for all the acts on the show. The producer didn't want The

Jackie and I with her album, Laurel Canyon, *for which I shot the front and back covers.*

Blossoms because they were black. He actually said that. Jackie told him that if The Blossoms weren't on, she wouldn't be on and she would tell all her friends, including The Beatles, to not do the show. Jackie won. To me, Jackie was my far wiser guide to the world of rock and roll.

The next hotel room interview was with Jimi Hendrix. He was staying at the Sunset Marquis Hotel. Fortunately he was in a suite, and his manager was there to let me in.

"Jimi's waiting for you in the bedroom." That's what he said. Once again, I thought nothing of it. *Yee Gads, what a baby I was.*

I entered the bedroom and he was sitting at the foot of the bed. He did not get up to shake hands. I can imagine how he felt seeing a young girl dressed in a blouse, plaid skirt, knee socks, and loafers approach him for an interview.

The truth is that I loved his music. I thought he was an extraordinary musician. My musical tastes were not reflected in how I dressed. When I was in work clothes I looked like a girls' school coed. When I was in casual clothes, I always looked as if I were ready to board a yacht. Too bad. That's how I was raised and I loved it. *Hmmm. I still dress like that!*

So there sat Jimi, bored out of his mind by me. His answers were short and mumbled. He made absolutely no effort to engage or be forthcoming. I didn't even care. I loved his musicianship, but every once in a while I had run into a musician who was not at all interested in talking to the press. Their record companies forced them to do it. Musicians were so submerged in their art that interviews didn't matter to them. He was one of those, and I was ok with it. It was late in the afternoon and I'd had a busy day. I was not surprised at all that we didn't click or had very little to say to one another.

I was going through the motions of doing a routine interview. The shame of it was that I was not interviewing a routine artist. I had interviewed tons of routine artists like the stupid groups The Left Bank (their hit was "Walk Away Renee" and they were the rudest people I've ever interviewed) or a group called the Swinging

Medallions (one-hit wonders—"Double Shot of My Baby's Love"—the absolute DUMBEST group of people I'd ever interviewed). It was all too bad.

I took my eyes away from my pen and paper to look at Jimi and ask another question. His head had fallen to his chest and he was in a deep sleep. I just sat there and watched him. Here was the hottest, most extraordinary musician of his time, two feet away from me, alone together in his bedroom, and he was O.U.T. I felt sorry for him.

And here, once again, is a classic truth about my naïveté at the time. I left Jimi sleeping sitting up on the edge of the bed, and walked into the living room where his manager was reading on the couch.

"Hi. Uh, Jimi fell asleep. I guess he's just really tired. Of course he needs his rest because he has a show tonight. I understand."

The manager looked at me and said, "Yes. Right." He went right back to reading, not even looking at me, and I just left the room.

It was years before I figured out Jimi had passed out on quaaludes. Someone had to explain to me what a quaalude was.

But, I WAS at the Whisky a Go Go on the Sunset Strip for his show that night, with Jackie, of course. I practically lived at The Whisky and The Trip, both clubs on the strip. Some rock show was happening at both venues every night. The other club that was popular was The Troubadour, but it was more folk-rock. It was where I saw the first shows EVER of Carole King, James Taylor, Linda Ronstadt, Steve Martin, Elton John, Judy Collins, Joan Baez, and so many others.

Jimi's opening at the Whisky was BEYOND the place to be that night. It was an incredible happening. The two good places to sit at that club were at a table in the front row, or a booth in the back. I chose the booth that night.

Jimi looked quite "refreshed from his nap" and started his act. No need to discuss how dazzling his talent was. I knew he'd set fire to his guitar at Monterey Pop, but I had no idea he'd do it at the Whisky. It wasn't that big a room, and when that guitar exploded in flames I can still remember jumping up on the seat of the booth and pressing my back against the wall as if that would save me. I was terrified.

"It's ok. It's ok, " soothed Jackie. "It will burn itself out."

Jim Morrison was a different kind of insanity. He was simply the sexist man I'd ever seen in my life. The first time Jackie and I saw him we were at the front table at the Whisky. His group, The Doors, was making their club debut because their first record, "Light My Fire," had become a hit.

The lights went out on the stage and in the club. The audience heard and felt movement among the crowd. We heard footsteps go up on the stage. We could hear musicians finding their instruments on stage. Then it went quiet. When the lights came on, The Doors were in place on stage. Jim Morrison's back was to the audience. They started playing, he started singing, and he never turned around the entire show.

He was dressed in tight black leather pants that looked like they were sprayed on, a black, sloppy knit sweater, and scuffed brown leather boots. His lyrics were poetry. The musical notes were ethereal. The rhythms were hypnotic. For almost an hour I stared at that perfectly-formed rear end, taut and toned. It moved to the music like an undulating wave. His thighs and calves were equally riveting. His soft, brown shoulder-length curls framed his head.

I have never lost those feelings for him. To have that kind of magnetism and NEVER turn to face an audience? Unbelievable.

He also hated to do interviews. I remember interviewing only Doors members Robbie Krieger and Ray Manzarek. I eventually sold my Jaguar to Robbie. They were nice guys and not all that weird.

But Jim and I were not through with each other.

One night Jackie was going to record at a studio called Sunset Sound. It was on Sunset Blvd. in Hollywood, and was located across the street from Blessed Sacrament Catholic Church. Her session was to start at eight p.m. We got there at 7:45 p.m.

All recording studios feature two areas—one is the studio space where the singer and band are and they sing and play into microphones; the other area is separated from the studio by a gigantic glass window, frequently almost the size of a wall. All the engineering and recording equipment is in that area. It's where the producer and engineer sit, along with any invited guests.

Jackie and I walked in the studio area and saw gigantic pieces of glass everywhere. The entire glass wall/window had been shattered. It was a horrific sight. Clearly, Jackie wouldn't be able to record, but what on earth had happened?

Well, Jim Morrison and The Doors had been recording all day and into the early evening. Jim was high on something and was very angry at the way he perceived the session to be going. In the middle of the session, he ran out of the studio. They had no idea where he went. In a few minutes he had come back with a gigantic statue of Mary that he had stolen from the Church of Blessed Sacrament. (Ironically, Jackie and I went to mass there frequently). He'd hurled Mary through the air and into the window. She was solid stone, and destroyed the window.

But that wasn't enough. He went back into the church and destroyed other figures of deities, and, taking even more, he came back to the studio and used the statues to smash walls, instruments, and engineering soundboards.

We'd missed him by minutes.

Wouldn't you know it? Jackie and I STILL were not through with Jim. This time it was Thanksgiving Eve. Jackie's parents, James and Jeanne, were from Kentucky. They were simple, loving, real people who influenced my life and filled it with love. They were very strict with Jackie and brought her up right. At one point she dated Elvis, and her mother made Elvis bring her back at ten p.m.

Jackie's mother had decided to teach us how to cook a turkey. Jeanne's ritual was to prepare the bird around Midnight, and then watch it cook all night, making sure it was basted, spoken to in dulcet tones, and coddled. (By the way, she taught me that the only way to truly tell if a turkey was done was if you shook its leg and it moved easily). *You're welcome.* Jackie and I were to stay up all night with her and learn.

Around three a.m., Jeanne decided the turkey needed more butter and she was out. Jackie and I had to go to the market! The only one open twenty-four hours close to the house was the Sunfax Market at the corner of Sunset and Fairfax. Today, another market, Bristol Farms, sits on the original site.

Jackie and I walked into Sunfax and started looking for butter. Mind you, there are not a lot of people in a market at three a.m., and particularly on Thanksgiving Eve. As we walked along the rows looking for butter, we passed the cereal aisle. Standing halfway down the aisle was Jim Morrison all alone. I stopped in my tracks and hit Jackie in the ribs. I whispered, "It's Jim."

We decided to walk over to him and say hello. I still had not recovered from my experience of seeing him at The Whisky.

As we walked toward him, we noticed that he was standing in front of the cereal boxes just staring and staring. We stopped and watched. Jim was transfixed by all the colors of the boxes. We could see his eyes rest on a box (for minutes at a time), and then move to another box and stare at that one. By now, I had heard of LSD and how people who took it liked to stare at colorful objects. This must have been what he was doing. He was thoroughly enjoying himself. I imagined that when he came out of it he'd have no memory of it.

I hated to leave Jim, but we needed to get that butter. Jackie's mother asked us to be quick. I really did NOT want to leave Jim. This time he was in a white t-shirt, jeans, and black leather jacket. Yum.

Darn if we didn't find that butter quickly. Before we left, I had to go back to the cereal aisle. He hadn't moved. I never saw him again. I wonder what he might have become. Drugs. So very sad.

There's soul and then there's S...O...U...L. Jimi's was electric. Jim's was ethereal, and James Brown's was deeply dark and alive, with a nasty beat. Before I was even out of college, his songs drove me crazy. I loved rhythm. In fact, I am a drummer. It has been my hobby since I was eleven years old. I taught myself how to play by listening over and over to a record, each time concentrating on one percussion part, like the high-hat cymbal or the snare. I would practice that part until I had it down perfectly. Gradually I would learn and add each part—snare, bass, ride cymbal, crash cymbal, tom, floor tom, until I had the whole ensemble going at once in perfect rhythm.

James Brown invented the syncopated beat that every Black soul band copied ever since. That beat drove me wild. Every time James was on a TV show I practiced all his dance steps. I had him nailed. Even kids at school would pay me to teach them how to do James' routines.

And then one night I went to the Trip nightclub to see James' show and interview him. This time Jackie wasn't with me. Most of my interviews were set up by individual publicists or publicists who worked for the record companies. While I still went to TV tapings and rehearsals to meet the recording artists, my columns and inter-views had gone from *The Hitline* to magazines Like *TEEN* (I was the entertainment editor), *Tiger Beat*, *16*, and many others. Publicists were calling ME now and pitching their artists. All that means, by explanation, is that James was expecting me after the show.

I was ecstatic watching James and the Fabulous Flames live. I knew every inch of the act, but seeing it up close was a dream. There were only two acts who ever really truly excited me this much live—James Brown and Ike and Tina Turner.

After the show was over, I was met by the publicist and led to James' dressing room. As usual, my wardrobe was exactly like a PTA lady. This time I had on a navy blue knit suit (skirt and jacket and blue and white striped top) that I bought at Bullock's Wilshire, the most conservative, society, white-bread store in Los Angeles. All my clothes came from there from the time I was born.

James' dressing room had a couple of his back-up singers and dancers in it, as well as some record company executives. I was so effusive about his performance that I could see he didn't let my outfit dampen his appreciation of my compliments. His outfit was a navy-blue sequined tux. In some weird world, we matched.

"I can dance just like you do," I said to James. Yes, that's what I said to James Brown! And, I repeat again, I had the "balls of death" as well as the confidence that I certainly could match him move for move.

"Oh, yeah? Let me see."

James Brown loved my dancing.

I went right into his routine. His eyes got wide and he had the biggest smile on his face. He started to dance with me, and everyone was gathering around us. We didn't need the music. The same beats were in our heads.

I stopped dancing after a few minutes. I thought that was the right thing to do. James shooed everyone out of the room except me. He took my arm and stood really close.

"Darlin', I'm goin' to San Francisco tonight. I have a show there tomorrow. I want you to come with me right now; get on my plane and stay with me," said James, that growl of a speaking voice in my ear.

Uh oh, I thought.

"I'm sorry, I can't do that. I have to work tomorrow," I answered politely.

He wasn't happy.

"Are you sure, baby?"

"Yes. Thank you so much for letting me dance with you. I'll never forget it."

I smiled sweetly and kissed him on the cheek.

Off I went, in my Bullock's Wilshire suit, ever the proper lady. I think what people or groups never understood, is that my unbridled enthusiasm for their art, be it acting, musicianship, or singing, was never about sex. I showed my total emotions because I loved their talent. I was 100 percent genuine and wanted nothing more than to tell them how incredible they were.

I actually think that the above paragraph is partly a lie. If I had ended up in a hotel room with a sober Jim Morrison, I might have just gone for it, but I never did anything like that.

AND THEN THERE WAS FRANK ZAPPA. He and I were attracted to each other's minds. His music was interesting, but I can't even name one song. He was just an extraordinary conversationalist and a real Renaissance man. He was interested in everything and was extremely intelligent. Most people create public personas. Frank was eccentric, all right, but with me he was just a person. He couldn't believe that I was a drummer. A highlight of my life was when he asked me to meet him at a rehearsal for the Mothers of Invention, his band, at the Whisky. They were opening that night. I went to the rehearsal, and he asked me to sit in on the drums so I could experience playing with the band. Yep. THAT happened. God bless you, Frank. You were taken way too soon. I hate cancer.

Drums with Frank. I still play all the time.

Chapter Three

BOBBY DARIN MY MUSICAL PRINCE

I deeply regret not sleeping with Bobby Darin. I've never been able to let go of that regret. We were perfect for each other. But let's go back, waaaay back.

When Bobby had his first hit record, "Splish Splash," I was still a kid who held her father's hand while crossing the street. I remember that Dick Clark's Caravan of Stars was coming to the Hollywood Bowl to do a concert featuring performers who had current hits at that time. Dick Clark was a well-known DJ and host of *American Bandstand*, a dance show I watched every single day. He also had a half-hour variety show on ABC featuring these sane artists like Fabian, Frankie Avalon, Bobby Rydell, Annette, Connie Francis, etc. I begged my father to take me.

My cousin, Leslie, and I were "chaperoned" by my father to the Hollywood Bowl. We were in a private box. There were tons of children there, as well as, probably, teens that could drive. As I look back, these parents really were good sports. It was my first rock concert, and I don't remember anyone on stage except for Bobby Darin.

He was wearing a black sweater with a white cotton collared shirt underneath and grey pants. He carried a jacket and used it "Frank Sinatra Style" over his shoulder. Of course, then, I didn't know what Frank Style was, but now I know that's what he was doing. Frank Sinatra and Sammy Davis were two of his idols.

Bobby lip-synched to "Splish Splash," and probably the B-side of the record, and then he was gone. I never forgot him.

Apparently, at that time, he and Connie Francis were in love, and her parents eventually killed the relationship. They didn't like him for her. Bobby moved on and married Sandra Dee. There will be tons more about Sandy in her own chapter. Wait for it.

In 1968, I was the entertainment editor of *TEEN* magazine. I also had zillions of rock music interviews published in other magazines. In addition, I had been appearing weekly for a couple of years as a rock news reporter on a live TV show called "Ninth St. West," in Los Angeles. I came on each week and told stories, gossip, news items, whatever you wanted to call it, on all the music stars.

I then got a call from Dick Clark, personally, asking me to quit the local show and do the same thing on a new show he was doing for the ABC network called, *Happening! with Paul Revere and the Raiders*. Of course I said yes. Who wouldn't want to be on a national show? I also knew Paul, Mark Lindsay, and Freddy Weller really well. We'd have a lot of fun.

Because I was now a regular on one of Dick's shows, I left *TEEN* and had my office at Dick Clark Productions on the Sunset Strip. In the late 60s, the Strip was alive morning, noon, and night with bands, stars, and just kids roaming the streets. There were night-clubs like The Whisky, It's Boss, and The Trip, where all the stars played. Every evening I went to one, two, or all three, catching acts and getting news for my segments and writings. The world had turned into long hair, granny glasses, denim, and drugs.

A word about Dick Clark: Yes, he was the same guy that I saw as a kid from *American Bandstand*. Did I take a moment to reflect on how odd it was that I now was working with him? Yes, but only for a second. It didn't have much of an impact on me. I was too busy charging ahead with my career.

What was Dick Clark really like? He was really smart, really nice, and sometimes he cut financial corners outside the law. Did he take payola in the form of having a piece of a record company that certain *Bandstand* stars recorded for? Yes, he did. Did I care? Not at all. Show business can be very dirty, and many, many men in it filled their pockets with lucre. Dick also transformed TV, did game shows, specials, employed thousands of people, and really contributed to the betterment of our pop culture.

HOWEVER, one day he asked me to do a commercial on *Happening* for Nair or Neet, a depilatory product for women. I was to do it live on the show every week. Well, people, if you are a regular on a TV show, and you are doing a commercial for a product using your face and your name, it's called an endorsement and you should be paid. I went to Dick and he refused to pay. I wasn't a hungry kid from Philadelphia trying to be nice to Dick to get my record played. I was a young adult on TV who belonged to a union, and I wanted my money. I reported Dick to the union and he had to pay. He was furious at me for not looking the other way and letting him fill his pockets again. To his credit, he didn't fire me off the show. He iced me out personally, but I stayed on the show till its run ended two years later.

Note: As soon as I became the TV editor of The Hollywood Reporter, Dick was my friend again. You get it. And it was ok with me. Through the years I covered every show he ever did, and I got special treatment (access to rehearsals and star interviews) and special VIP seats. Good on ya', Dick. I miss you.

Bobby Darin had changed his name to Bob. Because of the times, he had switched from slick singer in a shiny suit, to a folk singer with a guitar wearing jeans, granny glasses, and going without his toupee. He was in his "natural phase." I much preferred the other Bobby. Hippie Bob was what I called Darin Phase Two. Rock Star Bobby was Phase One.

"Hey, Sue!" called Dick one afternoon. "Come into my office and meet Bob Darin."

"How are ya, darlin'," he said, taking my hand. I noticed he was totally appropriately dressed for his "If I Had a Carpenter Phase" in jeans, a white t-shirt, jean jacket, and cowboy boots. He also, literally, was holding a guitar.

We chatted a few minutes about music. I told him the story of it being Jackie De Shannon, who told Bob Dylan to switch from acoustic to electric, and that's when his career took off. We liked each other's knowledge of music from the start.

The very next time I saw him was when I was at *The Hollywood Reporter* and he was in "Mack the Knife" Phase Three. The shiny suits had returned. He'd been nominated for an Academy Award for *Captain Newman, MD* (which he should have won), and he was playing to sold-out nightclub engagements all over the world. NBC had just announced they were doing a summer variety series with him, and I was flown to Las Vegas to interview him at the Hilton International Hotel.

Without question, the two most talented male performers I have ever seen were Bobby Darin and Sammy Davis, Jr. Each of them could sing, dance, act, do impressions, and play every instrument. They were dynamos on stage, and no one, to this day, has ever been able to touch either one of them.

Bobby's opening number was "For Once in My Life." It was a redo of the Stevie Wonder hit, but he put a new spin on it. Yes, it was a loud, exciting Vegas arrangement (think Frank Sinatra), but as it was playing, the horns came in and played the horn riff from Santana's "Everybody's Everything." I guarantee you, no one in that audience or any other, would have noticed, but I did. Knowing that Latin rock riff even existed, and sneaking it into a "Vegas-type" arrangement was something Bobby would do. The rebel in the jeans was still there. It was for his own enjoyment, and I "got it."

After the show was over I went to his dressing room. It was jammed with people, and I waited my turn to have time with him. He knew we were doing an interview, so, eventually, everyone would be asked to leave and I would stay.

By that time I had been in every "star" dressing room at every top Vegas hotel. They all were the same layout in various forms—a living room, bedroom, and bath. Some were more luxurious than others, some didn't have bedrooms, but they had pullout couches instead. This dressing room at the Hilton was built for Elvis Presley, so it was big and definitely had a bedroom (which was closed off only by curtains!).

Bobby and I talked for hours.

"I loved the 'Everybody's Everything' riff in the 'For Once in My Life' arrangement," I said at one point.

His eyes grew wide and then softened to true appreciation of kindred spirit.

"You're the only person who's noticed that," he said.

"Music is my life," I said, looking into his eyes.

There was a moment of lightly awkward silence, and I said, "I'm on the two a.m. plane." At that time in Las Vegas, planes went all through the night between Las Vegas and Los Angeles.

He got up and started walking to the bedroom.

"You don't have to go. You could stay over night," he said sweetly.

I knew what that moment was about. I remember getting up and walking to him, and literally looking at him, then the bed, and back to him. I was afraid. The only man I'd ever been with was my fiancé from college. I was not married, and my parents had drummed it into me that you do not sleep with a man unless you were married. Ok. So I did when I was engaged, but I THOUGHT we were getting married. That programming was instilled so deeply in me that I couldn't do it.

"It's ok," he said, so gently. "I'm going to get you a room in the hotel and you can go home tomorrow. There's no point in racing to the airport. And then he kissed me...REALLY well.

As I stood there, he went into the bedroom and then came out carrying a white t-shirt. "Here's my shirt. You're going to need something to sleep in."

I took the shirt and held it close. He made a phone call to the front desk. In a few minutes someone from the hotel appeared to take me to my room. I hugged Bobby good night and was led to a suite that had a round red velvet bed with a mirror on the ceiling, and a Jacuzzi bathtub in the bedroom area. And I was alone in it.

A few months later, Bobby was shooting his TV show at NBC in Burbank and I went to visit him. He was as adorable as ever. I loved his twinkling eyes. But, to me, he looked tired. I noticed that after each song he sang he would leave the set and go to a backstage area. There he would sit down and take oxygen from the very large, hospital-sized canister. I was now very concerned.

*I shot this of Bobby and Dusty Springfield on what
proved to be one of his last TV shows.*

About a month later, in November of 1973, he invited me into
his house on Heather Rd. in Beverly Hills. He was supposedly
engaged to a girl named Andrea Yeager, but she was nowhere to
be found. There was also another rumor that he and Sandra Dee
were going to get back together because they really did love each
other and were not happy being apart. My sources told me that
they had even picked out a house in Bel Air to buy. I was not going
to bring any of that up. I'd made up my mind to only talk about it
if Bobby did first.

We were in his den, and, as usual, listening to music and talking
about it. We could listen to the same record over and over, each
time only focusing on one instrument. It's an amazing way to listen
if you love music.

He seemed wistful, restless, and a little unsettled that night. It
wasn't that I didn't have a good feeling, he just wasn't as happy
as I'd seen him. The good news is that the oxygen machine was
nowhere to be found, but it didn't mean it wasn't there. I assumed
that if he wasn't performing, he didn't need it.

He brought up Sandy and said, "I'll always love her. She's the one."

I took his hand and told him that I knew that. "Please tell her. I
think she feels the same way about you. You really should do that."

He just looked at me and nodded.

After that moment I felt it was time for me to go. We hugged each other tightly and said goodnight. We made no plans to see each other, but, of course, we would. We always did.

On December 20th, I was concerned about Bobby when I arrived at my office. He'd been in the hospital for an infection caused by some dental problems. I really had a strong feeling that I needed to see him at the hospital right away. I called his press agent, Dick Taylor, and said, "I need to go see Bobby this morning. Can you arrange that?"

"Oh, Sue," said Dick. "Bobby died this morning."

"That's impossible," I said, like an idiot. "He just had an infection. How could this happen?" And then I couldn't stop crying.

I heard Dick's voice say, "Sue, he was really sick. He had a rheumatic heart. He wasn't supposed to live through his teens. It's a miracle he lived this long. I know he was your friend. You need to know that he was really depressed. He stopped taking his heart medications. He also didn't take the antibiotics he should have before going to the dentist. It was getting harder and harder for him to breathe. This is what he wanted."

It was almost too much for me to take in. I was just in so much pain. He was only thirty-seven years old. I still can't hear his music or watch him on screen without crying.

As the years went by, I held onto his t-shirt, and sometimes slept in it. When I finally met Dodd Darin, Bobby and Sandy's son, I gave him the shirt. Dodd told me he had nothing of his father's; that he was too young when it happened and nothing was really saved. Dodd was so grateful for the shirt, and I did the right thing. But, for me, I wish I still had it to sleep in. A world without Bobby just doesn't sparkle.

Chapter Four

SANDRA DEE LOOK AT ME—AND I DID

A lot of innocent, pretty kids, with no dreams of being movie stars, get shoved into the business by greedy family members who view them as cash cows. Money is the all-important thing; they don't give a damn about the welfare of the person and the star usually gets destroyed. That's what happened to Sandra Dee.

I have mentioned repeatedly in this book, that I was the "go-to" interviewer for press agents who represented people with problems. They knew I didn't want to hurt anybody.

Of course I grew up with Sandra Dee as *Gidget* (1959), *A Summer Place* (1959), and *Imitation of Life* (1959). I thought she was adorable and wonderful. In *Gidget* I learned it was ok to be a jock and play with the boys. In *A Summer Place* I learned that you NEVER slept with your boyfriend, no matter how many violins are swelling, because you will get pregnant and shame your entire family. In *Imitation of Life* I learned that it was always better to have your outfit match the couch, carpet, and drapes of the room you were in. Thank you, Ross Hunter.

By now it was the 70s. Sandy's career had cooled, and her marriage to Bobby Darin was over. It was not a great time in her life, and I was sure that a lovely story in the *The Hollywood Reporter* might help.

We met at the Beverly Hills Hotel in the Polo Lounge in one of the special booths near the back on the right side of the piano. Sandy was already there when I arrived. I was unusually nervous.

Instead of sweet, shiny Sandra Dee sitting there, I saw a troubled, aged before her time woman who had vodka and cigarettes for lunch. I was extremely upset—not disappointed. I was upset for her and what surely was not a fairy-tale life. She looked hard and worn, and so very fragile and sad.

I would ask friendly questions, and she would answer them. I even got to her to laugh a few times. When the waiter came to take our order, I ordered the McCarthy salad, and Sandy ordered another straight vodka. I had never seen anyone drink at lunch. She also chain-smoked throughout. I was trying not to gag.

The next time we saw each other was several years later at a party. She approached me and told me how much she loved seeing me on TV. (I had just done twenty-seven shows to promote a book). I was very touched by that. She was looking good that day. She was sober and celebrating her son's book (Dodd Darin her son with Bobby Darin). I was so happy she looked well. We had a terrific time at the party.

By this time, it had come out that her stepfather sexually abused her and her mother looked the other way because she still wanted the marriage. She used Sandy as a pack mule to support everyone and didn't give a damn about the abuse. I met her mother. She was scary. No. She was pure evil.

After Bobby died and I knew Sandy was not in good shape, I ended up at ABC-TV as director of daytime development. Sandy's money was running out, and I decided to go over to her house to offer her a job that paid a lot of money. I was still trying to help. I could have put her on *General Hospital, One Life to Live,* or *All My Children,* and the ratings would have skyrocketed. I know it was a comedown from her own movies, but if she needed to eat, she needed to eat.

Her house was a pretty traditional in the flats of Beverly Hills. Her mother, Mary, was a real estate agent, and had probably built up a decent portfolio. We ended up on the beige couch in the living room, and Sandy had her vodka in front of her. That was a bad sign. You can't drink that much and be a responsible worker. If she'd signed the contract, ABC would have put big money behind her and I had to have a reliable asset.

As I was talking to her, she sounded very enthusiastic and hopeful. Her mother was lingering in the background like the plague. We said goodbye and she told me she'd let me know. A few days later she actually did call and say she "wasn't up to it," but she thanked me profusely.

A few years later, Sandy's closest female friend reached out to me and said Sandy wanted to meet. Sandy wanted to write a book and she wanted me to co-author it with her! I was stunned and honored. She told me that I was the only one Sandy would trust to do it.

This time we met on a park bench somewhere in west Los Angeles. It was a beautiful sunny day, and Sandy looked beautiful and sunny. She also looked sober, and was talkative and friendly. At the time of our meeting, I was only writing original novels, and doing very well. It had never been my intention to "ghost" write or "co-write" anything. What that means, is that you get less money and put in more work. You can never tell how often your subject is going to show up, and it can be a very taxing job. Also, at the time we met, the book market was not looking for her kind of bio. I wanted to work with her very badly, but I wanted to make sure we could sell the book. Because I knew it wouldn't sell at that time, I turned down working with her. I hated doing that and disappointing her. I WILL REGRET TO MY DYING DAY NOT SAYING YES. How I would have loved to have spent months and months with her, hearing her truth. I had made a business and financial decision instead of an emotional one, probably for the first time in my career. I was right by the way, about the book not selling well, but thinking back I would have preferred those hours with her, even if we didn't make a dime.

After the book time, Sandy was living in an apartment near the Sunset Strip, and her son Dodd Darin was paying for it from his father Bobby's estate. Sandy's kidneys were failing from so much alcohol, and her lungs were severely damaged from all the chain smoking. Even with dialysis tubes and other medical procedures going on 24 hours a day, all Sandy wanted to do was die. She kept smoking and drinking straight vodka all through the dialysis and other treatments. I've never seen someone who wanted to die so much.

As a child, she was raped repeatedly by her stepfather. Her mother was her "pimp." She had no safe place. She wasn't allowed to get any treatment because she needed to keep shooting. Her only joy was her beautiful son. At least that was something, but not enough to make her want to live.

This gives new meaning to rest in peace. God Bless Her.

Chapter Five

THE MANSON MURDERS HOLLYWOOD HORROR YEARS- OLD SECRETS FINALLY REVEALED

July 28th, 1969

I was being dragged by Cass Elliot to go to the opening of a night-club called The Cheetah on the Santa Monica Pier in Los Angeles. I didn't want to go. The truth is that I was assigned to cover the opening for *TEEN* magazine. I had recently been named their entertainment editor. My job prior to that was at KFWB Radio, the hottest rock station in LA, where I was the editor of their weekly newspaper—the first rock music newspaper EVER in the U.S. I had kind of had it with being totally in the rock word, and was delighted to move to *TEEN*, where I could do "Young Hollywood" instead. All the "cool kids" were going to be there that night.

Everyone cheered when Cass and I walked in. It was like the party started at our entrance. Believe me, the party had already started. Sonny and Cher were there, and that was plenty.

I found the club noisy, kind of fun, but not that all that interesting. The Cheetah was a big venture for whoever backed it, and it was crucial that the most important young stars were there.

I noticed twenty-six-year-old Sharon Tate walk in with a weaselly-looking guy named Steve Brandt. Steve was a "hanger-on," a sycophant to stars, who inserted himself into their lifestyle before they knew what was happening. He was writing for Grade D movie publications, and completely dismissed by the legitimate press.

Watching people dance, drink, and get loud was not my kind of fun. If I was watching a music artist whom I thought had talent, volume was not an issue. Since 1965, I'd had to go review every rock act that was ever at The Whisky a Go Go and The Trip on the Sunset Strip. The famed nightclub Ciro's, dying without traditional Hollywood glamour, had been turned into a dismal spot called "It's Boss." Sonny and Cher and Ike and Tina played there.

I wanted to make this evening a short one. As luck would have it, Cass wasn't really into having a late night and wanted to leave early with me. There were so many people there that it was easier for the club to have trams drive the guests to and from the parking lot and the club.

Cass and I got into a tram, and we were the only ones there. We sat toward the back. In a few minutes, Sharon Tate and Steve Brandt got on and joined us in the back. I will never forget how Sharon Tate looked. First of all, even though it was July, Sharon was wearing a dark ranch mink coat and had the collar framing her face. She was breathtakingly beautiful. Her blonde hair color was exquisite, her cheekbones were perfectly prominent, her smile angelic, and her eyes a most beautiful light brown. When she smiled, because she was pregnant, she looked like a sweet angel, almost like not of this earth.

"Hey, have you met my friend, Sue Cameron?" asked Cass.

"Oh, so YOU'RE the one I read every day, answered Sharon, smiling.

"Thank you," I said. "I'm so glad you read my work, and congratulations on your baby."

"So what did ya think about the club?" asked Cass.

"It was ok, " said Sharon. "I'm just thinking about the baby, so these things don't mean much to me anymore."

"Where's Roman? asked Cass. Roman was Sharon's husband, Roman Polanski, the movie director.

"He's in Europe shooting, but he's definitely hurrying back so he'll be here when the baby comes in a few weeks."

She looked so happy and content.

"Why don't you come over some night? asked Sharon to Cass. "Friends are there all the time and we just play card games, listen to music. It's fun."

"I'd love to," said Cass.

August 9th, 1969

I was at home in bed, getting ready to watch the news. It had been a blistering hot day, one of those LA days where everything is so still that we call it "Earthquake Weather." It was stultifying, and so hot, that I was wearing absolutely nothing. I turned on the 11 o'clock news, and as I was walking to my bed I heard—

"ACTRESS SHARON TATE, FOUR OTHERS MURDERED IN BENEDICT CANYON."

I went ice cold and ran to get closer to the TV. I was in disbelief, and hurting so for that beautiful creature I was with less than a week before. *Four friends were there? What? What are the names? I was screaming inside my head. Was that the night Cass went to the house? Oh my God!*

I recognized the name, Jay Sebring, a very hip men's hairdresser. Other names came out and I didn't recognize them. Cass' wasn't among them.

The announcer started talking about the possibilities of this being just the beginning of targeted murders of people in Hollywood. I ran to every window and shut and locked them like someone was coming for me. I didn't care about the heat. I was terrified.

After a few minutes, I was calm enough to call Cass. She was totally freaked out.

"I was supposed to go tonight, and at the last minute I didn't feel well." She started to cry. "I knew Abigail Folger. I knew Jay. The baby! Do we know anything about the baby?"

"Everybody's dead. Hang up right now and lock all your windows and doors. We don't know what's going on. Call all your friends and tell them to do the same."

No one in Hollywood slept that night. We were terror-stricken.

Cass called my office around 11:30 a.m. the next morning and was screaming.

"Do you know what that son of a bitch John Phillips did? He called the police and told them I was the one who murdered all of them."

"What???"

"That's right. I was sitting here this morning, all my doors locked—just dazed. Suddenly there's a knock on the door saying it was the police. I opened the door and let them in. I thought, because I knew all the victims, they were going to see if I could help them. Instead, they accused me of the murders and wanted to take me in for questioning! Me? I asked them why they could possibly think that, and they said they had a tip. I just knew it was John. That bastard was so mad that I wanted to quit the group, it's the kind of thing he would do."

"This is insane," I said. "What'd you do next?"

"I called my lawyer and he talked to the police. I don't know what he said, but they left right after that and didn't accuse me any more," continued Cass. "I got right on the phone to John and let him have it. He was laughing his really sick laugh. He admitted he did it. He thought it was funny. I hate him."

"Now what?" I asked.

"I'm just going to sit here and figure out what I'm going to do to him."

Note: About a year after the murders, Steve Brandt committed suicide. He was so sick, he told everyone beforehand that he wanted to be with Sharon. It was the height of desperation of someone so wanting to be a part of something "important," (i.e. a Hollywood murder) that he just had to die to be involved. Just unbelievable.

May, 1972

Once again, there I was, happily sitting at my desk at *The Hollywood Reporter*, when I got a phone call from a top public relations company asking me if I would go to the California Women's Prison at Frontera to be part of a panel speaking to prisoners for "Career Day." The state of California was instituting a new program asking successful women in different fields to come to the prison to hopefully inspire inmates to want better lives. I had never been to a prison before (duh), and was very curious as to what it would be like.

On the day of the appearance, I was a little anxious as I drove about an hour out of Los Angeles to Frontera, a town I'd never heard of.

From their current website:

The primary mission of the California Institution for Women is to provide a safe and secure environment for primarily Level I/III female offenders. This mission is further defined by our responsibility to provide quality healthcare and institution programs specifically geared to meet the special needs of female offenders. Specialized programs include academic and vocational programs, pre-release and substance abuse programming, pre-forestry and camp training, an arts in corrections program, and a wide variety of inmate self-help groups and community betterment projects.

The California Institution for Women accommodates all custody levels of female inmates. In addition to its large general population, CIW houses inmates with special needs such as pregnancy, psychiatric care, methadone, and medical problems such as HIV infection.

CIW serves as a hub institution for the selection and physical fitness training of female firefighters selected for conservation camp placement. The institution also serves as a higher security facility for female inmates in Administrative Segregation.
Until 1987, CIW was California's only prison for female felons. It was originally called "Frontera," a feminine derivative of the word frontier—a new beginning. The campus-like design was in keeping with the 1950's progressive notion of rehabilitation.

I drove up and saw something that looked like a large high school campus. Nothing looked threatening to me. The walls were a little "high," with barbed wire, of course, but it didn't look that unusual. The entrance looked like you were going into a school, and there was a lobby with couches and chairs that were plastic and institutional. Nothing was really filthy, but it wasn't shiny and new. You knew the place in which you were standing was not where you go to be rewarded. It was eerie, and smelled faintly of banana peels.

A friendly, official-looking man walked toward me with an extended hand. "You must be Sue."

"How do you know that?" I asked. Was I tailed, profiled, secretly photographed?

"It's our business to become familiar with our guests way ahead of time," he said. "I'll show you to the auditorium."

He led me out of the lobby area, past desks with some officers, and into a room with a door—a big, thick, door with locks and buzzers. I did not like the looks of it, and I started to panic. The whole place just looked gray.

He buzzed me in and told me guards were going to go through my purse. I certainly understood their precautions, but I couldn't help but experience what being locked up felt like. The door slammed shut.

"I'm getting back out, right?" I said, making a feeble joke.

"Of course, Miss Cameron. All our guests get a little nervous coming in. Don't worry. I'll be near you all the time."

Truthfully, I remember going to the auditorium, meeting my fellow panelists, and looking out at a sea of faces of women and girls, all locked up for felony crimes. I recall them laughing at my jokes and being a friendly audience. I have a recollection of them being uplifted and inspired. After I was through, I wanted to get out and get back to my car as fast as I could. When I was on stage, I felt fine. I didn't know where I was. But, off stage, I knew exactly where I was. Being "locked up" was making me claustrophobic, and I wanted to go home.

"You were really wonderful," the warden said. "I've never seen anyone get through to the girls the way you did. I think you really raised their spirits."

"Thank you so much. It was obviously a different type of audience for me, but I enjoyed myself."

He had walked me back to the big door that let out to freedom, but he wasn't buzzing me out. I felt him grab my arm. *That's it, I thought. Ida Lupino and Mercedes McCambridge are coming for me any minute. I'm doomed.*

Suddenly, he nodded and the door opened. I felt my sweat lessen. We were back in the anteroom near the lobby, but he wasn't making any moves toward walking me there.

"I'd like to ask you something," he said, in a very serious tone. "We have some very special prisoners here who are in a solitary situation. They're not allowed to be in the regular prison population. I think they could really benefit by spending some time with you. If you have just an extra half-hour, I'd like you to meet them."

"Of course," I said, feeling flattered.

"Wonderful. Just follow me."

This time we went out another door and were outside on "campus." I could see building after building, some lawns, walkways— again—a high school. Very soon after we started walking he said, "By the way, I think you should know that the prisoners I want you to meet are the Manson Girls."

I stopped dead in my tracks. My body went into instant chills that I hoped he couldn't see.

"Absolutely not! They killed my friend, Sharon Tate!"

"Well, I certainly understand if you'd rather not do it. It IS an unusual request."

And then the reporter in me kicked in. How could I turn down meeting the Manson Girls? Who were they really? What were they like one-on-one? I remembered their faces so clearly from the news film. Could I really deal being face-to-face with Susan Atkins, the girl who killed Sharon and cut her baby out? Or Patricia Krenwinkle, who killed Abigail Folger and Rosemary LaBianca? Tex Watson killed Voytek Frykowski and the poor gatekeeper, Steven Parent, as well as Leno LaBianca. I knew their names instantly–the killers and the killees.

"Warden, I changed my mind. I think it's something I HAVE to do. But, tell me—I'll never be alone with them, right? Will I be separated by bars? Do their guards have guns?" I was asking questions a mile a minute.

"It will be very safe. You don't need to worry. I would never suggest anything to put you in danger. They are in a separate house with their own guards."

I followed him as he walked farther away from campus. As I walked I thought to myself. *Is my will in order? You're too young to have a will? My mother's going to kill me for doing this? I must be insane.*

In the distance, I saw what looked like a one-story "bunker" in the middle of a grassy field. It was away from every building. Attached to it was an outdoor area covered in wire fencing, like a complete bubble. I saw grass on the ground, but in it was a very worn path in a circle like a running track, only it was partly overgrown with weeds.

"That's their exercise area. There's no way out," the warden answered, anticipating my question.

We were now at the entrance of their building. This time the anteroom was much smaller, and the inside door to where they were was much bigger. I was greeted by guards with guns, and they asked me to leave my purse and all my jewelry with them, especially if I was wearing a necklace. Stripped of anything personal, I walked through a metal detector.

That's it, I think. They're going to strangle me with it so I'd better leave it with the guards. Mother of God, what I am doing?

The door was pure steel, and when it opened it was like the grind of a ship's hull hitting an iceberg. I know. *Titanic thoughts. Death and destruction. I'm doomed.* When that door slammed shut behind me, I thought I'd be locked up forever. It's a sound I will never forget because of its finality.

I was in a hallway and the warden was holding my arm. All the walls were white, and I could see a row of windows on the right side as I walked down the hall. Suddenly I was face to face with the Manson Girls. All three. All at once.

The warden let go of my arm and stepped back. Really?

We were in their "living room," if you wanted to call it that. There was bench and a few chairs. I saw an eating table, and I wish I could remember if there was a TV there. I can't remember. I think there was. In the back of the room was the door to their outside cage recreation area. To the left of the living room were three cells that didn't look hideous. Ironically, due to the isolation and the super-high security, I think they actually had better living quarters than the other, less dangerous prisoners.

Seated to my left was a very pretty young girl wearing a tennis sweater, jeans, and penny loafers. She had on light makeup and a flattering dark pink lipstick. She smiled at me and looked about as threatening as a hot fudge sundae. It was Leslie Van Houten, the homecoming queen. Even though my visit was an unplanned event, my knowledge of the Manson crimes was extensive, and I remembered very well that Leslie was not even there on the night of the Tate murders. From all accounts, she was forced against her will to go on the second night to the LaBiancas' house by Charlie Manson and Tex Watson.

"Hi," she said, extending her hand and smiling like a young Mary Tyler Moore. "I'm Leslie Van Houten. I really like your loafers. Are they Gucci?"

"Yes. I really like their clean style."

"I wish I had a pair," said Leslie. "They're so beautiful."

My mind imploded. I am discussing Gucci loafers with a Manson Girl who looks like Mary Tyler Moore. WHAT?????

I liked her immediately. Yes. There, I said it. I liked her. She was very sweet and her eyes were very intelligent.

I looked up and saw Patricia Krenwinkle standing about four feet away, observing the Gucci shoe conversation. She did not look like she cared AT ALL. Her eyes were cold and she was completely closed off. But, she wasn't walking away from me. I knew she was the one who killed Abigail Folger and Rosemary La Bianca in cold blood. She still looked very much like someone capable of another murder, but she didn't terrify me. I sensed she was under control and just curious as to who I was. I'm not saying I wasn't a little apprehensive, though.

I remember introducing myself and she said, "Hi, I'm Pat."

Nice to meet you didn't not seem appropriate, but that's what I said. I couldn't think of anything else. My "murderer-meeting" skills were not honed. It was a very cursory conversation, and her attitude didn't make room for more than that at the moment. OK by me.

Behind Patricia I could see a very nervous, obviously disturbed figure. Susan Atkins couldn't stop moving. She was pulling at her arms, shuffling her feet, and glaring at me, all at the same time. I was face to face with the girl who killed Sharon and her baby. There she was, three feet away.

I wanted to look in her eyes. I wanted to see that evil creature capable of those horrible deeds. Our eyes met, and I felt a fear that is indescribable to this day. Those eyes were the eyes of a totally amoral, unfeeling sociopath with no humanity...not even one cell of humanity. Her eyes were wide open, crazy, insane. There are no words to really convey what I saw. But I know it was what Sharon saw. Oh my God.

Susan was a young girl whose mother died and father abandoned her. She ended up having to take care of her younger brother and was shuffled among relatives. That's a sad story, but not an unusual one. A lot of kids have bad parents. They don't end up murdering people.

Susan Atkins was the most certifiably insane person I'd ever seen. It was so clear that there was no redeeming her. The death penalty should have been enacted upon her as I was standing there, as far as I was concerned. She was never going to get well. She ended up living way too long, in my opinion, and died of cancer in 2009.

I got away from Susan as fast as I could. My presence bored Patricia, so she walked away. But Leslie asked me to sit down and talk to her. It was like talking to a girlfriend about fashion, hit records, movie stars, and politics. It was shocking to me. The reporter in me wanted more, so when Leslie asked me if she could add me to her permanent visitor list I said yes. C'mon, people—one-on-one access to the most fascinating "character" in the most famous (still to this day) Hollywood crime? Of course!

I drove out to the prison to see Leslie many, many times. At one point, she asked me to write her book, and I was considering it. The more we talked, the more difficult it was for me to accept what happened to her life. Leslie was a very bright student who became the homecoming queen. She was from an average middle class family in the sweet suburb of Los Angeles called Altadena, who ended up in prison for life for murder. I just didn't get it.

Here's the story gleaned from her from many conversations we had through the years. She also wrote me long letters. Keep in mind that the Leslie I was talking to no longer had any drugs in her system and she was, and still is, dealing with what she did when she was a Manson robot. Also, these are quotes from numbers of conversations we have had.

"I was unhappy at home because my parents were fighting all the time," said Leslie. "I had no problem with school. I knew I was popular and I had a good time there. But I was also bored. I just felt that I wanted to get out. My parents were getting divorced; I was experimenting with drugs. I wanted to see what was out there.

I'd heard about San Francisco and the Haight-Ashbury area. I was attracted to the hippie lifestyle and the drugs. So I ran away to San Francisco.

One night I was at a party, and I saw a guy sitting in the corner of the room. He had short hair and he was playing and singing 'The Shadow of Your Smile' on his guitar. I went over and sat down to listen. He was really sweet. He was a little older, and he kind of reminded me of my father. I was really missing my parents. He talked to me in such a gentle voice. He made me feel safe. I was so lonely. He told me his name was Charles Manson.

He was asking a bunch of the kids to come live with him on a ranch. He said it would be beautiful; that we'd have plenty of food and we'd be safe. I didn't know then that he would be asking us to sleep with each other and him. I didn't want to sleep with him.

He would wake us up every day and line us up outside. He or one of his assistants, like Tex Watson, would drop a tab of LSD in our mouths every day. I didn't realize it then, but that's how he was brainwashing us to do whatever he wanted. He told us there was going to be a race war and that we had to get ready. Taking LSD every day really destroyed our minds. It caused such damage. I remember when we first went to prison, the doctors we saw had to show us pictures of the crime scenes. I had no idea of what had happened. It took over a year for all the LSD effects to wear off.

The morning after the Tate Killings:

Nobody had any idea what was going on. Word spread through the ranch that something big had happened, but we didn't know what it was. I had my morning dose of LSD, and then it was either Tex or Charlie who told me I was going out that night with some of the others. I can remember now that I didn't have a good feeling. I was scared and I tried to get out of it, but I couldn't. I still didn't know anything about what had happened the night before.

After it was dark we piled into a car and drove off. Tex drove, and I was there with Patricia Krenwinkle. I remember Tex saying that we were looking for a house where rich people lived. He finally stopped at a house where a boat was in the driveway. We all went into the house, and I remember Tex going after Mr. LaBianca and

Pat, taking Mrs. LaBianca. I stayed back in the kitchen. I did not want to be involved in what was going on. I opened the refrigerator and kept staring at the light. I couldn't stop staring. I was hearing horrible sounds coming from the bedrooms. I wanted to run. Then Tex came in and pulled me away from the refrigerator. 'You've got to go in there and kill someone,' he said. I said, 'No.' He told me that Charlie gave him orders to kill me if I wouldn't cooperate. Tex pushed me down the hall to the room where Mrs. LaBianca was.

Mrs. LaBianca was on the floor and Pat was stabbing her. Tex slammed me to the floor and told me to take the knife from Pat and kill her. I thought Mrs. LaBianca was dead already. That was the only reason at the time that I could stab her. I stabbed her 14 times. It was what Tex wanted, and he was going to tell Charlie if I didn't. Mrs. LaBianca was dead before I started.

Do I know if Mrs. LaBianca was dead? No. Do I know if Leslie REALLY thought she was dead? No. Is that perhaps a way she can deal with her actions? Maybe. Or, now that so many years have passed since our conversations, Leslie realizes she did actually help kill her. No one will know if Leslie actually killed her. Maybe she did. Maybe she didn't. Not even Leslie can know.

After all these conversations with Leslie, I can tell you that she has been a model prisoner. She has earned two college degrees, and she regrets down to her deepest soul the fact that she got involved with Manson, took the drugs, and ended up in the LaBiancas' house. She always told me she doubted if she'd ever get parole. It bothers her to this day that members of the surviving Tate family keep campaigning against her parole and showing up at hearings. Leslie had nothing to do with the Tate murders. Her story is a tragedy from the hippie movement and drug use. It's ALL tragic. Do I believe she should be given parole? Yes. And I understand everyone who disagrees with that. But they haven't met her and spent the time I have with her.

Note:

Through the years of these visits, I also had occasions to run into Patricia Krenwinkle. I saw her change into a better person. I saw that in some cases, prison could rehabilitate people to an extent. Does she deserve parole? Not on my or your life!

Susan Atkins remained as insane and scary as she was the first day we met. The death penalty would have been just fine for her. She died in prison of cancer.

Extra Tidbits:

The Manson Murder House was owned by Rudy Altobelli, who was Valerie Harper's manager at the time of the murders. When Valerie heard the address of the house, she thought Rudy had been killed.

Prior to Sharon Tate renting the house, it was rented by Doris Day's son, Terry Melcher, and his girlfriend, Candice Bergen. It was Terry who was Manson's intended victim. Manson was a singer-songwriter, and Terry turned down his demos, refusing to sign him to his label. Dennis Wilson of the Beach Boys is the one who introduced Charlie to Terry. Manson had no idea Terry wasn't living in that house. If he had been, he and Candice would have been the victims.

I once was at a dinner party with Doris Day and Ethel Merman (only four of us), at the home of Gus Schirmer, from Schirmer music. I tried to bring up the murders with Doris, and she turned to ice. I never should have done that. She stopped talking to me for the rest of the night. At a dinner party with only four people, that makes for a lot of silence. However, the silence was broken repeatedly by Ethel Merman, Queen of Broadway, who, happily decided to sing for her dinner and dessert and into the night. It was an incredible evening. After that, Ethel and I became pen pals for the rest of her life.

Right after the murder, suddenly it became a "status symbol" to have been someone Sharon Tate invited to dinner that night but you decided not to go. That's how sick Hollywood is for fame. If all the people who claimed to have been an invited guest showed up, Sharon would have had to have held that dinner on a football field. The ONLY one invited was Cass Elliot.

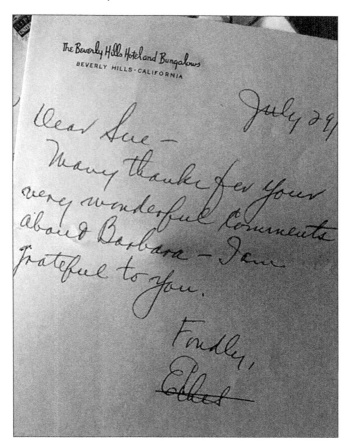

From Ethel with love.

Chapter Six

THE NELSONS OZZIE, HARRIET, DAVID, RICKY, TRACY, AND ME

Like most children my age, I watched the TV show *Ozzie and Harriet*. My father, (the step-father doctor, not Biodad, the Hollywood lawyer) wore sweaters just like Ozzie's cardigans. My mother wore an apron like Harriet's, although it was quickly discarded when she'd decide to do an impromptu strip number for any one of her four husbands.

I had the expected crush on Ricky Nelson, with his beautiful blue eyes and long eyelashes. I wasn't in my teens yet, but it was the thing to do, and I really did think he was one of the most beautiful male creatures I'd ever seen.

One day, my (Biodad) father took my cousin, Leslie, and me to the studio lot where *Ozzie and Harriet* was filmed. I saw Ozzie from far away as he was leaving the set. It was lunch hour, so when we walked onto the set no one was there. My father left us alone and we had the run of the stage. *Note: This would NEVER happen today.*

We walked onto the living room set, the fake front door and lawn area, the boys' bedrooms, and ended up in the kitchen. We were so thrilled to be on a real set. It was the first one I'd been on. The second happened about a year later when my father took me on the set of *Superman* with George Reeves, Jack Larson, and Noel Neill. I still remember being in a state of shock at meeting all of them. George was actually in his Superman costume. They were in a cave covered by boulders, and George Reeves said to me, "Pick one up." I did, and it was as light as a feather. Fake rocks. Who knew?

But now we were in the *Ozzie and Harriet* kitchen and I wanted a souvenir. I knew not to take anything visible. That would be stealing, AND I could get caught. I started opening the kitchen drawers. Nothing. I kept on. Finally, in the last drawer, I found some Coca-

Cola bottle caps. Clearly, they had nothing to do with what was on camera. I had to have a couple for posterity. I took them. Yes, I confess. They were the only things I ever "stole."

CUT TO: Rick Nelson's daughter, Tracy, starring on a CBS series called *Square Pegs*. She had a spectacular face that was a combination of her gorgeous father, Rick, and her beautiful mother, Kris. I remember when Kris married Rick and took him to her senior prom. I really was jealous. No kidding. I really was.

I didn't know at the time that unmarried Kris was pregnant and they had to get married. I'm sure they loved each other, but they were way too young. They also went on to have twins, Gunnar and Matthew, and later on Sam, just before they divorced. By the way, Kris was Kris Harmon, daughter of famed football player and announcer Tom Harmon, and the actress Elyse Knox, one of the most beautiful, elegant women I've ever seen.

When I saw footage of Tracy, I just thought (and still do) she was one of the most unique individuals ever. Her look was one-of-a-kind, her baby voice played against type and made her even more interesting, and, most importantly, she had real acting talent. She was all of seventeen years old, and I had to meet her. I knew I could advise her and help her career.

In my typical style, I just walked onto the set and introduced myself. They were shooting at a real high school somewhere in an unpleasant area of Los Angeles, and I just headed down there. We hit it off immediately. When I looked into her eyes I saw the soul of an old, wise woman. She was seventeen going on fifty. And the depth of her brain and understanding about life was unfathomable. When we parted, she invited me to her eighteenth birthday dinner given by her mother, Kris. Hmm. Kris. The girl who "took Rick away from me."

The dinner was held at a Moroccan restaurant called Dar Maghreb in Hollywood. You sat on pillows and ate food with your hands. Imagine my shock when I walked in and saw Tracy, Kris, and Tracy's *Square Pegs* co-star, Claudette Wells, waiting for me. Only FOUR at the party?

Kris and I got along well. I could tell from the conversation that she and Rick had a terrible marriage and an even worse divorce. Rick barely saw any of the children as they were growing up. I could also tell that Tracy just adored her father with all her heart.

I visited Tracy a lot on the set. Soon, I found myself a huge part of her life. She took me everywhere. I met her Harmon grandparents at their home in Brentwood when Tracy was recovering from some minor surgery. Her Uncle Tom was very polite and a little distant, much like his son Mark Harmon (Tracy's uncle) of *NCIS*. Grandma Elyse, or Nino, as her grandkids called her, was sweet, charming, well-mannered, and a true lady in every sense of the word. She really had the magic, and gave up her whole movie career when she married Tom.

There was always tension between the Harmon and Nelson families because of the quickie marriage that united the two clans. Drugs and cheating on the part of both Rick and Kris destroyed that marriage, but the in-laws on both sides didn't really want to know about why things fell apart. Ozzie was long gone, but Tom, Elyse, and Harriet never wanted to hear such things. They were a group of adults who learned how to put up a front for the public. Tracy told the truth.

Because Tracy and I were "frick and frack," I was literally taken in by "The Nelsons." They all confided in me separately. As I said, the Nelson and Harmon families put up good fronts, but there was usually a feud going on, only put aside by a holiday or family function. There were disagreements among all of them—Kris and her mother, Harriet and Rick, Rick and his sons, Rick and David, Tracy and Kris, Kris and her sister and brother. It was nothing like TV, yet, individually, I liked every single one of them.

Harriet Nelson was really cool. She was a vaudevillian and very world-wise. Believe it or not, she started smoking at thirteen, hung out at the wild Cotton Club in Harlem, had a brief marriage as a teen, and then she was the only girl who toured with all-male bands as a singer. There were no aprons for Harriet in her early years!

She fell deeply in love with bandleader Ozzie, and had two sons, David and Ricky. They started their radio show and then it went to TV. From the moment they hit TV, Harriet had to "be Harriet Nelson." She wore that apron twenty-four hours a day, even though she smoked like a chimney till the day she died. She always hid it from the public.

I first met Harriet when Tracy invited me to go on the train from Los Angeles' Union Station to Mission San Juan Capistrano for lunch, about two and a half-hours by train from Los Angeles. It was Mother's Day, and Tracy, Harriet, and I were celebrating. Harriet was a little more free when she was with just Tracy and me. She had a wicked sense of humor. The Harriet who exited the train was "public Mrs. Nelson." I saw she was not the hip band singer from the 30s. She was warm and welcoming, and really was Mrs. Nelson. She didn't have a dual personality. This wasn't a trick. She simply respected the Nelson reputation and her audience. She was a pro.

I watched as the people at the train station saw her and got excited. They treated her with true reverence and respect. In a sense, she was everyone's mother. Sure, you had the others like Donna Reed or Jane Wyatt of *Father Knows Best*, but Harriet was Harriet. She was the real thing on TV and in real life.

Harriet was also very aware that she had to be Harriet. When we arrived in San Juan Capistrano, we went to some country inn-type restaurant that looked like a little house. I remember it was surrounded by beautiful rose gardens. There was a long line out in front waiting to get in. I soon found out that we didn't have reservations, even though this was where Harriet and Tracy knew they wanted to go.

We walked to the front of the line to talk to the hostess, who, of course, immediately recognized Harriet. "Oh, Mrs. Nelson! We didn't know you were coming, but please wait here and we'll find a table for you right away."

The line people were watching this.

"Absolutely not, dear," said Harriet. "We'll wait our turn like everyone else. No one is more special than another." She then literally turned to the crowd, smiled, and nodded.

I had a fit because I was starving, but Harriet was correctly being Harriet. She truly meant what she said. She was a very fair and humble person, and waiting in line was the right thing to do. Harriet never considered being "Harriet" as a burden. It was an honor for her.

Off we marched to the back of the line. As soon as we got there, others waiting began to offer her places ahead in line. Again, she politely refused.

I have been hundreds of places with probably hundreds of famous people. I have never seen anyone treated with more reverence than Harriet Nelson.

I met David Nelson at his house one day during a brunch he and his second wife, Yvonne, gave. Tracy didn't like Yvonne very much, and told me that Yvonne was threatened by her and her brothers because she and David never had kids of their own. Yvonne had three children from a former marriage and was quick to have those children take the last name of Nelson. Those kids used to go all over LA (and probably still do) saying they're the grandchildren of Ozzie and Harriet and reaping the perks. The Nelson blood children didn't like this one bit. David was caught in the middle and he caved to his wife. David was not strong, but very nice, and easy to talk to. He was Harriet's favorite son, and everyone knew it—particularly Rick. That wasn't pretty either.

Tracy began taking me to Rick's concerts. The first one I went to was at Magic Mountain, an amusement park with a big stage just outside Los Angeles in a town called Valencia. Forget about Valencia. It was the first time I was going to meet Rick.

We went to the rehearsal and were given stick-on badges with Rick's face on them. During a break Tracy said, "Come on stage and meet Pop."

Pop, I thought. How funny. I wasn't meeting Pop, as far as I was concerned. I was meeting Mr. Gorgeous, someone I'd wanted to meet since I was ten or twelve. Tracy's father? Forget it!

Rick and Tracy that day at Magic Mountain.

Suddenly there he was, offering me his hand and looking straight into my eyes with those incredible blue eyes and that shy smile. It was simply a polite introduction and then he had to get back to rehearsal. He knew who I was from all my columns and magazine articles, and that made me feel really good. Meeting someone you've longed to meet for years can be disappointing. Meeting Rick was not, because he was as beautiful as I imagined. After going to more concerts, and spending more time with him, I found conversation difficult. He was so private and shy that he was barely forthcoming on any subject. I eventually learned that small talk wasn't for him. If you had a specific topic, preferably music, you could get a conversation going, but that was about it.

One day Tracy came to me and told me she wasn't feeling well. She was starring on a TV series called *Father Dowling*, for NBC. She said she'd been to a number of doctors but no one had any answers.

I didn't like how she looked. She was very thin, her eyes were sunken in, and her coloring wasn't good. I picked up the phone then and there and called the doctor who, at the time, was the best diagnostician in Los Angles, Dr. Mark Saginor. He said he'd see her right away.

Tracy went over to his office and called me the minute she was through.

"He took one look at me and told me I had Hodgkin's Disease. That's cancer. I have to do chemo, radiation, all of it. You just saved my life, you know. It was caught just in time," said Tracy.

To NBC and Fred Silverman's credit, they stopped production on *Father Dowling* and waited for her to get well.

Tracy faced it all head-on and triumphed.

Another time a crazy fan of Tracy's barged into my office brandishing a sword, threatening to kill himself if I didn't get her to come over to meet him. He wanted "to marry her." Fortunately, my assistant managed to notify me, and I called the Beverly Hills Police while she told the guy that Tracy was on her way.

All in a day's work.

The first week in December, 1985, Tracy's brothers, Gunnar and Matthew, were debuting their new band at a nightclub in Santa Monica, California. Tracy asked me to go with her. By this time I knew Matt and Gunnar well, and really enjoyed their senses of humor. As twins growing up, they used to wrap themselves up together to form a ball and roll around the house terrorizing their mother, Kris. It made her nuts.

When Tracy and I arrived at the table, Rick was sitting there with his new girlfriend, Helen. Rick had never seen his sons' band and it was a big deal that he was there. I had already accepted that he was pretty much an absentee father, so I was very grateful he had showed up for his kids. I remember telling him how happy I was to see him and how much it meant for Gunnar and Matthew, that he was there. He told me that he was glad the dates worked out because he was going on a month-long tour and this was the only time he'd be available to see them.

I sized up Helen, still jealous that I wasn't Mrs. Ricky Nelson (sort of). She was average in every way. I couldn't see much of a personality. She was nice, and not a talker—just like Rick. Then the band went on and conversation ended. The boys were terrific and Rick was very happy about it. When the show was over we all got up to go say hello. Gunnar, Matthew, and Tracy were really savoring the moment with their father, who was showing real support and love. That was the picture I was left with in my head when I went home.

December 31st, 1985:

I had a date with an executive from the TV producer Aaron Spelling's company to see my friend Helen Reddy sing at the Westwood Playhouse. Incidentally, Helen's opening act was a new comic named Joy Behar. I thought Joy was hilarious and loved Helen's show. Afterwards, we visited in the theater and then left. I remember that my date, who shall remain nameless, wanted me to go back to his house with him. I didn't want to go, but agreed to stay for one drink. We all know that scenario.

We arrived at his house and turned on the TV to watch the ball drop. Instead I was greeted with blaring news anchors saying, "Ricky Nelson killed in plane crash."

The evening was over. The Nelsons were over.

There were no cell phones at that time. Tracy was in Aspen with her husband, supposedly celebrating New Year's. I called Kris Nelson at her Brentwood home.

"Kris, It's Sue. Oh my God."

She was crying. "Come over here. We're just gathering here because we don't know what else to do."

"Where's Harriet?" I asked.

"David told her and he's with her. He took her to his house."

"What about Tracy?' I continued.

"It's terrible. Billy (her husband) found out on TV and had to tell her. They're flying in tomorrow morning. There are no planes out of Aspen right now."

"Is there anything that I can do to help? I know it's kind of a stupid question."

"Yes, there is," said Kris. "Would you go to the airport and pick up Tracy and Billy and bring them to my house in the morning?"

"Consider it done. I'll be there."

I got the flight number and arrival time and turned to my date and said, "Take me home."

So much for Happy New Year.

I was in a state of shock, just like the rest of the world, but I was also at the center of the family during a time of their greatest crisis. It was the beginning of a pattern that has followed me my whole life. Famous Family=Crisis=Me in the Middle.

Waiting for Tracy and her then-husband, Billy Moses, at the airport was like a bad dream. I simply couldn't believe Rick, and other wonderful people, had died. When I spotted Tracy coming toward me she was so pale she looked like she was inside out. Billy's arm was around her. We hugged and hugged. There was nothing else to do.

"Where are we going?"

"To my father's house," said Tracy.

Rick Nelson lived in a house off of Mulholland Drive. It was an infamous house because Errol Flynn lived there, and at one point, right after the actor John Barrymore died, the director, Raoul Walsh, stole Barrymore's body and propped him up on the couch. He called to Flynn to come into the living room and there was Barrymore, dead, but sitting in his usual spot on the couch.

I wasn't thinking about that story as we entered the house. It was around 11 a.m., but there was no light in the house. It was a dark house anyway, with wood paneling and cabin-like furniture.

Tracy walked to the den and I was face-to-face with David and Harriet. They were dazed, of course. We all were. I couldn't help but notice that I was the only non-family person who was right in that room, with America's most famous family at a time that was their most private and wrenching. Again, I couldn't help but recognize that things like this kept happening to me. Why was I always the one who was there behind the headlines? I truly believe God placed me there, over and over again. For whatever reason, I have been blessed with ability to help people, public and private, in a crisis. And, make no mistake, death is death, but when it involves a public person or family, it IS different. Certain skills are needed—planning, dealing with the press, and calling security. You have no idea.

I took a look at Harriet. She was sitting on a leather chair and her posture was not slumped over. She was ramrod straight, and she was staring straight ahead. All light was out of her eyes. I saw a woman whose heart was still beating, but she was gone. I'll never be able to erase that image.

The funeral was set for Forest Lawn, and on that day, after a very sad, heavy service, invited guests went to David's house for a reception. He lived in a ranch-style house in the San Fernando Valley. It was just an awful time. People were speaking in hushed tones. Harriet was still just sitting and staring. David and his wife were trying to be host and hostess to the guests.

The original host of the game show *Wheel of Fortune*, Chuck Woolery, was married to Teri, the daughter of David's wife, Yvonne. They were hanging out in an office behind the kitchen rather than joining others in the living room or dining room. For some reason I was in there with them and a few other people. Polite, insignificant conversation was going on, typical of the situation. Chuck was also David's very best friend. Suddenly, I was thirsty, so I decided to leave the office and go into the kitchen. As I walked into the kitchen the phone was ringing and ringing. There was no answering machine and no one was picking up. I decided to answer it.

"Hello?"

The male voice on the other end of the line could barely speak and sounded very upset. "This is so-and-so, I need to speak to David Nelson. It's an emergency."

"He's in the middle of hosting a funeral reception for his brother right now, this isn't a really great—"

"You've got to go to David and give him this message. I can't stay on the line. Tell him that Chuck Woolery's son was just killed in a motorcycle accident!"

And then he hung up.

Why me, God? Again? Now I'm at a funeral reception and I have to go tell David that his best friend's son is dead? And David has to go in and tell Chuck? Are you kidding me?

I searched for David and found him in the dining room surrounded by people. I grabbed his arm and said, "You have to come with me right now!" He was startled, but he went with me to the kitchen. He had a very confused look on his face.

"David, there's no other way to do this," I said. "I just got a call from so-and-so and Chuck's son, Chad, was just killed in a motorcycle accident. You have to tell him."

Picture David Nelson at that moment. He'd just put his brother in the ground about ninety minutes prior. His mother is destroyed and he's now in charge of everything. His face was a mixture of disbelief and absolute horror. He asked me the name of the person who told me, and as soon as I said the name he knew the story had to be true.

"Where's Chuck?"

"He's in the office."

David turned in what looked like slow motion to me. He looked like he was walking through water as he approached the office. The door was open and I saw Chuck and Teri talking, kind of smiling, and just getting through the day. The closer David got to the den, I found myself counting the few seconds Chuck had left before his life would be blown apart.

David walked in and the door remained open. I didn't hear the words, but I saw the blood drain from Chuck's face. Teri screamed. The door closed.

Since that day, Tracy Nelson has fought cancer five times and won. Billy divorced her. She had two wonderful children and we're still in each other's lives. Tracy Nelson is a warrior. Neither of her parents ever really was available to her as she was growing up. She is the most sensitive young lady I've ever known, and the strongest. What an incredible woman she has become.

As for Harriet, after the funeral she went home to her house in Laguna to die. Mind you, there wasn't anything physically wrong with her, but she was done. She gave away all of her beautiful bedroom furniture and installed a single bed against the wall with a cross hanging above it. A picture of Rick was placed on the simple wooden dresser. She had set up the room just like one in a convent. She laid down on that bed and waited for God to take her. She had to wait nine long years.

David died in 2011. His step-children are still claiming they're "real" Nelsons. The actual Nelson kids are still fighting over the estate.

My beloved Tracy is alive and healthy. That's what I care about.

Chapter Seven

ELVIS' WOMEN AND ME????
AND HOW MUCH I LIKE ALL OF THEM

The first time I saw Elvis Presley, I was running the underground music newspaper, the KFWB *Hitline*. Elvis was doing a concert at the Sports Arena, a stadium in Los Angeles, and I was going there to review him.

I remember, as a little girl, watching him on TV and thinking that he was too "blue collar" and not refined enough for me. I was TEN! What kinds of thoughts were those? But they were accurate. Whatever a ten-year-old thought sexy meant, I thought he was that, but I never would have brought him home to dinner. My parents would have thrown him right out.

My seats in the arena were very close to the stage, and I was, aside from being no longer ten, eager to see him in person. He did not disappoint me. He was a terrific performer who radiated sex and threw it back and forth between himself and the audience. I gave him a great review.

The next time I saw him he was in his white sequined jumpsuit phase. He was not yet fat, and he was opening at the International Hotel in Las Vegas. It was the very first time he had ever played Vegas, and it was a HUGE deal.

By this time I was a daily columnist for *The Hollywood Reporter*. In today's internet world, where any twit can write a page online (and there are millions of them) and call themselves a columnist or reporter, in the 70s there were only three or four columnists who mattered, and I was one of them. Every movie studio, TV network, record company, agent, press agent wanted me to do a story on their clients/stars. I could go anywhere in the world and it would be paid for. I remember one time I wanted to get to London, and

I found out which actors were shooting in London. I saw that Kirk Douglas was shooting something, so I called the studio funding the movie and said I wanted to interview Kirk. Done. I had a first class airplane ticket and a paid-for hotel room, and a car and driver to take me where I wanted to go. Long way of saying that it was no shock that I was invited to cover Elvis' Vegas opening.

I had also become friends with Cass Elliot at this point, and she told me that when she saw him in concert one time, he invited her back to his hotel room. She was hoping it would be for a rendez-vous. Instead, she watched as he took out a gun and shot all the TV sets in the suite.

I saw Elvis. He did NOT invite me back to his suite, but he was very sweet and shy.

The day he died, I was very, very sad. He did it to himself, but it didn't have to happen. There were too many people around him using him to make money.

Some time in the 80s, I made the acquaintance of a writer who "ghosted" (wrote for people without using his name) a book for Priscilla Presley. One afternoon he asked me if I'd like to have dinner that night with Priscilla Presley. I'm not sure why he did it, but he had cleared it with her beforehand and she said she wanted to meet me. She had read my column many times and felt I wasn't going to use her or break confidentiality. After all, it was just dinner!

In order to stay away from crowds, Priscilla picked a kosher restaurant in a Jewish section of Los Angeles on Pico Blvd. It was called Milk and Honey, and I'd never heard of it. So, tell me now, would you ever think that you'd end up in a kosher restaurant with Priscilla Presley? I learned very early on in my career to stop thinking like that, because my adventures took me to the absurd and back.

Priscilla is a very nice, very guarded person. She is also very shrewd, and had to become so very quickly, because people immediately started to try to use her to get close to Elvis. As Mrs. Presley, at such a young age, she had to grow up fast. She was a kid, a virgin, thrown into his madness. She had no privacy; no time to grow up naturally. Rightfully so, she was wary of everyone and what they wanted. And, as the mother of Elvis' only child, the pressure was even worse.

I can well imagine how unprepared she was to have him surrounded by his male pals. I also imagine she felt somewhat like a trophy. I suspect early on that she figured out he got her, used her, and put her on a shelf. I doubt that any woman of his was treated any other way. It was the times; it was life with a gigantic superstar. But, they truly loved each other. I absolutely believe Elvis' intention was to be a good, loving husband. And, certainly, Priscilla's love was true. Did they get a divorce because Elvis found out about her affair with her martial arts teacher? Yes, but for God's sake, Elvis hadn't paid any attention to her at all. He never really delivered on his vows to be a good husband, and he definitely was never faithful. I'm totally on Priscilla's side.

Priscilla never mentioned Elvis that night. Conversation was in general about show business, life, books, and music. She was lovely, and very beautiful. Amazing eyes.

I have had other occasions to spend time with her through the years at charity events. For a while we were on the same board. Priscilla is the ambassador for the Dream Foundation, and does a tremendous amount of work. I saw her in action at those meetings. She's smart as a whip and sees through everything. Nothing gets past her, and she's very protective of her life. I like her very much.

These women are out of order. For those of you keeping track, Priscilla was first. When they got a divorce, Elvis became engaged to a legitimate beauty queen named Linda Thompson. The next one up was Ginger Alden, who was engaged to him when he died. I met Ginger before I met Linda.

I met Ginger Alden in the 80s. She was another great southern beauty. Actually she had the same coloring as Priscilla. Ginger was adorable, accessible, funny, and a person who enjoyed life on a daily basis. She had a very successful career in commercials, and she wanted to transition into being an actress. Could she act? I didn't care. She was beautiful, good in interviews, and everybody wanted to meet her because she was the one in the house when Elvis died. They were engaged and he died six months later.

"I can tell by the look on your face that you're about to ask THE question," said Ginger. "Yes, he really was dead when I found him. I get it all the time. Don't feel bad about asking me. I saw him dead on the floor. I was concerned when he didn't come back from the bathroom, so I went in and there he was. I called one of his TCB guys for help, and as soon as they saw he was dead they pulled me out of there as fast as they could. They needed to deal with the situation. It was crazy and awful."

"It was drugs, I presume," I asked.

"I never saw any. I'm not kidding. I'm telling you the truth. I was 18 years old. I had no experience in anything. Elvis never took any pill in front of me. I had no idea!"

I helped Ginger meet a bunch of Hollywood producers and casting directors, and her big break came when she was asked to do a screen test for a TV show called *The Colbys*. It was a spin-off of *Dynasty* starring Charlton Heston. *Dynasty* was so hot, and I knew if Ginger managed to get the ingénue lead on *The Colbys* that she'd have a real career. She didn't get the part. She came in second of the three girls who tested. I was quite sad about it, because had she gotten the part it really would have benefitted her the most.

Ginger hung around Hollywood for a while, but if you don't get parts quickly, people lose interest. She ended up going back to New York, falling in love with a great guy and having a son. Ironically, her husband of twenty years died of an unexpected heart attack the same day Elvis died. Wow. I don't even know what to make of that. Neither does Ginger. I really like Ginger and we still stay in touch.

Linda Thompson was a twenty-two-year-old Miss Tennessee at the Miss Universe pageant. She too, was a virgin. I think that was Elvis' specialty. They were together six years, and Linda had to leave because of the drugs. It broke her heart to leave him. I also believe that Elvis was much more "present" during his relationship with

Linda. Even though Linda was young and innocent, just like Priscilla and Ginger, she had a sense of self early on. She was strong and demanded the right treatment from him. The demands weren't necessarily verbal. Her behavior was different than the others.

Even though Linda was engaged to Elvis, married to Bruce Jenner (mother of their sons Brandon and Brody), and married to hit record producer David Foster, Linda never lost sight of who she was and what her value was in a relationship.

One could call her a "steel magnolia" from the south, and she IS that. But she is also a compassionate, loving, smart, humorous broad who is totally unpretentious. She gets "the game," plays it spectacularly, but she also lives in a compound of houses in Malibu where it's all family, all the time. Her brother, Sam, who was one of Elvis' bodyguards (and then became a judge) even after Linda left, lives on Linda's property with his wife. Her father lived with her until he died. Linda makes canned jams from the fruit in her garden. I can't tell you how "down home" she is, yet she doesn't mind a Gucci purse...or twelve.

Linda is a statuesque blonde, very unlike Priscilla and Ginger. She's much more outgoing. Although she and I were at large Hollywood parties and more intimate "Girls Night Out" dinners for years, we'd never said more than a lovely hello and a Hollywood hug. Then one night, Kathy Hilton, Paris's mother, gave a dinner party for a friend of Linda's and mine. Linda and I ended up sitting side by side at the head of the table. She was late, and rushed in and whispered in my ear, "I was at an estate sale. I just couldn't leave. The deals were too good."

We exchanged more pleasantries, and then, not being able to contain her excitement Linda said, "I just have to show you what I bought. I don't want to make a scene, so I'm just going to open up my purse."

Inside was a sixteen-karat emerald ring surrounded by diamonds.

"Is it too much?" she asked teasingly.

I adored her on the spot. Of course it was too much. But it was hilarious and she knew it.

"I can't help but notice your necklace, too," I said. It was about 15 diamond eternity bands on a chain.

Linda Thompson

"All my dead boyfriends," she said, tugging at them. "Bless their little hearts." (In her "exaggerated" southern drawl.)

And even though this is the Elvis chapter, if I'm talking about Linda Thompson, I'm talking about Bruce Jenner's ex-wife. All the girls in our group knew Bruce wanted to be a woman. It was common knowledge for more than 15 years among us. To Linda's credit, she NEVER outed him directly; she never initiated any discussions.

Bruce revealed his desire to transition early on in Linda's marriage, but after their two sons were born. She was devastated.

She didn't want a divorce, but there was no other choice. She also handled her sons by Bruce exceptionally well, always trying to put Bruce in the best light and salvage their relationship with him.

BLESS HER BIG HEART.

And, Elvis, you really lost three great women. What a shame.

Chapter Eight

PERRY COMO—MY FATHER'S FAVORITE SINGER. AND MY?

Perry Como? Why on earth would I be writing about Perry Como, a man who not only was my father's favorite singer, but my father's age! Every week my father would sit there and watch *The Perry Como Show* and I would be bored out of my mind.

And then one day I met Perry. He was the cutest, cuddliest teddy bear with the sweetest eyes. There was magnetism in person that never was captured by the TV screen.

I was at a press party for one of his TV specials and something just clicked when we met. I was just out of college. He was "theoretically" OLD. He was married. He had children. But he didn't look old to me. He was almost angelic. We talked for a while, and then he was whisked away. That was ok. He was working and needed to talk to everybody at the party.

About a month later I received a call at my office desk.

"Hello, this is Mickey, Perry Como's road manager. Mr. Como is coming into town and he'd like to send a car for you around 6 p.m. Where will you be?"

I gave him my home address and hung up. My heart started pounding. This was far too adult for me. *What was going to happen?* I had no experience in this sort of thing.

The car arrived on time and took me to the Beverly Hills Hotel. Mickey was in the lobby to greet me. "Perry's waiting in his bungalow for you."

His bungalow? Oh, God.

I was ushered into his living room and saw a table for two set up. Perry immediately stood up from the couch and greeted me with a kiss on the cheek. There was a full bar and a menu ready.

Whew! I thought. Dinner. Good. I can do this.

Mickey left us alone right away. I have no idea where he went.

I have no memory of our conversation or what we ate. I simply remember the mixed feelings of terror and excitement.

When dinner was over I didn't know what to do. God bless Perry. He could see I was an inexperienced, lovesick kid. He took my hand and led me to the bedroom. Now I realize I could have protested, choked, fainted, whatever, but I just glided along with him. He was wearing slacks and a sweater. I was wearing clothes. That's all I know.

The bedroom was so large that it had a sitting area, and that's where he took me. We sat on the couch in front of a TV and he said, "Let's watch some TV." I was so very grateful that that's what he did. He took off his shoes and put his feet on the table and I did the same. We found a show we liked and then he took my hand held it for the next two hours. He knew I was afraid, and he wasn't pushing for anything.

After a couple of hours it was clear that it was time for me to leave just because it was the right thing to do. We put our shoes on and got up. He walked me to the door and pulled me to him. I was right. He was a cuddly bear. It felt so good in his arms. And then we kissed. And kissed. I loved it. He was gentle and sexy at the same time.

When the kisses ended, Mickey materialized out of nowhere, and took me to the car.

This pattern of Mickey calling and sending a car each time Perry was in town continued for about two years. I remember being in Perry's dressing room at CBS when he was shooting a Christmas special, and his coming into the dressing room in between takes just to kiss me. I must say it was a little weird making-out with Perry and then watching him sing "Ave Maria." I remember hearing the word around town that I was "Perry's Girl," and being treated differently by his producers. It didn't feel cheap.

My favorite time of all with Perry was in November of 1970. A car picked me up and brought me to Capitol Records Studios.

Perry surprised me by bringing me to his recording session. When I arrived he was in the studio with the musicians. As soon as he saw me he came in and whispered, "This is for you."

My heart melted. He walked into the studio, stood at the microphone and cued the orchestra. And then he sang, "It's Impossible." *Oh my God.* My heart still aches every time I hear it.

I remember another time when he was shooting a special at NBC, and I asked him if I could bring my parents to watch him shoot. I couldn't believe that I was going to give my father (doctor, not Biodad) the gift of meeting his favorite singer.

Just before we got to the studio, Perry fell from a set and hurt himself. By the time I got to him he was in a wheelchair and I was suddenly at his feet, holding his hand, asking if he was ok. I'd forgotten we were in public AND MY PARENTS WERE THERE!

He assured me he would be ok and said he was going to be x-rayed and not to worry. Mickey showed up and wheeled him away. He gave me a look like, "I'll get back to you."

And then my mother said, "Well, dear. How long has this been going on?"

Oops.

Chapter Nine

VERONICA LAKE A MYSTERIOUS BLONDE TO NEVER FORGET

Veronica Lake was one of those mysterious 40s movie stars, very sexy, and famous for her long, blonde hair that covered one eye. It was called her "Peek a Boo" hairstyle. She had an amazing career for ten or more years, and then disappeared from sight. The only reason I knew who she was, was that my mother would watch her movies sometimes. Even at a young age, I could spot that star quality.

Cut to 1970, and Veronica Lake had come out with a book about her life. Naturally, since I had a reputation of being a respectful journalist, and one who not only knew stars from all eras, but would treat them well and write a beautiful story, I was asked to interview her. This time the interview was at Musso and Frank's restaurant in Hollywood. I usually did interviews at Musso's, The Brown Derby, and The Beverly Hills Hotel.

Musso and Frank's opened in 1919, and I had been going there since I was a child who could barely walk. I was known there by the owners, all the waiters, and every bus boy. My father started taking me there on weekends when he visited me. It was one block away from the Las Palmas Theatre (which my father owned), and was very convenient.

The restaurant had all dark wood booths, faded landscape wallpaper, and a brass coat rack at every other red leather booth. It looked like a restaurant in New York in the 20s, and it has never changed to this day.

This has absolutely nothing to do with Veronica Lake, but everything to do with Musso's. Thanks to my father, I loved restaurants. My haunts were his haunts—Chasen's, Musso's, Greenblatt's Delicatessen, and Ah Fong's, the Chinese restaurant next door to

Greenblatt's. Ah Fong's was owned by the actor Benson Fong—think number one son in the *Charlie Chan* movies. Benson's waiters were out-of-work actors like Harold Fong, who also ended up in whatever Chinese movie was shot in Hollywood.

My father was always doing deals, but I never noticed because he set me up doing an activity while his meeting was going on. For instance, at Ah Fong's I would sit in the kitchen with Harold and the other waiter/actors, and shell Chinese peapods. At Musso's I was at the stove watching them make flannel cakes.

A flannel cake is a paper-thin crepe-like pancake the size of a dinner plate. They were so thin, that an order consisted of three of them on top of each other on the plate. They were doused with melted butter and served with a separate silver container of warm maple syrup on the side.

There were two tricks with flannel cakes:
1. Make sure the batter was thin enough or the cake would be doughy
2. Ask for extra melted butter so you could lift up each pancake and distribute butter and warm syrup evenly.

I had been going to Musso's since I was two years old, and flannel cakes were my favorite. I still eat them today.

One day, when I was about ten or eleven, I ordered the flannel cakes. They were brought to the table and I said to my father, "They don't look right."

"What do you mean? he asked.

I tasted them.

"They are too doughy. They were made by a different chef. I don't want them."

My father called the manager over to the table. He was our buddy. "Susie says the flannel cakes are different."

"No, sir. They are the same," said the manager.

"No they're not," I said, in my most adult voice. "They're too thick. It's not the same recipe."

"But it is," continued the manager.

"Then it's not the same chef," I said. I WAS TEN, MIND YOU!

And then the manager looked down at the floor for a second and took a breath. "I can't believe this. Our chef died ten days ago, and not one customer has noticed the difference until now. We didn't want to alarm our customers because the chef was so loved. Your daughter is the only customer we couldn't fool."

By the way, I still have the "Palate of Death."

Veronica Lake was sitting at a table with her press agent. She had on no makeup, wore a scarf over her head, and she was wearing a grey sweatsuit. Gone was the slinky femme fatale who steamed up the screen. In its place was a woman who very clearly had abused alcohol horribly and led a miserable life, and now some kid in her early twenties was doing an interview.

"I hated Hollywood. I hated that they made me wear my hair that way. I wasn't a person, I was a commodity," said Veronica. "I was being suffocated here and I had to get out."

"I understand completely," I replied. And I did, because I had been studying stories about Kim Novak, my favorite movie star, since 1956, and I knew the routine. It was not unusual for Hollywood to take young blondes with the magic and then try to coop them up.

She was so grateful that I "got her."

"I was afraid to do this interview. You're so young to even know who I was. Sometimes I wonder if anyone remembers me," continued this fragile, terrified bird.

"I've seen ALL your movies. *I Married a Witch* was my favorite," I answered.

"Mine too!" She smiled her first smile and I could see her eyes start to come alive just a little bit.

She was forty-seven at the time of the interview and looked like she was in her 70s. That's what alcohol does to people. My heart was breaking, but at the same time I was so happy that I was giving her some joy. I think Veronica Lake was one of the most broken human beings I've ever seen.

"You know, I'm getting my star on the Hollywood Walk of Fame right after lunch," said Veronica, with some delight. "Would you like to be there with me?"

"Of course! I'd love to."

When lunch was over, we walked down the street to where the star ceremony was. For those of you who don't know, the star ceremony is a big deal, with fans all over the sidewalk cheering the star, an emcee on a microphone introducing other stars and dignitaries, tons of photographers, and the star surrounded by friends and family. After the speeches and the unveiling, there is a big celebratory reception.

Veronica and I arrived at her star. Standing next to it was the announcer from *Laugh-In*, Gary Owens. There was NO ONE else there except for me. It was the saddest Hollywood event I've ever

Veronica Lake gets her star with Gary Owens
and me by her side.

witnessed. Veronica Lake was a star with the same stature as Marilyn Monroe or Lauren Bacall, but it was 1970, not 1940, and she was all but forgotten.

We looked at the star and then at each other. Gary congratulated her. One photographer, the only one to show up, asked us to kneel down on the star. Gary, Veronica, and I knelt down and a photo was snapped. That's it. End of ceremony.

Now what?

Veronica reached into her purse and brought out a copy of her book.

"I want to sign this for you."

"Please," I said.

She wrote: *Dear Sue, Here's hoping our first meeting won't be our last. Love, Veronica.*

She was dead of alcoholism three years later. We never saw each other again.

Chapter Ten

MOTOWN MAGIC, MADNESS, AND MURDER

I have always felt I was a Supreme, a Temp, a Top, a Vandella you name it. I think, for a certain generation, we all fantasized we were members of those groups. We would secretly dance in our homes, perfecting the moves. There's a reason wedding DJs and bands always use Motown in their repertoires. No matter what the age, if the party is lagging, put on some Motown and it will jump to life.

But, as usual, this kid, because of being a reporter, got right into the middle of Motown.

Let me say that Berry Gordy is an absolute genius, both in musical taste and marketing. Let me also tell you, that when Motown started to hit it big in the U.S., Berry couldn't break into the British market at all. The singer Dusty Springfield, a huge Motown fan, headlined an engagement at the Brooklyn Fox Theatre and was introduced to the "supporting acts" like Martha and The Vandellas. Dusty also had her own weekly variety show on the BBC then (one of many), and could do whatever she wanted. She was as big a star in England and Europe as Michael Jackson was at his zenith. They had to book who she said. The first person she insisted on booking was Jimi Hendrix. No one had ever heard of him there. But then after she saw the whole Motown sound in Brooklyn, and loved it so much, she returned to England and ordered the BBC to do an entire Dusty Does Motown Special. She broke Motown worldwide.

My personal introduction to Motown was when The Supremes came to town to promote their first new single. I was still at KFWB radio then, the top rock station in LA. At that time, record companies ORDERED artists to go to the top radio stations in each city they visited to promote their records. They would meet with the DJs, program director, and, in the case of KFWB, me, so I could interview them and take pictures.

I liked Diana, Mary, and Florence. They were so new that each thing they experienced in Hollywood was like watching them taste ice cream for the first time. KFWB was located on Hollywood Blvd., and they had never seen it before. After our brief introductory interview was over, I offered to show them Hollywood Blvd. They just wanted to walk around and see the stores.

Off I went, now considering myself the "Fourth Supreme," as we hung out and went shopping. There we were, walking along Hollywood Blvd. with no bodyguards or security. People recognized them and waved, but it was just fun. What an innocent time. No guns, no celebrity assassinations, no stupid TMZ or the Internet.

"Look! There's Frederick's of Hollywood," exclaimed Diana. "We've got to go in there!"

Frederick's was infamous as a lingerie store for hookers. Really. They had lace panties with no crotches, a few tasteful whips in pastel colors...crazy wigs...well, you get the drift.

In we went. The girls went wild. They loved it. They were grabbing lingerie and teasing each other and giggling like the kids they/ we all were.

Then we hit the wig department. Remember all those Supremes wigs? Well, they thought it would be funny to try the Frederick's wigs on me. Within seconds they had found a duplicate of the Diana "bobb" wig and placed it on my head. I looked "just like her."

"I want it," I said. "I just have to wear it right now."

I walked out of the store wearing that wig and "joined the group."

A couple of days later, I was to do the official interview. They were staying at a hotel called The Beverly Hills Comstock. I knew it wasn't really in Beverly Hills. It was on Wilshire Blvd., more toward the suburb of Westwood, but the hotel was close enough to Beverly Hills to appropriate the title in its name. It really was a glorified motel, comprised of a few stories built around a pool. They had chaises and round tables with umbrellas and food service outside. When I arrived, Diana, Mary, and Florence were sitting under an umbrella having lunch. They had on makeup, sunglasses, and extravagant bathing suit cover-ups. They looked every inch the part of "Hollywood stars," and they were basking in it.

They never knew they weren't in Beverly Hills. They weren't aware their hotel wasn't the real Beverly Hills Hotel. I was going to do nothing to burst their bubble. As someone who had been born and raised in Los Angeles, and been going to the real Beverly Hills Hotel since I was a child, I wanted them to have their moment. I was really happy for them. They were just ecstatic that they had "made it"—at least to them, this was "making it." The future of true suites at hotels like the Ritz in Paris or entire floor of Caesars Palace in Las Vegas were not even in their lexicon as yet. They were kids from the projects who never, ever thought they'd really make it out. Bravo to them.

The rest of the Motown gang, namely the groups—The Temptations, the Four Tops, The Miracles, etc. were forced to play black nightclubs longer than the Supremes. It was easier to break out three pretty women into the white arena. Motown invited me to all the shows of their acts, and I would frequently find myself in scary areas of town. I didn't care because I had front-table seats to watch up close the amazing Temptations and Four Tops. I was insane about their songs and choreography, and would watch show after show. All of those men were very nice to me and treated me with the same respect I gave them. I loved their artistry. I was never that wild about Smokey Robinson and The Miracles. They just didn't do it for me. They were too "soft" for me.

I also loved Marvin Gaye and Tammi Terrell. The writing team of Nick Ashford and Valerie Simpson wrote their hits like "Ain't No Mountain High Enough" and "You're All I Need." When Tammi Terrell died suddenly from a brain aneurysm, the rumor was that she was beaten badly during an argument by Temptation lead singer David Ruffin, and that he was responsible for her death. I hated him from that moment on. It was later revealed that Tammi had always had brain issues from birth. HOWEVER, the beating, in my opinion, exacerbated what was there and strongly contributed to her death. God took care of David. He died of a cocaine overdose a few years later.

Note: "Ain't No Mountain High Enough" was written by Nick Ashford and Valerie Simpson for Dusty Springfield. Once Berry heard it, he forbade them to send it to her. He wanted it for "his" Diana.

One day, I got an invitation from Diana Ross to come to The Daisy, a private club in Beverly Hills. She was introducing a new act she wanted people to see. Of course I went. It was the Jackson Five. It was the first time they had ever sung for a live Hollywood audience.

Note: Nothing to do with Motown, but I also received an invitation from Atlantic Records to go to the back room of the nightclub Studio One, to see their introduction of a new singer named Bette Midler. Little did they know I'd seen her at the Continental Baths in New York City. That night at Studio One, Bette literally became a Hollywood Star. The same thing happened when I was invited to the very first shows of Carole King, Steve Martin, James Taylor, and Elton John at the Troubadour. How lucky I was to have experienced that history first hand.

At another point in my Motown saga, I received an invitation to the "Sweet Sixteen" party for Berry Gordy's daughter, Hazel, at Berry's house in Beverly Hills. I didn't even know her, so I figured it was just going to be a big blow-out with lots of press. I was right. The house and grounds were filled with people she didn't know. I think she had at least a few friends her age there. It was mostly a tax-deductible promotion party for Motown. I remember that most of the party was outside, and there were floats in the pool made out of flowers and candles. It was very beautiful. Most of the guests were not allowed in the house. I noticed some security guards around. I had fun hanging with other members of the press who were cool, as well as some of the Motown people. It was just your "average" Hollywood party.

At the climax of the party, all the guests were asked to go to the front gate by the street. Berry escorted Hazel down the driveway and, parked at the end, for all of us to see, was a brand new T-Bird. It was really hot and Hazel was thrilled.

Once that gift was given, it signaled the end of the party, and most of the guests lingered by the car and waited for the valets to deliver their cars. I have no idea why I didn't give my ticket to the valet to get my car. Instead, I walked back into the pool area. What a fateful choice.

Almost no one was in the backyard. I truly can't remember why I went back. Maybe I was hungry or thirsty and wanted a little something before leaving, I don't know. Within a couple of minutes I heard a commotion by the house. I was at least 200 feet away, but I heard loud, agitated voices. I don't remember hearing any screams. Then some guard ran past me as fast as he could go.

"What's happening?" I asked loudly.

"There's been a murder," he yelled.

Swell. There I was, alone by the pool. The reporter in me wanted to go as close to the house as I could. What an exclusive! But my survival instinct kicked in and I thought maybe I'd just better slowly edge my way back to the gate and get out.

By the time I got back to the gate, the few people left noticed that something was very wrong. I saw the guard talk to the lead parking guy and then head back to the house. There were some other press people there, but they just weren't as on the job as I was. I went over to the parking guy and asked him what he knew. He said that some young man working there had just stabbed the houseman to death. I'm saying stabbed, because I never heard any shots, and I think stabbing was what I remembered at the time. It was over forty years ago, so don't hold me to the actual method of death. But the man was dead, and dead is dead.

The next morning, I raced to the office at my usual nine a.m. time and wrote my column. The headline was something like "Murder at Berry Gordy's Party." Mind you, I also wrote great things about the party and how pretty Hazel's T-Bird was. It was simply a factual account of a party that just happened to end in a murder. I had never been to one of those before!

My column came out on the east coast about five or six a.m. the next day. I always read the *Los Angeles Times* before I went to the office, and I was surprised there was no mention of the murder. By the time I showed up for work at nine a.m. west coast time, my phone was ringing off the hook.

"Sue Cameron," I answered.

"This is George Stromberg calling from Motown. Mr. Gordy is very unhappy this morning."

First, for purposes of this book, George Stromberg is a fake name, but I'll stick with it. "George" was the Motown enforcer. The Jewish mafia bought a huge interest in Motown when they needed an infusion of cash, and George was put in place as a vice-president. I had actually met him at parties and liked him very much. He was funny and charming.

"I'm sorry to hear that Mr. Gordy is unhappy. I had a really nice time at the party," I said.

"Did you happen to notice there was no mention of the incident in any paper or on any TV or radio station?" asked George.

"I saw it wasn't in the *Times*, and I thought it was odd, but I didn't pay any more attention."

"Well, Sue, we thought we got to all the press outlets to kill the story, but we forgot about the trade papers and you ran it. Now it's out there. Mr. Gordy insists that you have lunch with me today. He would appreciate it if you would cancel anything else you had planned. Do you understand me?"

Yikes, I thought to myself.

"Where would you like to meet? I asked, praying that it would be a public place so I wouldn't meet the same fate at the houseman.

"Meet me at Harry's Bar in Century City at one p.m."

"OK."

Oh, God. Now what?

Needless to say, I was a little apprehensive going into Harry's Bar. It was not the first time that George and I had had lunch. I always had a good time with him, but never forgot his position and duties for Motown. He was waiting for me when I got there, smiling, standing up and extending his hand. We made some polite conversation and then he switched the subject.

"Remember that song from *Mahogany* (1975) that Diana sang called 'Do You Know Where You're Going to?'" he asked.

"Of course," I replied. "I love that song."

"Do you remember that originally the Motion Picture Academy wouldn't allow it to be nominated? They said it wasn't eligible because of some rule?"

"Yes," I answered again.

"Do you remember that for the first time in the history of the Academy they held a special meeting and changed the rule so the song could be nominated?"

"I do. That was quite amazing," I said.

"Yes, it was," replied George. "Some legs were broken, but we got it done."

Hail Mary, Full of Grace ran through my head. I said nothing. And then George continued with a smile.

"We at Motown want to think of you as a friend. We don't like surprises like what happened in your column. Can we think of you as our friend from now on? It would make us very happy to feel that way."

Without any hesitation I said, "Motown can always think of me as a friend. I promise you."

And then he ordered grilled swordfish for both of us. I tried so hard to eat that "friendly fish."

Forty-eight hours later, a gigantic, beautifully wrapped present arrived at my office. It must have been four-foot by four-foot square. I opened the card and it said, "From your friends at Motown."

It was a brand new, state-of-the-art biggest TV set made at the time. I took it home.

One month later, another box arrived from Motown. I think this time it was a stereo or tape recorder or something cool electronic. These "friendly" monthly gifts went on for years and years. They eventually calmed down from big items like electronics and jewelry, to advance copies of all their records. They also never missed a Christmas as well.

Eventually, George died of natural causes. I still really liked him and was sorry he was gone.

Note: LITTLE SUSIE AND "THE MOB"

In addition to what you've just read, the first time I met a mobster was when I was about eight. His name was Mickey Cohen, and he "owned" Los Angeles. My father was friendly with him because he worked for the mob lawyer, Jerry Geisler.

One night when Mickey and my father were coming out of a supper club/bar on the Sunset Strip, Mickey was shot at in a drive-by. Mickey was wounded and my father hid behind a car. That did not deter his friendship with Mickey. I first met him at Schwab's Pharmacy on the Sunset Strip where all the actors and stars hung out. All I remember is that he had on a light-colored suit and a fedora. He was nice to me.

The next time I saw him was when I was ten or eleven, and my father took me to a strip joint to see Mickey's girlfriend, Liz Renay, and his other girlfriend, "Miss Beverly Hills," perform.

Yes, that's how my divorced father spent his custody time with me.

Years later, when Paramount announced it was going to film The Godfather (1972), it was a huge deal. I was at The Hollywood Reporter. One thing a movie company never wants is for a reporter to print a scoop before they are ready to announce. My source called me about five minutes after Diane Keaton was cast. Almost every actress in Hollywood wanted that part. I put it on the front page right away. We went to press, and the next morning I had scooped everyone. Paramount was furious. They called me; they sent letters. Too bad for them. I did my job.

What they didn't know is that my source was Mario Puzo, the author of The Godfather himself. A friend of mine was having an affair with the married Mario, and I was at his house in Malibu (which Paramount paid for) all the time.

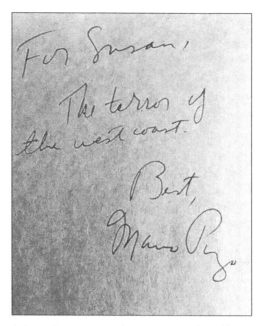

Mario Puzo wrote this to me. I adored him.

Mario kept me abreast of all the happenings. According to Mario, the LA mob was very unhappy they had no control over the movie, but the Teamsters Union did because they represented many of the crew members. The Teamsters threatened to strike and stop the movie unless a "made man, i.e. mob member" who was an actor was cast in the movie to keep an eye on things. Paramount acquiesced and cast a guy in a pretty big part who was, indeed, a member of the mob. I will not tell you his name.

At the end of shooting, when Mario's lease was up on his house. He had to go back to New York. Just before he left, he gave me the red plastic Olympia portable typewriter on which he wrote "The Godfather." Wow!

Several years later, after I'd had three books published, some "questionable" people came to me about writing a book on mafia wives who become heads of the families because their husbands are in jail. It was a great idea, and I wrote the book. When the book draft was "shopped around" at a very famous book convention in Europe, the Italians found out about it and killed it. No publisher would buy it.

Word of that "killed book" got around, and one day I received a call from an agent I knew asking if he could take me to lunch. I said yes, and met him a few days later. The conversation was benign in the beginning and I couldn't figure out why I was there.

"Listen. There's something I want to talk to you about. I know what happened in Italy. I represent Donnie Brasco, the FBI under-cover agent who joined the mob. I'm sure you saw the movie."

"Yes, I did."

"I'd like to put you on the phone with him because I think a book should be written about his wife and what she went through when he was undercover. I'd like him to let you go to their house and interview her. He's a little hesitant about letting his wife do it, and I thought that if you both talked, he'd see how legitimate and smart you are, and you'd only do something worthwhile."

Yikes, I thought.

"He still has death threats, so he uses different names and untraceable phones. I'm going to give you a number that is only good on Wednesday from noon to three p.m. Los Angeles time. Call it. Identify yourself and ask for Mr. Richards, said the agent.

"OK. What's the number," I said, my knees knocking.

Before Wednesday came, I talked to some friends and advisors and everyone told me not to do it. It was more like, "Are you insane? There are hits out on these people!"

I called the number. A very gruff voice answered the phone and said he was in an airport and he only had a few minutes to talk. I had almost no time to even get into the subject.

"Look. My wife is very nervous and she's changed her mind. She doesn't want to do this. I don't want her to do this. Do you under-stand? We are not doing this," said "Mr. Richards."

"I certainly do understand, and thank you for your good work with the FBI."

Then I hung up the phone and noticed the beads of sweat at my temples.

Chapter Eleven

CAROLE KING THE QUEEN

Carole King has the biggest ego of anyone I've ever known. When you first meet her you can actually see her wait for you to say, "You are the greatest contemporary songwriter who ever lived. " And you know what? She is. And, I was happy to say it. Her ego is well-warranted.

Some time in the very late 80s, I received call from the premiere public relations guru, Pat Kingsley. She told me that Carole King wanted to become an actress, and asked if I could advise her. Duh.

Carole King truly is a musical talent beyond all expectations. Of course I would meet her. We met in a tiny open-air market in Venice, California. Wooden tables were set up in the parking lot, and waitresses came by to take your order from all the fresh product. It was very "Carole King."

Even though Carole came from a traditional middle-class New York Jewish city upbringing, she was, and is, a genuine hippie. She's the real deal. She worries about the environment and many other causes, and puts her money and power where her mouth is. She's the most organic person I've ever known.

We were polar opposites. I want caviar, not granola. But we connected on the level of music and art. When her hands touched piano keys, my soul melted. She has such strong hands. At one point I just asked her to let me photograph them on the keys. The pictures were very special.

I can remember one day being in her apartment on Riverside Drive in New York, and she wanted to try out a new song. Her hands hit the chords and I couldn't help but say, "Those are Carole King chords." Those of you who know her music understand exactly what

Carole in front of the infamous Tower Records when her album was released.

I'm saying. So did Carole. She was very aware of her talent and what was specific and unique to her. Unmistakable chords; unmistakable voice. Incomparable composing.

To be in Carole's inner circle was to be awakened in the middle of the night when she would call from her Idaho ranch, or wherever she was, with the words, "I just wrote this. Let me know what you think." Then through the phone would come that artistry being played just for you. It was stunning, and a privilege.

Regarding her acting, Carole took lessons and was quite serious. Any casting director, executive, or producer I called would meet with her. Naturally, she's Carole King! But those meetings rarely translated into parts. Carole did a couple of small movie parts, and a play in Los Angeles, and she was good!

The pinnacle of her acting career was when she starred in the musical, *Blood Brothers*, on Broadway. She was just terrific.

My favorite time was when Carole was asked by the women's prison in Frontera, California to go sing. I deliberately didn't tell her that I'd been there many times visiting the Manson Girls. As we drove up she told me she was very nervous. I told her it would be all right.

We were met by a different warden, who didn't recognize me, thank God.

"Where are we going?" asked Carole.

"We're just going to one classroom and you can just take out your guitar and sing a couple of songs," he answered.

"Are there murderers in the class?" continued Carole.

"Yes," answered the warden.

Carole shot me a look of panic.

After going through the process of purse searching, wanding, and metal detectors, we were led to the classroom.

Carole walked in and everybody applauded. When the applause died down, two girls from the back shouted, "Hi, Sue!"

Carole in front of the women's prison the day she met the Manson girls.

Carole's jaw dropped and she looked at me like she'd seen a ghost.

"What was that?' she asked.

"Oh, it's just the Manson Girls saying hello to me."

I'm surprised she didn't drop her guitar.

Along the way in this acting journey, Carole decided to make another album. She had met, on Broadway, a very sexy talented young man named Paul Hipp. He turned Carole on to really studying electric guitar and being a little more "rock." She was having a great time, and she asked me to work on that project.

We ended up at Capitol Records, and the album was called *City Streets*. It was not my favorite, because I don't think it was the true Carole. I think she was heavily influenced by Hipp and lost sight of herself.

Carole had an idea to shoot the album cover in Harlem. She really wanted to break that softer hippie stereotype, so, off to Harlem we went IN A LUXURY MOTORHOME! Yes, we were very conspicuous in that thing, parked in a terrifying area. We had hair and makeup people, plus the photographer and his staff, all standing in front of crumbling brownstones, with overgrown weeds.

I cannot tell you how uncomfortable I was. We reeked of money and privilege. I thought we were going to be shot any second. I remember looking down on the ground and seeing tiny white and blue plastic objects. There were so many that it almost looked like snow. I asked someone what they were.

"Crack vials," he replied.

Oh my God.

During all of these adventures, Carole welcomed me into her personal and musical families twenty-four hours a day. I think she knew I felt like an outsider, but she was inclusive and warm, and I tried so hard to be comfortable with bass players sitting on cement. Whatever. I did my best.

The time came to set up the publicity for her album. Capitol Records had a good department, and my experience in setting up campaigns was quite extensive. We had offers from every major TV show and magazine because it had been several years since a new Carole King album had been released. I was thrilled!

I remember approaching Carole in the studio with the good news of this publicity avalanche and she said, "I'm turning everything down."

I couldn't believe what I was hearing. There was no way the album would be successful. She was signing a death warrant, because it was 1989, not 1970. Everybody had to promote his or her product.

"But I saw Paul McCartney on *The Today Show* yesterday plugging his new album," I said, hopefully.

"My fans will come to ME," said Carole defiantly, displaying that well-deserved, but in this case, not well-served ego.

The album died on the spot. Shortly after, so did our business dealings. I was sad about it, because I loved her talent and I enjoyed our time together.

A few years later, Carole was being Carole again, and she signed with the music manager Peter Asher and went on the road again doing what she does best. I was so happy for her. She deserves every accolade.

A SPECIAL NOTE:

Dusty Springfield was Carole's favorite singer. She told me many times that Dusty was the best interpreter of her songs she'd ever heard. When Dusty was struggling with breast cancer, Carole and Carole Bayer Sager wrote about five songs for Dusty to sing. I got a call from Carole (King) asking me to send the demos to Dusty and see if she would record them. I told her Dusty was getting weaker. Carole said that she would set up an entire studio in Dusty's house and come over to London and produce the songs herself. She told me that her biggest dream was recording a duet with Dusty.

I received the demos and listened before I sent them to Dusty. I couldn't stop crying. The songs were so beautiful and so perfect. I decided to send them to her with a note so she'd get a surprise in the mail. I called the day after I knew the CD would arrive to give her time to hear them.

I told her on the phone how much I loved the songs and asked if she was happy with them.

"I haven't listened to them. It makes me too sad." And then she paused, and I heard her try to compose herself. "I can't sing anymore," said Dusty, one of the greatest voices in the history of music. Her breast cancer was very advanced now, and I wanted to curl up and die with her at this news.

"You know that Carole (King) wants to come over to your house and set up so it's easy for you," I said, trying not to cry with her (yet).

"I am terrified to meet her," said Dusty. "Her talent is mindboggling. Even if I could still sing, I'd be afraid because she would be there. I wouldn't have been able to do it anyway."

Carole was devastated by the news. I've never recovered from losing Dusty.

Chapter Twelve

SONNY AND CHER WE ALL PLAYED IN THE SAME SANDBOX

When Cher was under fourteen years of age, she would sit in her school daily, dreaming of a better future. She lived in the San Fernando Valley, a lower class area of Southern California. By the way, there are both good and bad areas of the valley, although some people like to think there are no good areas (except for Hidden Hills and Calabasas areas). At any rate, Cher lived in a really bad area.

Her very beautiful showgirl mother named Georgia, much married and much loved, had Cher with some Armenian guy named Sarkissian. He never stayed around. Georgia and Cher were very close, and when Georgeanne, a new little sister came along, the three were just as close. Georgeanne's father was a Mr. La Pier. No one ever saw him, but both girls took his last name because it was a nice one. However, all of the financial and parental responsibility was on Georgia. It was a very difficult life for them.

All Cher ever wanted to do was be a star. She practiced signing her autograph on page after page of her lined school paper.

Now picture me at one of the top schools in Los Angeles with parents who kept asking me, "Would you like to be a lawyer or a doctor?" I had a phenomenal back-up network of family support, and I was going to go to USC, one of the best private universities in the country.

But, my mother was also like Cher's mother, Georgia. She was a hot number and ended up having four husbands by the time she died at ninety-five. My biodad was a theatrical producer and lawyer, and my step-dad was an obstetrician gynecologist. I was lucky, because my mother's marriage to the doctor lasted forty-six years, and I had tremendous personal and financial stability. Cher was not so lucky.

Here's what happened in 1965:

I was in my senior year at USC and was a journalism major. I was one of the section editors of the *Daily Trojan*, and life was cool. For fun, once a week I went to KHJ-TV to dance on a show called *Hollywood a Go Go*, an *American Bandstand*-type show hosted by a DJ named Sam Riddle. On *Hollywood a Go Go*, people who had hit records would come on the show and lip sync their hits. This weekly crazy music escape from USC amused me highly. It was a whole different world from sororities and football games. I still dressed, of course, like a woman lawyer, even though I was dancing on a hip show. All my clothes came from the snobby, exclusive store Bullock's Wilshire.

The show was live, so everyone always showed up an hour early. One day I saw two "creatures" walk in. It was a young man and girl dressed in bobcat fur vests, jeans that were tied at the waist, and some kind of Indian boots on their feet. They also had on headbands. The guy's hair was almost as long as the girl's jet-black straight hair. The girl had a slightly large nose and crooked teeth, but you could tell she was something special immediately.

No one in the room would talk to them. We had never seen anything like them. The girl kept grabbing the boy's hand for reassurance. I found out their names were Sonny and Cher, and they had a local hit record called "Baby Don't Go" that was beginning to pick up some national traction. I knew the record and liked it.

They looked liked nice "fish-out-of-water" people to me. To this day, I still feel that way about the real Cher—total fish out of water no matter where she is. Sonny overcame that.

As weird as I thought they looked, the girl had style. There was just something about her. I decided to go over to say hello. Not one person had gone near them since they arrived.

"Hi, my name's Sue. I think your belt is really cool."
"Thanks," said Cher, looking down.
"And my name's Sonny," he said, offering me his hand.
"I just realized 'Baby Don't Go' is yours. I like the song."
"I wrote it," said Sonny proudly.

"Cher, where are you from? Are you LA people?"

"Yeah. I used to be in the Valley, but me and Son (HER grammar, I assure you) just got an apartment in Hollywood. It's like a dream."

"I'm so happy for you. Have you ever been on TV before? You seem a little nervous," I asked Cher.

"I want to throw up. I'm not kidding."

"Do you want me to show you where the bathroom is here?"

"Yep."

And that's how it all started—over vomit. And it wasn't the last time.

Six months later, after my USC graduation, I was at work in my new job. I was the editor of the first underground music newspaper—The KFWB *Hitline*. Ironically, it was the rival radio station to KHJ where I danced. I was also now on KHJ's live Saturday night TV show, *Ninth Street West*, doing a rock and roll gossip report because I ran into everyone who ever had a hit record almost on a daily basis. First, because the actual recording artists themselves had to come by the radio station to personally thank all the DJs for playing their records, and second, as part of my job I went to every TV taping of all the rock shows such as *Shebang, Shivaree, Shindig*—so many. Everyone knew the kid with the notepad and camera, and I knew them.

One morning as I arrived at work, I walked through the lobby of KFWB and I saw Sonny sitting and waiting. He was just in jeans, a white t-shirt, and a jean jacket. Sonny's other job was what's called a "record promotion man." He had to meet each week and bring all the new single records and personally play them to every program director of every rock station in Los Angeles.

"I can't believe you're still doing this job, " I said.

"I'm not giving up this job yet. Cher and I need the steady money. I'm recording some stuff with her alone, too. We just did a Byrds cover called 'All I Really Wanna Do.' She sounds great on it. Tonight we're cutting a song called 'I Got You Babe.' I think it could be the one. I'll bring you copies. I can't quit this until I know we're safe."

Sonny, Cher, and me—kids in the same sandbox.

Sonny and I got along well. He was a sensible businessman. He was unrefined, a total bull-in-a-china-shop, but he knew how to get the job done. I always liked him because he was unpretentious and never forgot that he was a truck driver from a very tacky Los Angeles blue-collar suburb. When he died and I sat in front of the TV watching Cher give her eulogy, it was one of the most surreal moments of my life.

It's funny to me as I write this that I never actually thought the words Cher—Fish out of water; Sonny—Bull in a china shop together. They were true in the beginning and remain true today.

Well, Sonny was right about "I Got You Babe," and even Cher had a hit single on "All I Really Wanna Do." The explosion had happened.

Sonny and Cher's first public appearance was a daytime event held in the parking lot of the Hollywood Palladium Theatre. I think it was just a record signing. By now, Sonny had quit his job as a promotion man, and Cher's "long-lost father" was trying to get into her life. He smelled money and all of a sudden decided to be a "loving father." Cher had security to keep throwing him out. Everyone was very new at everything. It was before the Vegas and big arena years. That was when Sonny made some deal with the mob to own part of Sonny and Cher. At that point, a man named Joe Di Carlo was suddenly everywhere with them.

But, on that day on Hollywood Blvd., in the early years, I was invited to go and sit at Sonny and Cher's table. The truth is, they barely knew anybody, and they knew I was safe. Cher's mother, Georgia, was there that day, and was so proud of her daughter. It was sweet to see. I liked Georgia instantaneously. Sitting at their table that day was almost like sitting at a high school graduation.

The next big deal for them was to do their nightclub act at a club on the Sunset Strip called It's Boss.

It's Boss was actually the old, glamorous, legendary Hollywood nightclub, Ciro's, where I'd actually danced with Gene Kelly at Liza Minnelli's wedding reception to producer Jack Haley, Jr. The club had fallen in disrepair and had closed. Then a couple of promoters put a fast coat of paint on it and began booking rock artists in there. They were trying to take business away from the Whisky a Go Go, and we all knew the club would fail. The first artists I saw there were Ike and Tina Turner and The Ikettes. The promoters were so cheap that they didn't even give patrons tables and chairs. They had couches and pillows everywhere, and I remember sitting right under Tina's nose for that whole, extraordinary show. I was so blessed to repeatedly have had these experiences.

Let's return to Sonny and Cher. They did have an act, but they'd never really played anywhere "big." It's Boss was a big deal. I knew Cher got really nervous before performing live, so when she arrived at her backstage dressing room, I was sitting on the couch waiting for her. She was in a new costume, a navy-blue denim striped suit with hip-hugger pants. I loved it. It looked so cool. Deep down I wanted to look cool like Cher. I also knew it was useless to try because that's not who I was or would ever be.

"Oh!" Cher exclaimed running over to hug me. "I'm so glad you're here. I'm freaking out."

"You have more than one hit record, people are going to love you. You'll feel it the minute you get on stage, I promise. You'll be great."

Then Sonny came in the room and Cher immediately went into the bathroom and locked the door.

"Oh, God," said Sonny.

I had seen this when we'd been on the same TV shows together, so it wasn't unusual. Cher always felt more comfortable locked in bathrooms. Sometimes her best friend, Paulette, might be in there, and sometimes not. This time Cher was in there alone.

The reason this bathroom thing was an issue, is that Cher got tremendous stage fright, usually throwing up before going on, and she would lock herself in the bathroom until, well, until. If she did it before a live TV appearance, she had to come out at a certain time. But this night at It's Boss, it may have been a live nightclub act, but there were no TV cameras there. It wasn't being broadcast. She knew she could be late.

Sonny just walked out of the dressing room. He hated constantly having to beg Cher to come out of the bathroom.

I stayed and told her through the door that I was there in case she needed me. They were supposed to go on at 8:30 p.m. It was now 7:30 p.m. I'd occasionally try to make some casual conversation with Cher through the door, trying to be encouraging. Sonny came in at 7:45 p.m. with a forty-five minute warning. Cher said nothing. Sonny came in every fifteen minutes, yelling louder and getting more agitated each time. Cher would NOT answer him.

Each time he would look at me and just shake his head.

At 8:30 p.m. she was still locked in the bathroom. She was really terrified. It was her first big live show. She knew all the industry people would be there judging her. She wasn't trying to cause any trouble. It was real fear.

Then Sonny burst in like a rocket on fire. "Cher, God damn it! Come out of the damn bathroom! The band's on stage, we're ready to go." And then he knocked on the door, practically beating it down.

Cher was still not answering him.

"OK. That's it! I'm going to go get the guys to knock in this door," screamed Sonny. "I'm not kidding!" He slammed the dressing room door behind him.

I walked over to the door.

"Cher? Listen. He's gone. It's just me here. I know you're scared, but it's going to be ok. It really is. You know you have to come out and do the show. Please open the door," I said.

Cher opened the door, came out and hugged me.

We were standing there chatting when Sonny stormed through the dressing room door with his muscle men.

Without saying a word, Cher walked out of the dressing room with Sonny and me trailing after her.

I took my place next to her mother at a front table. Yes, a table. The couches were gone. The mob "participation" in the Sonny and Cher machine was first being felt.

Their band, led by guitarist Don Peake, struck up the first chords of their opening number, a cover version of "Walkin' the Dog." Cher knew just how to move to that sexy R&B beat, and all eyes were on her. It was their very first big public show and the dye was set—all eyes on Cher and who's that guy standing next to her.

After that, Sonny and Cher not only "owned LA," but, because "I Got You Babe" became a national hit, they were "stars."

The first thing they did was buy a "fancy house." In their mind they bought a mansion, but, instead, what they really bought was a tract house in the valley. They weren't sophisticated enough to know that. They were "REALLY new money," and they went for this all-white house that may or may not have had real marble all over everything. They were so excited about the house that I was invited over to see it.

Everything was white—floors, walls, furniture, light fixtures—it was one of those late 60s houses trying to look expensive—and it was indistinguishable from all the others on the block. There was no way I was going to rain on their parade. They had come from living in absolute dumps, and this was probably the nicest house they'd ever seen. I was genuinely happy for them.

But, of course, some things never change. Sonny was the one who showed me around the house, and when we got to the master bedroom, Cher was there with her best friend, Paulette, and they were packing because Sonny and Cher were going on their first big tour. They were going to do some national TV shows and play some clubs.

And what does that mean? Touring! Cher is terrified. So what happens? Cher and I hug and then she and Paulette lock themselves in the master bathroom because Cher doesn't want to pack, because she doesn't want to go. Truly, I just start laughing. There's that look on Sonny's face again! This time I just leave. Cher doesn't have to go onstage in this case, so, as far as I'm concerned, she can remain happily locked in the bathroom as long as she wishes.

When a rock artist became "hot" in the late 60s, suddenly every person around them became hot. Sonny and Cher's managers, Charlie Greene and Brian Stone got the front tables at clubs on the Strip. Sonny and Cher's driver would drive up and down the Strip, and, if he knew you, he'd just throw a marijuana cigarette in your car as a present. Everything revolved around the Sunset Strip because of the music. Big acts would be playing there or watching other acts play every night. I was there because I was interviewing the acts and reviewing the shows. Did Elmer Valentine, owner of the Whisky, let me in the minute I came to the door and bypass the whole line? Yes.

Power and access came from three areas: you were the rock star; you were the drug dealer; or you were a powerful member of the press. Obviously, I was number three.

I was, and still am, totally against drugs. I once saw a friend of mine light up a marijuana cigarette in his own home, and I picked up the phone and called the police to report him. He grabbed the phone out of my hand and hung up.

"What are you doing? Are you nuts?" he screamed.

"If you smoke that cigarette you will become an addict and end up on heroin," I replied, reciting exactly what I learned in school. And you know what, I still believe marijuana is a gateway drug for addicts.

What I noticed was that the more famous Sonny and Cher became, the less Cher saw of Sonny. She was ecstatic that her dream was coming true, and she much preferred to hang out with her girlfriends in her bedroom. Cher's bedroom always has been where she spends most of her time. And, as time has gone by, and success increased, her bedrooms have also increased in size and design.

The next house they moved to was a truly beautiful "old money" traditional home in Bel Air, a gorgeous, exclusive park-like area near Beverly Hills above Sunset Blvd but not the Strip. It was a home that belonged to the actor Tony Curtis. I was over there because I was invited to a birthday party for Chastity. The Mediterranean home was situated on a lot of land, and, as I recall, the party was a circus theme in the backyard. The home inside was decorated beautifully and traditionally, but it was still comfortable. Cher, more importantly, was also comfortable in this house.

But the Sonny and Cher star was still rising with big Vegas deals, a couple of low-budget movies, and TV shows. It was time for the next house—a legendary mansion called Owlwood in Holmby Hills. One family originally owned the ten acres, but then they sold one of the mansions to actress Jayne Mansfield, who was famous for building her pool in the shape of a heart and having her name written in tile on the bottom. Another home was owned by the swimmer/actress Esther Williams. The family kept the original 12,000 square foot home, but later sold it, ironically, to Tony Curtis. Once again, Sonny and Cher bought a home from Tony Curtis.

Sonny and Cher, Movin' On Up.

Owlwood was a masterpiece that looked like a place where royalty would live. There was so much beautiful wood paneling, curved staircases it looked like a museum. When I was invited to see this house by them, my jaw dropped. They kept it exactly as elegant as it was, but they literally roped off the formal living room with red velvet ropes on stanchions as if it were a museum and you couldn't touch. I doubt they ever went in there. I guarantee you, Cher never came out of her bedroom.

All of their success led to the huge TV hit on CBS, *The Sonny and Cher Show*. My press career kind of followed theirs. When they left rock for TV, so had I. I had become the TV editor and daily columnist for *The Hollywood Reporter*. It was my job to cover all TV shows. We laughed about it.

Sonny and Cher and Carol Burnett both shot their shows at CBS. I was always at Carol's on Fridays because she shot her show then, all in front of an audience. Also on Fridays, Sonny and Cher shot their opening and closings in front of a live audience.

On Wednesdays and Thursdays Sonny and Cher shot all of Cher's solo numbers and the sketches.

I was on both sets weekly for years. Do I have to tell you how many times Cher still locked herself in her dressing room? By this time, Sonny paid no attention at all because he had his own dressing room, away from hers. He also no longer had to go get her. They had stage managers for that. I still laughed about Cher in her room, but I also still had empathy for someone who has such stage fright. It is real for Cher. She was not ever trying to be difficult.

No one in Hollywood was surprised when they got divorced. It is very true that Sonny's hard work and pushiness helped make Cher a star. But, no one can "make" someone a star unless that unique star quality is there in the first place. Cher was really tired of being ordered around and used like a workhorse. She wanted control of her career.

Sonny was lost. His whole life was Cher, and he was smart enough to realize that the entertainment business was not a good place for him to stay. Sonny was a nice guy who had the mentality of the truck-driver, which was that he would work hard and get a check. I know he was absolutely shocked by the success of Sonny and Cher. We would talk about it. Sonny and I always had very honest talks, and I liked him. He wasn't a Harvard man, but he didn't pretend to be. He was a guy off the street who persevered. When he became mayor of Palm Springs, I could see that as a good position for him. He was a man of the people. When he was elected to congress, truthfully, I was horrified.

Now single, Cher moved on to a new Egyptian mansion on Benedict Canyon in Beverly Hills that was perfect for her. She was in her Egyptian goddess persona at that time and it was a match from heaven. Yes, she still spent a lot of time in her bedroom, but she also, out-of-the-blue, decided to have a "garage sale" from so many of the houses and things she had collected over the years. I went to it and bought a fur coat given to her by Gregg Allman. I looked very good in it.

I was also on the set of the taping of Cher's first special with Elton John and Bette Midler. I knew Elton and Bette through Dusty Springfield. The taping of that show was one of those moments in history when each star was at a career zenith. The electricity in that room could have lit up all of Times Square in New York. It was extraordinary to have been in that studio at that moment in time.

One of the biggest reasons that I have kept celebrity friends, is that I am very loyal. So many people try to use celebrities to make money. One time, ABC wanted to make a mini-series about Cher's life. I got a call from them because they knew I had known her for many years. I took the meeting with the ABC executives and found out what they were up to. Then I called Cher and told her about the project. I explained that she was in "public domain" and that they could do it without her permission. However, they wanted her to executive produce.

"Tell them you couldn't reach me," she said, knowing full well that her non-response would kill the project. Smart move on both our parts. It was never made.

Cher has been brilliant about her career. She, herself, will be the first one to tell you that she is an uneducated person in terms of schooling, but she's the smartest "street smart" person I've ever known. She has managed to remain a relevant, Oscar-winning star, and live concert act for seven decades.

And, whenever we see each other we clasp hands and jump up and down like the teenagers we once were.

Chapter Thirteen

THE O.J. SIMPSON AND THE HOLLYWOOD MADAM HEIDI FLEISS SCANDALS THE GOOD, THE BAD, AND THE UGLY

The two biggest scandals in Hollywood in the past twenty-five years were the OJ Simpson Murders, and Madam Heidi Fleiss and Her Hookers. Naturally, I was right in the middle of them. I liked them both so much, until one of them became, in my opinion, a murderer.

Let's talk about OJ first, because murder trumps hookers every time.

Yes, in my opinion, and from private knowledge, I believe OJ killed Nicole and Ron. Let's just get that said and done.

OJ and I both went to USC, but we didn't meet until we were guests on the same TV show. I found him adorable, magnetic, and sexy. He was also sweet and funny. We really hit it off and had a few lunches. There was absolutely NOTHING romantic between us. We just laughed at the same things. After the lunches tapered off, every time he'd see me having dinner in a restaurant, he'd always send over a bottle of champagne. I was impressed by his manners.

In 1985, I met an actress named Tawny Kitaen. She had just starred opposite Tom Hanks in *Bachelor Party*, and she had a terrific screen presence. She had voluminous red hair, a smile that could rule the world, and a personality to match. In person she just radiated. It was one of those instant friendships where you had to see each other every day for coffee, lunch, shopping, whatever.

I quickly found out that Tawny was a rock and roll chick who had made some "kind of" soft porn movies—the kind that actually were shown in legitimate theatres. In her house she had movie posters from these movies showing herself in various states of "undress." We were such polar opposites that it just worked. I really like "colorful" characters.

It took a few months for her to confess to me that she was OJ Simpson's mistress, girlfriend—whatever word you wanted to use. I was really shocked, not only because I knew him well, but because I knew how unhappy Nicole was that he cheated on her all the time. I felt bad that I now knew who he was cheating with and that she was my friend.

Nicole, by the way, was very cold to me each time we met. Maybe she was just always suspicious of women OJ greeted warmly.

One day I went to Tawny's house and a white Bronco SUV was in her driveway. (This was still the late 80s.)

"It's a present from OJ!" said Tawny proudly.

I was happy for my friend that she was happy. I must confess to you that I adored Tawny so much, I threw my values and judgment out the window. I did absolutely nothing to discourage her from seeing him.

"How'd you like to spend a couple of days at the Ritz Carlton in Laguna, all expenses paid?" asked Tawny.

"Really?"

"Yes. OJ's paying for everything and he invited you to come with me. You know how much he likes you. You and I would have adjoining rooms."

"Great! I'd love to," was my now-shameful response.

The Ritz Carlton in Laguna is a five-star resort that sits on a bluff overlooking the Pacific Ocean. I had stayed there a number of times myself and really loved it. Of course I wanted to go again.

Two days later, Tawny and I hopped into her white Bronco and drove down. Our rooms were beautiful and were directly on the ocean.

"Order anything you want on the room service menu, get a massage, do whatever. It's all on OJ," Tawny said brightly. "I'm going to go meet OJ and I'll see you later this afternoon."

And here's how innocent I was and am. "You mean OJ's here?" I am telling you that I literally thought he was giving us a present. I had no idea he was going to be around.

"You must be kidding," said Tawny. "He and Nicole have a house right next to the hotel. He's just going to tell her he's leaving to play golf. He has a room here for us."

Stupid, party of one.

In a few hours Tawny was back and we were on her bed.

"I don't really like having sex with OJ," revealed Tawny.

First, I was stunned by the candor. Then I couldn't come up with a response. "I'm sorry" didn't quite cut it.

We then just watched a movie on TV.

At seven p.m., Tawny's phone rang. It was OJ. He wanted to have drinks with the two of us in the bar. Okay, then.

He was waiting at the table when we arrived, and you could feel the buzz of the room just because he was there. It was always that way. We ordered drinks and were having casual conversation.

"I want to go to law school and become a lawyer," said Tawny, out of the blue.

The first thought in my mind was, *Fantastic. I'm glad you want to do something of value with your life.*

"You? A lawyer? Are you crazy?" said OJ. "You don't have what it takes to do that!"

Tawny completely deflated AND accepted that she would fail. I saw OJ's control technique right before my eyes. It made me very sad.

After the Ritz Carlton weekend, OJ gifted Tawny with some beautiful jewelry. I can't remember what it was right now, but I do remember that it was the jewelry that Nicole found in its jewelry box as she searched OJ's dresser drawers, thinking it was a present from him and then never receiving it. I was shocked when it came up at the trial and it was jewelry she wasn't supposed to find.

At another point, OJ gave Tawny a miniature poodle puppy named Spike. It upset me, because I knew Tawny would not really be available to take care of him. She was always flying off with OJ, shooting a movie on location, or off with some musician. Two months into puppyland, I told Tawny that I wanted to take Spike. She wasn't caring for him at all.

"Good. I love him, but I'm just not around. Thank you."

I drove Spike over to my mother's house. She treated him like a little king and he lived a glorious, pampered long life.

Shortly after the Ritz Carlton in Laguna trip, Tawny and I went to New York and shared a room at the Ritz Carlton on Central Park South. It wasn't necessarily planned that way. I had a business trip and Tawny was going to meet producers and see some rock singer I'd never heard of. There certainly was no reason to stay faithful to OJ!

The afternoon of the day we arrived, New York was hit with one of its biggest snowstorms and power outages. There Tawny and I were, in a pitch black, cold room with no available hot food and no elevators, in one of the most expensive hotels in New York. And what did we do? We decided to go for a walk down Fifth Avenue. That was not smart.

As I look back, the trip was funny because of the similarities and the role reversals. In Laguna, Tawny was at OJ's beck and call and she went to his room. In New York, the rock "boy" did whatever Tawny wanted, and she had HIM waiting for her at a different hotel.

It's important for me to say that I adored Tawny. I don't adore my behavior of being complicit in hurting Nicole by helping Tawny and OJ. That behavior was not right. I was really young; it was all so "hot" and so wrong. I will always regret it.

The last time I saw OJ with Tawny was when I was moving to a beautiful condo on the Marina Peninsula in Los Angeles, about 250 steps from the sand. OJ and Tawny were literally helping me move. Think about OJ's strength and arm reach for a second. He could take two giant boxes and put one under each arm and just GO. He also hung up all my heavy mirrors and paintings for me.

The OJ I knew, up until 1994, was kind, helpful, and respectful to me at all times.

And then Nicole Simpson was found viciously murdered, almost totally decapitated, etc. No more details of that. I, and the whole world was shocked. But I only knew OJ cheated. I had no idea he was a horrible physical and mental torturer of Nicole. Almost immediately people were saying he did it. I defended him to everyone who talked about it to me. I simply couldn't believe that someone who was a personal friend, who only showed me kindness, could be a murderer. How could someone I really liked be a killer? How could I not notice any signs?

I called Tawny right away.

"Oh my God this is awful," she said. "He is so upset. All his friends are turning on him. I gotta go, but don't you ever mention what you know about us."

That night I had a dinner reservation at a restaurant called Eclipse. It was the current hot Hollywood restaurant. Just as I was getting ready to leave the house, the Bronco chase began on TV. (OJ and Tawny had twin Broncos.) I grabbed a portable TV and took it to the restaurant.

When I arrived, the author Jackie Collins, and Allan Carr, the *Grease* producer and Cass Elliot's manager (until she died), were already at the table. They were ecstatic that I brought a TV. We plugged it into the wall, and soon about sixty diners were crowded around. It was just unreal.

Eclipse restaurant, because of the trial, became like a cafeteria each night for all the OJ trial reporters and lawyers. I, too, went there several times a week. Robert Shapiro, F. Lee Bailey, and Johnnie Cochran, CNN reporters, especially Larry King, were there. Dominick Dunne from *Vanity Fair* and I shared dinners. All of us were appearing as "talking heads" on news shows. The OJ trial was a "show-within-a-show," meaning that because it was on TV, the public saw that, but everyone on the TV met each night for their own games. It was completely insane.

I called Tawny right after they arrested OJ and she said, "Cathy (Randa, OJ's assistant for years) is getting messages to him. He is crying in his cell. Call her. Tell OJ you care." I did. Sorry to say.

Within a few days, as evidence came in, I had to let go of any thoughts of his innocence. *What was I thinking before? I was blinded by my past experiences with him.*

One night, somewhere between his arrest and the beginning of the trial, I saw an interview with Nicole's best friend, Faye Resnick, on Connie Chung's TV special. She was strong, believable, and was the most outspoken of anyone proclaiming OJ's guilt. I admired her courage and thought she was quite special. I wanted to meet her.

A mutual acquaintance set up a lunch for us in Beverly Hills. It was like we'd known each other for years. I told her how much I believed her story and saw her strength. We became really close friends, and still are to this day. We see each other all the time.

Here's what Faye told me:

"Nicole and I were best friends. I knew all the times OJ beat her up. I saw the pictures. I kept begging her to leave him and move out. She was terrified of leaving. He was constantly telling her he was going to kill her. It was how he kept her there as long as he could. She finally filed for divorce and moved to the Bundy condo. I moved in with her. He would call her day and night and scream, either saying 'I want you back' or 'I'm going to kill you.' It was horrible.

"Shortly before her murder, she began an affair with a really close friend of OJ's who is a very famous football player. I told her over and over again to not date him. It would be a red flag for OJ. I told her I believed that he would kill her. She said to me, 'I know he's going to kill me and get away with it,' but she wouldn't listen. She wouldn't stop the affair.

"At that time I was abusing cocaine and wanted to get well. After that conversation with Nicole, I checked myself into rehab. I knew when I left that she had plans to see the football player the next night. I was really worried, but I had to go to rehab and get better.

"When I was called to the phone by one of the directors of the rehab center, I knew Nicole was dead. I thought to myself, 'He finally did it, he finally did it.' I wasn't surprised, but I was devastated. I'd lost someone I loved very much."

Faye and I are now friends forever.

"Allegedly," when the football player, who was going to Nicole condo, heard the news, he suddenly went to the airport and left the country.

When the trial was on, Faye and I would watch every day, talking on the phone from each of our homes, and then we'd meet on the trial lunch breaks at least three times a week at La Scala in Beverly Hills. Faye's' closest friend, next to Nicole, was Kris Jenner. In fact, Kris and Faye shared an apartment after Kris divorced Robert Kardashian. Faye and Kris made up the nucleus of those "west side" women who the public thought just went to the gym, had coffee, and lived lives of leisure. Through them, I had a pipeline to everything. And, if you remember, NONE of those women testified at the trial. The only one was Cyndy Garvey, someone who was "on the outs" with the girls, and who was even more ostracized for testifying.

One of the biggest rumors, and I will say "rumor," "alleged," and "unverified"—was that the reason the trial was moved from Santa Monica (where it should have been) to downtown Los Angeles, was that lawyer Marcia Clark was "seeing" married Los Angeles District Attorney Gil Garcetti and they would be in closer proximity that way.

Faye, who continued to speak out and call OJ guilty, received constant death threats. Her apartment in Beverly Hills was broken into three times. She had people following her. Defense lawyer

Johnnie Cochran (who absolutely used race to get OJ off) did everything he could to make sure she wasn't called as a witness.

OJ was declared "not guilty" (which doesn't mean innocent) by a jury of Black women who thought he was sexy. Period. So stupid to move it to downtown. So stupid to allow a jury of Black women.

Several months after the O.J. trial ended, Faye and I were approached by a battered women's shelter called Interval House to host a fundraiser for them. We were delighted to do it, and picked a date about three months away. As we started to plan the event with Connie Armijo, an event planner and caterer to the stars who is one of our favorite people in the world, the civil trial of O.J. started.

Our fundraiser was planned to be at a huge estate next door to the Playboy Mansion. We got Larry King to emcee, hired a terrific band, and planned extraordinary food by Connie. We sent invitations to all our friends, and Larry sent out some too.

On the day of the party, we had absolutely no idea that the O.J. civil trial would have a guilty verdict rendered. That happened in the afternoon some time, and all of a sudden our phones were ringing with people asking to come to our party. It accidentally became the ONLY party that ever happened to celebrate his finally being found guilty.

Three hours later, people started pouring in, and Faye and I looked at each other and said, "Who's that? Is he on your list? Is she on your list?" In poured prosecuting attorney Christopher Darden, Kato Kaelin, some of the witnesses, the reporters who covered the first trial. It was insane. I seem to remember Marcia Clark and Kris Jenner being there, but I can't be sure. It was an explosion of joy with people crammed so tight you could barely move. Everyone was cheering. Connie had to triple the food orders at the last minute. What a happening! And to be the co-host of it? When Faye and I walked on stage with Larry King, it was magical. The band ended up playing until midnight, and we all danced like teenagers.

Tawny Kitaen and I lost touch after the murder trial. She moved back to her hometown in Orange County, south of Los Angeles, married a professional baseball player, had two kids, and then they divorced. She still lives there and goes by her real first name of Julie.

Kris Jenner is richer than God, and has worked really hard to get there.

Faye and I still eat at La Scala, and I love her.

OJ's finally rotting in jail. (Well, he was, until he was disgustingly paroled.)

Nicole's still dead.

In the middle of all of this, my second novel was released. It was called *Love, Sex, and Murder*, and it was a juicy tale about a Hollywood murder and DNA. It was NOT written about OJ, at all, but it was one of the first novels to really delve into DNA. The press pounced on me. I was suddenly one of the OJ "experts," and I was on every talk show you could imagine, and more than once. I had a platform to pronounce him guilty as often as I wished.

About a year and a half after he was pronounced not guilty, I was taking a redeye flight to Miami to go on a cruise. I was waiting at the gate and I saw OJ walking toward the same area. I turned to ice. There was no way he didn't watch those shows, and he had to have heard what I said about him. I was literally terrified he'd see me and hurt me.

He kept walking toward my gate and I realized he was going to be on the flight. I hid in a small crowd of people as far away from him as I could. He still walked with that OJ strut, and you could see him looking around, waiting for people to recognize him and "cheer" OJ. It was pathetic, but it made me furious that he thought for one second that anyone would talk to him. No one did.

It was time to start to board. He was in a seat about ten feet away from the little area where they take your ticket. I was going to have to walk by him.

Please, God, let him be in first class and go ahead of me.

I raised the collar of my coat as far up as I could. I turned my face away and put my head down as I walked by. Then I was in my seat. Waiting. And waiting, as the line of passengers came down the aisle. I had an aisle seat.

Please, God, don't let him have to walk past me.

And then I saw him coming down the aisle. I took my coat and literally put it over my head to cover my face and body. I had just enough room for half an eye available to see where he went. He sat in the aisle seat three rows ahead of me.

I flew all the way to Miami with a coat over my head.

* * *

In 1993, my first novel, *Honey Dust*, was published by Warner Books. It was a sexy Hollywood expose about three generations of a family vying for control of a movie studio. What was particularly interesting, was that each generation was headed by a woman. This literally was the book Jacqueline Susann, author of *Valley of the Dolls*, predicted to me that I'd write. It had seventeen sex scenes in it.

As incredible luck (or blessing from above) would have it, my book came out the same week that Madam Heidi Fleiss was arrested for running one of the hottest Hollywood hooker businesses in years. Since my book was a Hollywood novel, I began getting tons of calls from TV, newspaper, and magazine press to comment on it. I quickly realized that I was being forced into being an expert on hookers, and the Hollywood actors who used them.

The absolute truth was that I had never heard of Heidi Fleiss before the scandal broke, and I had no knowledge of hookers.

Within forty-eight hours of this breaking, I was at a Hollywood party at the Beverly Hilton Hotel and Heidi was there. It was another "And God Delivered Unto Thee" moment. I went right over to her.

"Hi! I'm Sue Cameron, and I want to thank you for helping me make my book a hit. All the press I'm getting is because of you."

"Hi, Sue," said Heidi, extending her hand. "I've been watching you on TV. You're good."

"And I think you're very smart and enterprising. I'd love to talk to you more."

Heidi, at this time, had thick brown hair, a good smile, clear skin, and pretty eyes. She was wearing a simple black pantsuit and black pumps. She had on very little jewelry.

"Why don't you come to my house tomorrow for lunch?" said Heidi. Duh.

Her house was a rented pseudo-mansion on Tower Rd. in Beverly Hills, almost on the top of the mountain. It was very modern, but looked a bit rundown. It was not neat, but not a mess at all. She greeted me in a typical athletic daytime outfit of gray cotton pants, a t-shirt, and a hoodie. We sat at the pool that overlooked the hills and the city and ate tuna salad.

We started talking and discovered that we grew up three blocks apart in the beautiful upscale Los Feliz area of Los Angeles near the Greek Theatre and the Griffith Park Observatory. We went to the same grammar school and junior high schools. Both of our fathers were doctors at Cedars-Sinai Hospital. (It was my mother's second husband of 46 years who was the doctor and who really raised me.) It was shocking. We really hit it off—the madam and the reporter. Who knew? I really liked her frankness.

"I was bored with school at a really early age. I learned the subject matter so quickly, my mind wandered. My parents were hippies, even though they became affluent. There was no discipline at all in my house. We kids could do whatever we wanted. I quit school to make money. I liked money. That was my interest, and I wanted to make it. I knew how to set up business structures. I knew I'd be successful. I have so much money now. Almost every day I hold fistfuls of it," said Heidi.

"Fascinating," I responded, wondering how she got from bright student to the hookers and the Beverly Hills house and then possibly jail. There was obviously much more to the story.

"Wait here. There's something I want to give you."

She was back in less than a minute holding an audio cassette in her hand.

HEIDI FLEISS
1270 TOWER GROVE DR.
BEVERLY HILLS, CA 90210
USA

Beverly Hills 2
9465 Wilshire B
Beverly Hills Ca

Heidi sent me lots of evidence.

"I want you to take this home and listen to it. It's a photographer I used to work with (name deliberately withheld by me). I think he had something to do with this. You can hear it on the tape. He wants in or something. He keeps calling me and bothering me. I want you to have this evidence. Don't worry. I have many copies of the tape. Let me know what you think."

"I will," I said.

"Would you like to meet me tomorrow night at Chaya Venice restaurant at six p.m.? I'll show you how it all works. Just don't write about it. My case is pending."

"Of course not. I'll see you there." My heart was pounding. Who gets that kind of invitation?

Venice, California is a beach town for primarily wealthier, artistic, non-conformists. There are funky/beautiful homes on the strand/boardwalk, and there are some real fleabag starving artist and bums' areas. It's a real mix.

Chaya Venice is a very chic, expensive sushi, Pacific Rim restaurant a block away from the beach. It is dark and loud, and their food is great. It occupies the bottom floor of a building that has condos on the top floor.

When I walked in I couldn't find Heidi. Eventually I went to the area in the back and there she was, in a corner booth, sitting with four gorgeous girls in their 20s. And when I say girls, I'm not saying hookers. I'm saying beautiful, well-groomed girls who looked like they were still in college majoring in political science, or they were recently-graduated interior decorators, or new assistant buyers for Gucci. You get the picture. I was absolutely floored. If Heidi weren't sitting with them, I would have thought it was "Sorority Girls Night Out."

I honestly think my eyes were bugging out of my head, because I could see Heidi looking at me and laughing.

"Here. Sit next to Tiffany," said Heidi.

"Hello, Tiffany. Nice to meet you."

"Hi," she said, in the voice of a breathy thirteen-year-old.

Tiffany looked like a cross between Christie Brinkley and Grace Kelly. If she hadn't opened her mouth and spoken, I would have bought the picture. But I'm sure it was very successful with men.

We made some small talk, and in seconds I could see that Tiffany's IQ matched her voice. And then I just point-blank asked her why she was working with Heidi.

"I'm getting money so I can go to law school," she said with a straight face.

I kept my cool. I found out she lived in a state close to California, didn't hate her parents, and hoped to go back home to live when she was finished in California. She was so stupid, and so sincere, that I liked her. She just didn't have a clue.

I turned my attention to Heidi.

"Why did you pick this restaurant?"

"Because I own a huge condo upstairs. My brother lives there, and this is what I call my home. Very few people know about it. The house you went to is work, but I sometimes sleep there, too. Tonight I am sending the girls out from here, that's all. I also want to spend some time with my brother later. I'll probably sleep here tonight," she answered.

Then a waiter came and she ordered lots of appetizers. Clearly, the girls couldn't commit to dinner because they never knew when they would be leaving. Heidi's phone rang like crazy.

"What's going on with your case?"

"I hired Anthony Brooklier as my attorney. He'll get me off. Look him up and you'll see why I hired him. The whole thing was a set up."

"What do you mean?"

"Do you know who Madam Alex is?"

"No," I answered.

"She was the biggest madam in town, and I worked for her. (*Note: I am so naïve I thought she was her assistant or secretary. It NEVER occurred to me that Heidi was one of her hookers.*) Alex was getting older and getting sloppy. She wasn't running the business right. She could be making so much more money. She paid off the cops weekly. It all was inefficient. So, one day I was alone in the house and I just took her black book. I called everybody and told them I was opening my own business with even better girls. I went to bars and clubs every night to find girls. And I wanted my girls to be very special-looking. I had to have the prettiest, classiest girls in town."

"Well, you succeeded," I said. "But what went wrong?"

"The police came to me a few weeks into my business demanding the same payoff Alex gave them. I refused. I wasn't going to give anybody a cut of anything. The cops went back to Alex and told her. Together they came up with a sting. It was a set up. They waited just long enough for me to get comfortable, and one night I sent girls to meet some rich Arabs at the Beverly Hilton Hotel, and they were undercover cops. That was it. I was arrested."

"What do you do now?"

"The one thing I don't do is break the code," said Heidi.

"What code?"

"A madam never reveals the names of her clients. I've had so many calls from my clients offering to pay my legal bills or whatever I need. It's really hush money, but they don't understand that I'm not going to talk. Can you imagine what my black book is worth?"

"Actually, yes. I can also probably guess a lot of the names that are in it," I replied.

"And you'd be right," she said with a smile.

"What's your next move?" I asked.

"Now that my name is so famous, I'm going to merchandise it. I just rented a store on Hollywood Blvd., and I'm going to sell a line of lingerie called HeidiWear. In one week, I found the store. I found a cheap factory in downtown LA with existing t-shirts, underpants, tops, pants. I had a logo designed and they are heat-stamping it on all the products as we speak. You're invited to my opening next week. Will you come?"

"I wouldn't miss it for the world."

I still have the HeidiWear she gave me as a present the night of the opening. The store was jammed. She also already had mail-order catalogues printed and being distributed that night.

A few days later my phone rang. It was Heidi.

"Wanna have some fun?" she asked.

"What EXACTLY do you mean?"

"I'm taking you to lunch today," she said, laughing. "Meet me at La Croisette at one p.m. (fake restaurant name). It was the number one Hollywood lunch place for actors and executives. She picked one p.m., of course, because the place would be at its busiest, and we'd have a larger audience.

When we walked in and stood by the maitre 'd, you could feel the place start to quiet down. Our table was at the very back of the restaurant, so we had to walk by everyone. All eyes were on us and you could hear a pin drop as we moved. I loved it. Sometimes I really like to stir up some trouble, and this was a beaut. When we sat down, people gradually began to resume their conversations, but in a more quiet manner. The waitress took our order and then left.

"Our waitress is one of my girls, and if you look toward the front of the restaurant at 'John Doe's' table, she's meeting him at his home after lunch to have a three-way with his wife. Now let's go through the whole restaurant from left to right starting with 'John Doe 2' at the 10 o'clock table. He only likes Asian girls who pee on his chest. Moving on to 'John Doe 3' at 11 o'clock (a studio head). He's actually impotent, but I set up things for him to watch—whatever combo he wants."

I didn't know what to do with myself. She continued this "sex-athon" describing almost everyone in the restaurant. It ranked right up there with one of the weirdest experiences of my life—one that could never be anticipated, and one that was thoroughly enjoyed. *Great gosh almighty!*

I have no idea what I ate for lunch, but it certainly wasn't a person.

Yes, people, Heidi went to jail. But she was right about the prostitution charges. That never was an issue. She made one very bad mistake in all her businesses—she didn't pay taxes. They got Heidi and same way they got Capone.

I actually went to the trial one day. Heidi was mugging for the cameras and was very arrogant. It wasn't pretty. When lunch recess was called, I went to the cafeteria. I was seated by myself at a table, and a very elegant-looking Candy Bergen-type woman with perfectly-coiffed blonde hair who was wearing a classic suit and silk scarf asked if she could sit with me. I remembered her because she was sitting behind me in the courtroom.

"Hi, I'm Sydney Barrows. May I sit with you?"

"Of course! You're The Mayflower Madam. I hope I didn't offend you by saying that."

"It's fine," she said. "There's nothing I can do about it."

Sydney Biddle Barrows, of the very wealthy, blue-blooded Biddle Family in New York, created a gigantic scandal several years prior to Heidi because she, too, was a madam. Sydney graduated from the Fashion Institute of Technology and had a hard time getting a job because no one believed she needed one. She started doing temp work, and one day ended up as a receptionist at an escort service.

"I enjoyed the work. It was not boring at all. I stayed on and began to help groom the girls. I was raised with impeccable manners and style, and made a real place for myself there. I'm good in business. I eventually just took over the company," said Sydney. "I set up a real corporation and ran it well. I paid my taxes. That's where Heidi slipped up. I flew in from New York to support her."

"How did you get caught?"

"The man who owned the office building where my office was kept raising the rent higher and higher. He knew what my business was, and it really was blackmail. I finally told him that enough was enough and he reported me to the police."

"But you never were convicted," I said

"I had a very good lawyer, and I paid my taxes. My attorney simply told the judge, in whatever legal language was needed, that if a trial went forward I would take the stand and name every client I had. That was the end of it, but the impact on my life was still very difficult. My reputation was ruined, my family was embarrassed. No matter how good I showed I was in business, it was difficult for me to get a job for any company. I had to create my own career as a speaker, consultant, and author."

Let me say here that Sydney is such a kind, loving person. I admire her and I'm so glad we are friends. I see her every time I go to New York.

As for Heidi, she went to jail and has had a horrible time. Drugs and plastic surgery have ravaged her face and soul. She lives in a tiny town called Pahrump, Nevada. Her phone rarely rings.

What a waste of a brain.

And Tiffany never went to law school. She went back to her hometown and her original name.

THE NOTE TO END ALL NOTES: In addition to the Debbie Reynolds side of the "Eddie Fisher Tree," I am also family to Connie Stevens and her two daughters, Joely and Tricia Leigh Fisher. In fact, many times ALL of us have been together for holidays and vacations. At one time, Connie owned a lot of houses that she rented out. She had a house in the Coldwater Canyon area of Beverly Hills that was rented out to three flight attendants. They were behind in their rent so many months that Connie called the police to have them evicted. Those girls ran out so fast after the police showed up, that they left behind a number of things. When Joely went by to see the shape of the house after the police left, she came upon a black book. Yes, the girls were Heidi's girls, and that book not only had all the names of each client, but what each client liked sexually. Of course I have a copy. It was really fun holding it up during talk shows. I still pick it up occasionally late at night. It's so amusing.

Chapter Fourteen

CAROL BURNETT, CARY GRANT, AND ME

My senior year of college couldn't go by fast enough. I was so ready to go out and conquer the world. I remember sitting in a boring class, taking out a piece of paper, and writing a list of what I wanted to do. I remember some of them:

Be a columnist
Write for national magazines
Have my own radio show
Guest on talk shows and maybe get my own
Be a reporter on TV
Write a book
BE CAROL BURNETT

Yup. That was pretty much my list, and I had completed it all, with one exception, by my second year of working in Hollywood. I know. Pretty amazing. I can remember being twenty-one years old and walking to a newsstand, looking at all the magazine covers and seeing that I had stories in five national magazines at once. It was unreal, yet, to me, totally expected. I never thought I wouldn't do my list.

But about that Carol Burnett part...

I had always loved comics growing up. Most of them were men, and I could imitate all of their characters. Carol Burnett was the first woman I had ever seen in the variety format. She could do great characters and I loved her.

I also knew another thing. I had no acting ability. I could mimic anything; I could create and write any character, but I didn't have the stomach to be judged through the Hollywood machine. Sue Cameron, the writer, would be just fine.

Carol and I ran into each other at CNN recently.

My *Hollywood Reporter* position, yet again, allowed me to meet anyone I wanted, and I wanted to do an interview with Carol Burnett. It was set up instantly.

I went to CBS TV City at Beverly and Fairfax, where she shot her show. She rehearsed Monday through Thursday, and then shot the dress rehearsal and the "air show" on Fridays. The show that people would actually see would be an edited version of the best of each of those shows. Sometime a sketch might play better in one version or another.

I was there on a Wednesday because she had more time to see me. I went to her dressing room, and the first thing she did was introduce me to her husband, Joe Hamilton, who produced the show. At that time, they were a very happy, successful couple. I also quickly recognized that Carol was equally, if not more in charge of her show, and that Joe spoke for her so she could always be the good guy. She WAS and IS a "good guy," but it also was smart business.

Carol had a two-room dressing room. One room was really private, where she had her hair and makeup done and got dressed. The other was like a den where she would receive people, friends could hang out and watch the show on a TV monitor; food could be sent in. I remember that I actually interviewed her in her private room. She was sitting on a high director's chair. Truthfully, I don't remember a thing I asked Carol or whatever she answered. I was so excited to be on that set to watch someone do the one thing on my list I was never going to do.

Digression:

My father, an entertainment lawyer who, right out of law school worked as an associate for the mob lawyer Jerry Geisler, also loved live performing. As a "hobby," he bought the Las Palmas Theatre, a legit stage house in Hollywood and put on plays...some of them big plays that went on to Broadway. The famed producer Ross Hunter, who did all those Lana Turner-Sandra Dee movies, was an intern for him, as was a former nightclub bouncer named George Schlatter, who went on to win multiple Emmys as the producer of Laugh-In. Both Ross and George loved that "Little Susie" ended up at the Reporter.

Because my parents divorced when I was a year-and-a-half, my father had weekend custody of me. A portion of EVERY one of those weekends was spent by me sitting in the audience of that theater while my father worked in his office.

I don't mean sitting watching shows with audiences. I was sitting in an empty theatre observing, even under the age of six, how a show gets put together. I was absorbing a project from the time a play was picked, the audition process to get the right actors, the rehearsals for both musicals and dramas, the song and dance rehearsals, the direction, lights EVERYTHING.

By the time I was about twelve, and I didn't figure this out until I was a little older, I had learned to be able to tell what made a project work or not. I could tell easily whether or not there was a good script that was miscast, or misdirected...whether the score was good or not. If something failed, I could pinpoint the problem because of my education and experience. I could also repeatedly, while shows were running, see what played well with audiences. A story or a show is always a combination of writing, direction, and casting. Knowing how the pieces did or did not fit is what taught me how to be a critic.

As a critic at The Hollywood Reporter, when I reviewed a TV show, a play, a movie, a nightclub act, I ALWAYS knew the reason it didn't work, and I said so. I will toot my own horn and say that I think I was an experienced and knowledgeable person who wrote intelligent reviews. I am grateful that others knew that too, *so when I criticized them, they knew it was to be helpful. It was because of the real-life education and experience of growing up at the Las Palmas Theatre.*

All that time I was observing in my father's theatre is why I fell in love with the *Carol Burnett Show* and went EVERY Friday for years to see both the rehearsal and air tapings. Carol, her cast members, Bob Mackie, the costume designer, Peter Matz, the musical director, the Ernie Flatt dancers, special material writers Ken and Mitzie Welch, all made me a part of the family. I loved all layers of putting on that show. And, it was as close as I was going to get to the Carol Burnett portion on my list. I loved being there each week.

Most of my friends guested on Carol's show, so it really was a party for me. Shooting on the next stage (and you could go between stages if you went to the ladies' room and switched exit doors), was the *Sonny and Cher Comedy Hour*. It was a Friday night spectacular for years in my life. I kept running back and forth.

Carol Burnett had two favorite actors Jimmy Stewart and Cary Grant. I liked Jimmy very much, but Cary Grant was, and always will be, my ideal man. Jimmy had already guested on Carol's show, and she and her husband were friends with Jimmy and his wife, Gloria. But, even though Carol was a huge TV star, she had not yet met Cary.

One day when I was on the set of her variety show, I told her that I had received an invitation from the singer Peggy Lee to a cocktail party at her house to celebrate her new album. Peggy's press agent told me that Cary Grant was going to be there. I told Carol, and she told me she'd received the invitation too. We were both hysterical that we were going to meet him. This was the only time I can remember where I "fanned out" over a celebrity. Cary Grant could have been the King of England as far as I was concerned. He was that special to me. I'm sure I got that from my mother, who, every time one of his movies was on, she would grab me and have me watch while she drooled.

Carol and I made a pact that whoever showed up first would be on the look-out for Cary. Peggy's house was a beautiful one-story modern house in the hills of Beverly Hills. The entire living room opened onto a patio with a view of the city. It was breathtaking. Everything in the house was white.

I arrived first and seated myself on the very pretty white living room couch and waited. Peggy Lee, by the way, couldn't have been more gracious, and was even a little shy.

The front door opened and in walked Carol. She said hello to some people and quickly joined me on the couch where we awaited our prey. We were on a caper. She was facing slightly toward me and away from the front door. One by one, stars entered. No Cary. After about thirty minutes of waiting, he walked in the door. He was wearing a slightly shiny grey suit, white shirt, grey silk tie. It all matched his hair. He was, indeed, the most elegant sight I'd ever seen.

"He's here! He's here!" I stage-whispered to Carol, who started to bounce up and down. "He's going to the bar. C'mon," I whispered. "It's time. Let's go over there!"

I got up and looked at her. She wasn't moving.

"Get up! What's the matter with you?" I said, eager to meet our prey.

"I can't," said Carol, with an odd look on her face.

"What do you mean you can't? I said. "It's Cary Grant! He's here. This is our moment"

And Carol replied, "I can't get up! I wet my pants!!!!!"

And, at that moment, I left Carol sitting in her damp underpants and went right to the bar and introduced myself to Cary Grant.

Yes. He was as charming as you would imagine. He looked right in your eyes and made you feel like the only person in the room. He offered me a martini. It was just like the movies.

As for Carol, I don't know how she did it, but a few minutes later she came to the bar.

As Joan Rivers said, when I told her this story, "What happened to Peggy Lee's couch?"

Carol has gone on and shown the world what a wonderful dramatic actress she is as well. She has conquered all fields of entertainment and dealt with divorce, substance abuse in her family, and most tragically, the death of her daughter, Carrie. She has done all of this with great dignity and grace.

Every time I run into Carol we hug like it's a magical Friday all over again. I love her.

Chapter Fifteen

JOAN RIVERS MY BELOVED SISTER/BITCH

"Joan Rivers just moved here from New York and she'd like to invite you over to her house for lunch tomorrow," said Frank Liberman, her press agent, on the other end of the phone.

"I love Joan, I'd love to come."

"OK, It's one p.m. at 1022 Coldwater Canyon. It's a steep driveway. Be careful."

I thought Joan was the funniest white woman whoever lived. She was fearless, and because she'd lived in New York we'd never met. I had heard she'd been itching to come to LA to broaden her career in TV and movies, and I was really looking forward to meeting her.

Her rented house was the typical decent, California ranch house. It was on Coldwater Canyon, which most people think is a good address. In a way it is, because the houses are beautiful and it's in Beverly Hills. But to actually have your house be directly on Coldwater Canyon facing the busy street is not the place to be— unless you are behind huge gates and have tremendous acreage. There are exceptions to that, like the estates of mogul Barry Diller, and Debbie Reynolds and Carrie Fisher's property. Their estates merely had a driveway and gate on Coldwater, and then you'd drive through the property to get to the house and guesthouses.

At one time, Bobby Darin and Nancy Sinatra each lived on side streets, and in later years Ellen DeGeneres had a huge property off Coldwater as well.

"Welcome. I'm Archie. I used to be a professional ice skater, but now I work for Joan. She met me after a show I did in Central Park and she befriended me. Please follow me."

I love Joan.

I sat there in the early American-decorated living room for a few minutes, and then another "host" arrived. His name was Warren. He was studying to be an actor, and both Warren and Archie were Joan's assistants. I soon learned that Warren was also Joan's maitre'd when she did comedy shows at Ye Little Club in Beverly Hills. Later on, Warren Burton became an Emmy-winning actor on a soap opera.

"Hello, hello, hello! said Joan. "It's so nice to meet you."

She grasped my hand and was so warm and open.

"I want you to meet Melissa. She's having a little party right now. We've decided to do Halloween early."

Joan held my hand as we walked down the hall to a play area, and there were children chasing each other in costumes. Melissa was adorable.

Joan and I campaigning for a presidential candidate in the 80s.

"Come. Let's just sit down at the table and talk over lunch."

She never let go of my hand as we walked.

We entered the dining room and a man was already sitting at the table. He immediately got up and introduced himself.

"I'm Edgar Rosenberg, Joan's husband."

"And you're a producer," I said, much to his delight.

That afternoon, I fell in love with both of them.

For the next forty years, we were really close friends. I learned that Joan was really a shy fragile bird/bookworm when she wasn't performing. I learned that Edgar's biting English wit was totally equal with Joan's. I learned that they loved each other, but also had some problems.

I was totally embraced in their orbit, and was present at dinner parties, holidays, vacations, and shows, as well as private lunches and dinner with Joan, and separate ones with just Edgar.

Note: Although nothing untoward ever happened during my separate dinners with Edgar, I knew that if Joan ever divorced him I'd want to marry him. I don't think Joan ever picked up on that, but Melissa did.

I stayed in Joan's 62nd St. property in New York on numerous occasions. When she did the red-carpet broadcasts, E! would put her up in a nearby hotel and I'd go there and watch the actual show with her, as we all would make cracks and write those lines down. I was present at many of her tapings at E! I was with her in Vegas, Tahoe, Reno—everywhere she played. I'd spend Sundays with Joan and Edgar and myself in bathrobes reading *The New York Times* and having room service. I saw her right after her mother died. Her father went into the hospital for a serious heart issue, and then Joan's mother fell ill. Joan fought with her mother. Her mother died the next day and her father lived—and married his hospital nurse. When Joan told me her favorite movie star was Kim Novak, I had Kim fly down from Oregon, go to a *Fashion Police* taping, and then have lunch with Joan. I was with her on the first night of her Fox Late Night Show (and also at the end). At one point, years after Edgar died, she was very interested in possibly moving to the San Juan Islands off of Seattle, and asked me if I wanted to live there with her.

We would text and email constantly. I've saved all of them. Losing her was like losing a body part I'd never get back.

And, speaking of losing her, let me state here and now that Joan was absolutely murdered by medical incompetence. I'm happy Melissa settled, because it gave her peace of mind, but don't think for one second that those doctors and their licenses are safe.

Let's go back and reminisce a bit.

"Hi, it's Joan. I'm at Caesar's Palace and I'm taking orders. What do you want? Soap, towels, shampoo?"

"I really need a blanket this time," I said, at home in Los Angeles. To Joan, every hotel was the best place to "shop."

"Edgar! screamed Joan. "Pack the blanket!"

Joan, a few months after living on Coldwater Canyon, knew somehow it wasn't in the right place and called me. "Where's the best place to live? I know this isn't it."

"Bel Air. That's the only place for you," I answered.

Joan and I took many boat rides around Lake Tahoe during her many engagements there.

Joan bought one of the most beautiful places in Bel Air on Ambazac Way. It was a Georgian Colonial that Joan decorated like a classic East Coast Vanderbilt-type house.

The first dinner party in the Bel Air house consisted of Vincent Price and Coral Browne, Roddy MacDowell and his boyfriend, and another famous actor and his wife. Joan's table was camera-ready for *House Beautiful.* We sat down and Roddy's friend realized I was a member of the press. He had just received a bad review on his singing act in *The Hollywood Reporter.* I knew nothing about it.

First course: lobster bisque was served. Joan lifted her spoon and we started to eat. I was next to Edgar. I loved him from the moment I met him. Suddenly the singer jumped up and started to yell at me. I guess I represented all press. He was drunk and it got louder. Then he lunged across the table to hit me. Joan put down her soupspoon. Edgar blocked the blow. Roddy grabbed the kid, took him outside and locked him in the car.

Second course: filet mignon with whipped potatoes and glazed carrots. I was still shaky and decided to go to the ladies' room. I opened the door and the wife of the unnamed actor was face down on the floor, passed out from some substance. I ran back to the dining room and announced it. The woman's husband ran to the bathroom and revived her and they left. Back to the dinner table. The filets were now cold. Joan threw her fork across the room. "F--k it. I'm ordering pizza."

On the first Thanksgiving at the Bel Air house, the fireplace backed up and we were evacuated due to smoke!

The Bel Air house backed up against the golf course of the Bel Air Country Club. It was a restricted club no Jews allowed. Joan's great love was her rose garden in her backyard, and she tended to them every day. The only problem was that wayward golf balls were constantly coming over the hedge and either hitting her or the roses. I was with her in the backyard one day and a ball went whizzing by. Suddenly a man in full golfing regalia stuck his head over the fence and asked for his ball back. Joan picked up the ball and yelled, "You Nazi! Your balls are mine!"

During what turned out to be some of the last days of Joan's talk show at Fox, I was concerned about Edgar's health. He was producing the show while fighting with Barry Diller, the head of the network. He didn't have good color and looked like he was in pain. I actually grabbed him backstage and locked him in a bathroom with me.

"What's wrong, Edgar? You've got to tell me. You don't look good."

"I have gout, an ulcer, some heart issues, and a couple of other things. I'm on so many pills. Don't worry. I'll be all right," he said.

The last week in July in 1987, I ran into Edgar at a Hollywood restaurant on the Sunset Strip called Le Dome. It was shortly after Fox had canceled Joan's show because Barry Diller, who owned Fox, ordered Joan to fire Edgar as executive producer and she refused—so Diller canceled the show.

Edgar came over to my table and said, "I need you to promise me something."

He seemed very serious.

"Of course," I said.

"Promise me that you will always be there for Melissa."

"You know I will be. You all are like family to me."

"Good," he said, and then he walked away.

On August 12th, 1987, I woke up in the middle of the night crying because in my dream Edgar was dead. I saw it. I felt it. But, it was a dream, right?

In the morning the feelings would not go away. I carefully debated telling Joan about them, but I didn't want to bother her. She was about to go into the hospital to have knee liposuction.

On August 13th, I flew to Carmel to stay at Kim Novak's house. It was glorious in the woods. I stayed in a cabin on the property.

On August 14th, the phone rang in the cabin. It was Kim's husband.

"Isn't Joan Rivers' husband a friend of yours? he asked.

"Yes."

"He just killed himself."

I ran to the main house crying. They let me in and put me on the living room couch and wrapped me in a blanket.

"I have to get to Joan, I have to get to Joan."

Without going into tons of details, I was in Joan's house four hours later. She and a few friends were sitting in Edgar's den. Joan just looked at me and nodded. There wasn't much to say. We all were in shock.

"Sit. Sit," said Joan.

We went through the funeral, where Joan picked out all the Rodgers and Hart songs Edgar loved, and then, for the next several nights, Joan and Melissa "sat Shiva" in the Ambazac house, and a rabbi came each night to bless them and do a little service.

Joan used a different lavish caterer each night and the buffets were dazzling. She knows how to entertain beautifully. But, I would watch Melissa, still in college, walking from room to room a little glassy-eyed in her faded jeans, white shirt, and penny loafers with white socks. It was THE traditional East Coast college uniform.

Joan hung back. She greeted people, but she kept disappearing into the kitchen or breakfast room. One night I followed her there. She was leaning up against a doorjamb.

"How could he do this to Melissa?" she yelled. "How could he be so cruel? God damn him. I'm so angry. He did this to his little girl!"

I was grateful she could let herself go in front of me. I've never seen anyone so angry.

About two weeks after Shiva was over, Joan and I were sitting in the Bel Air kitchen. She was in a robe and slippers, crying softly. "No one wants me. All my bookings have been canceled because they think a widow can't be funny. I'm off all the dinner party guest lists because I'm single and the wives think I'll go after their husbands." She paused for a second, Kleenex over her nose, and said, "I know. We'll go Jewish skiing! Go home and pack and come right back."

"What's Jewish skiing?" I asked.

"Don't ask."

In a few hours I found myself on a plane to Deer Valley with Joan and Melissa and a hairdresser (our beloved Max D'Fray). Shalom Slolom.

Jewish skiing means you start by taking your hairdresser with you. You get up around nine, have room service in your two-bedroom chalet, and then get dressed to ski. A golf cart takes you to an inside heated ski room where skis are put on you and you walk out onto the slopes. There you are met by your private instructor. Max and Melissa were good skiers and they went right to the black diamonds. Joan and I stayed on the bunny hill. I also fell off the ski lift into a pile of snow. Only my eyes and hat could be seen. Joan had me dug out.

"That's it!" she said after two runs. Time for lunch.

As we went to the restaurant at the bottom of the slope, Joan asked, "Have you ever done snow angels?"

"No. What's that?"

She proceeded to lie down in the snow and show me.

"C'mon. Let's do it together."

That was a great moment.

We did one more run after lunch, and then we went back to the chalet where masseuses were waiting for us. After that we took naps, and then Max did our hair so we could go out to dinner. After dinner you go shopping. I remember that Joan and I bought sparkly men's ties that

Jewish skiing with Max, Joan, and Melissa.

looked like a costume for the Temptations. Hers was shocking pink and mine was shocking blue. It's all just repeated on the next day.

Reminiscing again, when Melissa turned thirteen, there was no religious ceremony. Joan decided to have a very chic lunch at L'Orangerie, the most expensive restaurant in L.A. Just before the dessert was about to be served, Joan went up to the mic to congratulate Melissa. Edgar was standing there with her. Joan turned to Edgar and said, "I guess this is as good a time as any to tell you. Melissa isn't yours."

Now I want to clear up the Johnny Carson thing once and for all. Even Joan never told the whole story because she still revered him. I never did. I knew he was a snake.

When Joan became the permanent guest host on *The Tonight Show*, Johnny was thrilled. It was his idea and he okayed it. She was doing great, and her ratings kept building. Her contract was renewed and then renewed again for—I don't know how many times.

But then she started getting better ratings than Johnny on her Monday night stint. Edgar called NBC, as he usually did, to talk about the contract renewal. His call(s) were not returned. He wrote letters. Nothing. He and Joan were puzzled. She loved doing the show and really wanted badly to be renewed. Silence from NBC. Her option expiration date was very close. She was confused and upset. Only then, when there were no offers or discussions coming from NBC, did she begin to explore going somewhere else.

What Joan never told anyone was that Johnny had ordered NBC NOT to pick up her option. He was jealous that her ratings were higher, and he was going to dump her.

And, by the way, that was confirmed to me many years later by the wife of head of business affairs at the time. It is ABSOLUTELY WHAT HAPPENED.

Joan called Johnny just before the announcement of her Fox show. She was still trying to be polite. Johnny made a big deal that she didn't call him, but she did. He was very mean, and hung up on her.

Joan was also very aware of who people really were. She told me repeatedly that, while she always appeared to be friendly toward Kathy Griffin, that, "Kathy is just waiting for me to die so she can have my career." I've never seen such brown-nosing as Kathy hanging around Melissa on both coasts after Joan died. Believe me, Kathy didn't leave *Fashion Police* on her own accord. That's all I can say.

Another thing you need to know about is Joan's generosity. She supported MANY people, and she never talked about it. One day I was in New York with her in her dressing room, and a four-inch-high stack of checks were sitting her for her to sign.

"Look at this. It happens every month. I can't let people starve."

Passover and Thanksgiving were two very important holidays to Joan. I was blessed to have spent many with her. While my religion doesn't celebrate Passover, I was always game for a "Joan party."

For one of the first Passovers when Melissa moved into her Pacific Palisades house, Joan had a theme. I walked into the living room and saw handsome, hunky waiters wearing those large black furry hats that Hasidic Jews wear. They also had on wigs with the pigtails. As if that weren't funny enough, they were serving "Pigs in a Blanket." That's a no-no at any time in the Jewish religion—but Passover? I howled.

A VERY HAPPY "RABBI JOAN."

I sat next to Joan at the table, and she spent the entire dinner fobbing her food off on me. She kept filling up my plate with hers.

"I'm not hungry. Eat this. I don't want anyone to know," said Joan.

Joan had a bad relationship with food. She was maniacal about being thin and simply wouldn't eat. She would eat almost an entire can of Altoids mints in 24 hours. Hmmm. I actually did see her eat an egg once in forty-two years of friendship.

The next year at Passover, because I knew the joke of it, I did something very special for Joan as a hostess gift. You probably don't know that Joan was the keeper of many of her friends' ashes, including Vincent Price and Coral Browne, Roddy MacDowell, and others. She loved her ashes collection.

Before I left my house, I crumpled up bits of eight-by-ten size printer paper and burned them in an ashtray. I then put them in a baggie and tied a colorful ribbon to it.

I walked up to Joan in front of everyone at the Passover cocktail hour, held up the baggie and said, "Here's your hostess gift. I brought you Elizabeth Taylor's ashes."

A hush fell over the room.

"This is really Elizabeth Taylor?" asked Joan, wide-eyed and hopeful.

"No, but I wanted to give you a gift you'd remember."

She doubled over laughing.

At the next Passover I came in a copy of the Oscar dress worn by Charlize Theron that Joan had ripped apart on *Fashion Police*. It was pink satin and had a very large white volleyball-sized flower over each nipple.

From the moment of my entrance I heard that low, almost growly chuckle emanate from Joan.

My favorite times with Joan were actually us sitting side by side somewhere in the world, no makeup or hair, each quietly reading a book. She looked like she might be a librarian from Anywhere, USA.

September, 2014
I had seen Joan forty-eight hours earlier at a *Fashion Police* taping.
"I'll be back next week and we'll have dinner," she said.

I was in my house when there was a newsflash that something had gone wrong with a medical test and she was being rushed to a hospital. My first thought was plastic surgery gone wrong, because I had told both Joan and Melissa that I thought she was doing too much anesthesia and weakening her system. Melissa agreed with me. Joan pooh-poohed both of us.

I called the house-keeper in New York and she knew nothing. I called the LA house-keeper and got the same response.

I called Sabrina, Joan and Melissa's assistant for decades, and left a message. I saw Melissa and Cooper on the news boarding a plane for New York. So I just waited and prayed.

I finally got a hold of Sabrina, who could tell I was totally panicked. By this time they all were in New York.

My Charlize Theron Oscar dress.

"Look, we don't really know anything. She's in a coma and the doctors have to do a lot of tests. Try to breathe. We're all in bad shape. Just wait for the test results."

"But what was she doing?"

"She was just having an endoscopy to look at throat nodules. That's it."

"Listen, Sabrina, please tell me how long she was down without oxygen."

"Maybe twenty minutes," was her reply.

I knew Joan's life was over, but I refused to really take it in. You don't come back when you've been deprived of oxygen more than six minutes.

Blessed Sabrina was my lifeline. I was getting reports, but no one was really saying or confirming.

Two days later I got this call.

"It's Sabrina. Are you driving right now?"

"Yes."

"I want you to pull over and turn off the engine."

I knew.

"It's time for you to come to New York to say goodbye to Mrs. R."

"I'll be there tomorrow. Oh God, Sabrina!"

Thanks to Melissa, Joan's last days in the hospital were spent in a beautiful, huge room, decorated by event planner Preston Bailey, who did Melissa's wedding. Things from her own bedroom were brought there so it looked like home. There were dusty rose roses in vases all over. She had her own lace comforter and all of her European linens. It was Joan's boudoir and it was fit for a queen. She looked beautiful and peaceful. I held her hand and talked to her repeatedly. For me, she will never die. I think I'll probably never laugh again, but if I really can't, I'll remember back to the time when my friend, Phoebe Snow, was in a coma and I thought if maybe Joan spoke to her it might help. Joan called and I held the phone close to my friend's ear so I could hear Joan's words of encouragement, "Wake up, you stupid bitch!"

Joan's hand was warm as I held it, and her heart was beating. A machine was breathing for her. I was alone in her room. Melissa had the hospital cordon off a corner wing of the hospital. Joan was in one room. Melissa and Cooper used another one to sleep in. Down the hall was a "catered green room" where Joan's invited guests would sit and wait their turn to say goodbye. It was handled so beautifully by Melissa.

I looked at Joan in her hospital bed with a tube coming out of her mouth. Except for the tube, she appeared to be camera ready to do a show. It was unfathomable to me that a body and person who seemed so alive didn't have a brain to match. Of all people. Joan, with that brilliant mind.

I told her I loved her and tried to talk about fun times. I believe people in comas hear you, and that has been borne out by my experience with mediums. I knew she was hearing every word.

I leaned over and put my lips next to her ear and said, through tears, "Wake up, you stupid bitch."

FUNERAL

Joan's funeral was set for five days after she died. I was already in New York, and normally I'd be thrilled to play in New York for five days, but, obviously, not this time. I kept going into hysterics and taking to my bed.

And then I was given an assignment from Melissa and Sabrina. Lots of friends from Los Angeles would be flying in over the coming days, and they asked me to look out for them and schedule activities for them to do until the funeral. It was a blessing.

We all were connected via our phones and I'd give them the agenda and we'd meet by the fountain in front of the Plaza Hotel at 59th and 5th. A typical day might be going to the Met, followed by lunch at Sarabeth's, a nap, and then dinner at Shun Lee West. All of us being together certainly saved me, and I think it helped everyone else too. We were in such a state of shock, so shattered, so angry, and so unbelievably sad. There are no words to describe how horrific it was.

The day of the funeral we met at the fountain again and walked the two blocks to the synagogue on Fifth Avenue. There were security guards; we had to show an id; there was special seating. It was a BIG deal.

Joan's closest "real" friends, meaning non-celeb (sort of) were seated correctly in the second and third rows. Melissa and Cooper were in front of us with Sabrina and Melody.

Behind us were Donald and Melania, Rosie O' Donnell, Whoopi, Kelly Ripa, Dr. Oz, Diane Sawyer, Kathie Lee and Hoda, Bernadette Peters, Kelly Osborne, Tommy Tune, Alan Cumming, Andy Cohen, Steve Forbes, Sara Jessica Parker, Carolina Herrera, Joy Behar, Michael Kors, and Paul Schafer.

Our group sat on the "bride's side." The speakers—Howard Stern, Cindy Adams, and Deborah Norville were on the "groom's."

The funeral was funny and elegant. It was made for a star, and Joan would have loved it. Truthfully, I'm sure she was there. Hugh Jackman and Audra McDonald sang, as did the Gay Men's Chorus. (Joan had the Gay Men's Chorus perform at her house every Christmas Day for years.) When the ceremony was over and we filed out into the street, Fifth Avenue was closed off from traffic and a gigantic bag pipes band played. It was perfect.

The reception was held in Joan's beautiful apartment, and every second of being there was unbearably painful. People were making polite conversation, the hors d'oeuvres were beautiful, but there was no Joan. It was awful to go through.

I spotted Kelly Osborne just standing in the middle of a room staring off into space. She was in total shock. I went over to her.

"You know Joan loved you very much, Kelly. She talked to me about you all the time. She so believed in your talent. She wanted you to do musical theatre."

Kelly grabbed me and started crying.

"Joan was like my grandmother. I did everything she said. Her advice was so good. I am going to study to do theatre. She loved you very much too."

We just held each other. There was nothing else to do.

Several minutes later I went back into the foyer and saw Barbara Walters holding on to a drape and talking to a wall. I don't say this in any disparaging way. You HAVE to understand how devastating all this was. No one was in his or her right mind.

What broke my heart the most was seeing her grandson, Cooper, trying to be brave and saying hello to people. Cooper was Joan's reason for living, and she was his. I just hugged him. No words came out of my mouth.

And, Melissa was magnificent throughout. She was trained by the best and performed her role perfectly. Away from people her sorrow was incalculable, but when she had to do her family duties, she was "top drawer."

Note: Just trying to inject some humor. Did you know that Joan, Barbara Walters, Cindy Adams, and Judge Judy went on many vacations together? Think about it.

While all this Joan activity was going on, we tried to do our best to get through it. That's what you do. But if you don't allow yourself to mourn, collapse, or do whatever is needed to deal with the loss, it hits you when you least expect it. Six months after the loss, I felt my chest cave in. I was coughing and choking. I couldn't breathe. I coughed so much that I broke my ribs and ended up in the hospital. I found out that when there is a chest problem, it is about having to deal with grief. I swallowed all that grief in order to get through everything. Eventually, it came out in a way that almost crippled me.

As I was lying in the hospital I heard the words, "Get up, you stupid bitch."

I got up, Joan. I got up. God love you.

Note: I went to see a very legitimate, respected, psychic medium named Marla Frees a few weeks after Joan died. She came right through with all her energy. I asked her if she'd seen Edgar and she said that he was in a small library with books, and that he stays there and reads all day. She said she didn't go in there. I know that that room. Joan was talking about Edgar's library that was in the Ambazac house and was recreated in its entirety in Melisa's house in Pacific Palisades. That's where he is.

Joan went on to tell me how tired she was at the end. She actually said, "I was so tired of being Joan Rivers. It was such an ordeal to keep the machine going. I'm exhausted, exhausted. I don't want to be Joan anymore."

I said, "It was medical malpractice. I want to kill your doctor."

"Don't bother," said Joan. "She'll get a reality show, and that'll kill her."

At one point, early after I returned to LA for the funeral, I went to the Santa Monica Pier just for a change of scenery. It didn't work. All I remember is holding on to the railing on the pier and crying my eyes out. Joan described seeing me on the pier. Absolutely NO ONE knew I was there...but Joan.

"All I care about is that Melissa and Cooper are happy. I know she's doing well, and I gave her this life. I didn't like doing reality television, but I did it for Melissa. I wanted her to have a safety net. The only downside of being dead is that Melissa can't hear me when I yell at her now," said Joan.

(I told that to Melissa who said, "Believe me, I hear her. I hear her.") I do, too.

As my session with Marla was wrapping up, Joan asked if my feet fit into my shoes now. That was extraordinary. One of the last things we talked about was a foot operation I was about to have to remove a bone spur so I could wear all my shoes!

She then went on to describe something Melissa gave me after she died. It was a silk scarf Edgar wore for black tie. She even knew the drawer it came from. Melissa told me it was the only thing she kept of his after he died. I'm so happy it's in my house now.

Joan also was at her funeral. She said she had no idea how loved she was; that she couldn't believe it and never knew. She also added that if she had spoken, her speech would have been funnier than Howard Stern's!

One of the things Joan and I loved the most was going out on boats. We used to do it a lot when she played Lake Tahoe. She told me she was spending a lot of time on boats and letting the wind flow through her hair. She said she doesn't care now if it gets messed up. She loves wearing no makeup. She's free. I need to concentrate on her happiness rather than my grief. I know we'll be together again one day.

Chapter Sixteen

RITA HAYWORTH TRAGIC SWEETNESS AND THE GOLDEN GLOBES SCANDAL

Rita Hayworth's father raped her repeatedly throughout her pre-teen and teen life. Sound familiar? The pattern repeats and repeats in the childhoods of sexy movie stars. Eduardo Cansino came from a dancing family and, naturally, he put little Rita in the act. Her disgusting father took the act to Hollywood and she was discovered and ended up a movie star.

When Rita was signed by Columbia Pictures, they decided she had a very low hairline, and she suffered through hours and hours of electrolysis to remove it. It's fascinating to look at the before and after pictures. But that's not what this chapter is about.

The Golden Globes have always been popular with Hollywood, but it has only been in the last ten-to-fifteen years that the public has really caught on to the fun. It used to be the best private party in town. The awards were held at a hotel, usually the Beverly Hilton, and there were no cameras. It had a full bar, a beautiful dinner, and people felt free to drink as much as they wanted and behave in any way they wanted.

I had been going to the Golden Globes since the mid-60s, when they were held in the old Coconut Grove nightclub at the Ambassador Hotel. My biodad was the lawyer for the Globes, so I just went with him every year. When I became a member of the press, I received my own invitation. When I became TV editor of *The Hollywood Reporter*, I was moved to a front table.

One night in the early 70s, I was seated at the front table at the Beverly Hilton with the producers Ross Hunter and Jacques Mapes. Ross was responsible for all those Lana Turner-Sandra Dee movies, as well as the hit, *Airport* (1970). He was a really wonderful guy, and friends with all the female movie stars. And, incidentally, worked for my father as an "errand boy" early on in his career.

The show was going along just fine, and then Rita Hayworth came up on stage to present the next award. She looked a little disheveled and seemed to have trouble with her balance. When she opened her mouth to speak, it was clear she was drunk out of her mind. It was not funny. She was in a room of ALL of Hollywood, and about to make a big fool of herself.

Instead of sticking to the speech, which was on the podium in front of her, she moved to the side and started talking. It was nonsensical talking, but we could make out the words that she felt like doing the striptease dance *from Pal Joey* (1957). In seconds, she was dancing and stripping and tripping, and really humiliating herself. The audience sat there in stunned silence. It was just awful.

With that, Ross Hunter, ever the gentleman, jumped up from his seat, ran onstage, and "gracefully" eased Rita off to the wings and behind a curtain.

It was a horrifying moment, and Rita all but destroyed her reputation.

By morning it was the talk of the town.

"Hi, Sue, it's Rick Ingersoll calling." He was Rita Hayworth's publicist and the first call I received at the office the day after the Globes.

"Hi, Rick. I bet you're not having the best day. I'm really sorry."

"I was wondering if you'd like to have tea with Rita this afternoon at her house?" asked Rick.

Are you kidding me????? I thought. *I get access to the subject of the biggest story in Hollywood right that second?*

"I'd love to," I answered.

"She's very nervous and upset. I'm asking you to come over because I know you respect true movie stars. Honestly, we need a good story to counteract what happened."

"Rick, I completely understand. It would be my pleasure."

At three p.m. I was ringing Rita's doorbell. She lived in a beautiful house behind the Beverly Hills Hotel. It's funny, as I write this now I wonder why I never called Ross Hunter to tell him I was meeting Rita. Oh well, I'm sure he read my story.

"Welcome," said Rick, as he opened the door. Rick was a handsome man with silver hair. He had, in my opinion, a very tasteful public relations company. One of his partners represented Princess Grace; Rick represented Carol Burnett, among others. I liked working with them. The reason they were so good is that they all were trained by and worked for major movie studios before going out and forming their own firm.

Rita's house was very traditional, with formal antiques and elegant furniture. I never asked if she owned it or if it was a rental. It all just seemed very chic.

Note: Rita had once lived in a smaller house on Palm Drive in Beverly Hills, where Jean Harlow died.

Rita was seated on the fluffy, English-rose patterned living room couch that had three sections arranged in a "U." A full tea service was on the coffee table in the center. Rita was on the right, I was seated on the couch to her left, and Rick sat on the third couch opposite Rita. In addition, I noticed that another press agent from Rick's firm was standing behind. I'm sure it was all set up to make her feel safe.

She was wearing a black suit (with skirt, not slacks) and a white silk blouse. She had on very little makeup, and her hair was combed beautifully. She looked like a well-groomed society lady, the exact opposite of what she looked like the night before. She also looked like a prop, but I understood what was going on.

"I'm so very happy to meet you," I said, extending my hand. She took mine in hers and I could feel her shaking.

"Would you like some tea? she asked.

"Yes, thank you. I take it with milk."

"Ah, just like in London," she said.

Her hand was shaking even more now as she poured. I felt so sorry for her. Here we both were doing this performance to erase a scandal. I was happy to be a very willing participant. She was yet another star pulled from a rough family situation into world-wide press, crazy boyfriends and husbands, and now the mother of two children from different ex-husbands. Her career was on the wane, and my heart was heavy as I went through the motions of an interview. I asked her the easiest, most bland, non-controversial things possible. That was part of the unspoken deal. I knew I was going to go back and write a beautiful story, without any mention of the Golden Globes. I was giving Rita a band-aid, and I was honored to do it.

At that time, no one knew anything about a condition called Alzheimer's. People thought Rita was a bad drunk. Instead, she was one of Alzheimer's earliest public victims. Eventually, her daughter, Princess Yasmin Aga Khan, came to Los Angeles and brought Rita to her home in New York to live with her. Yasmin provided round-the-clock caregivers. Rita was finally diagnosed correctly, and Yasmin made sure that her mother's reputation was corrected by sharing that she had Alzheimer's.

Several years after Rita's death, I met Yasmin for a drink at the Tower Hotel on Sunset to do a story on the Alzheimer's Charity she'd set up in her mother's honor. Yasmin was as beautiful and lovely as her mother. Princess Yasmin suffered another tragedy when her only child, a son named Andrew, died at twenty-five in an unconfirmed suicide due to addiction. To this day, she still raises money to fight Alzheimer's and lives her life with the same dignity she has always had.

Chapter Seventeen

HELEN GURLEY BROWN AND JACQUELINE SUSANN MY SOUL SISTERS

On a night in 1956, when my parents went out to dinner, and the housekeeper was in her room, I snuck into my parents' bedroom. For a week, prior to their dinner engagement, I saw my mother sneaking around the house holding a book that was covered with a hastily-made brown paper bag book cover. I just had to know what she was hiding. Their room had a very glamorous doublewide chaise, and when I entered I saw that my mother had just left the book on it. Fool.

I sat on the chaise and took off the brown cover. The book's title was *Peyton Place*. It ended up on the bestseller list for fifty-nine weeks, and sold over twenty-million hardcover books. That was astounding for 1956. I turned it over and saw a photo of the author, Grace Metalious. She was a smart brunette, wearing jeans, a plaid shirt, and tennis shoes, and she was sitting at a desk that was clearly in a cabin in the woods.

If you're reading these stories, no matter what order, you are beginning to see a theme of me, the child, who saw certain people in certain photos or films or movies, who, for some odd reason, ended up affecting my life. What makes it so unique, is that my profession afforded me the opportunity to meet and become friends with almost all of them.

Not Grace. She died of alcoholism at thirty-nine. Had she not, I would have found myself in that cabin, I assure you.

Peyton Place first put the idea in my head of writing novels. I had already been involved in every grade as a kind of chronicler of events for the school paper. It was what you were supposed to do. But, *Peyton Place* took to me another level. Grace Metalious joined those "East Coast" women with whom I identified and admired. It played into that strong desire to go to college in the East.

In 1958, Rona Jaffe, another smart brunette who I also met later on, wrote a book called *The Best of Everything*. To this date I'm still friends with one of the actresses in the movie, Diane Baker. Again, I loved the book, and I was drawn to what it represented. It was a different generation from mine, but I was heading right in that direction.

In 1962, I read a book by Helen Gurley Brown called *Sex and the Single Girl*. Helen also was a smart brunette. It was good for me to see successful brunettes as role models. If you went to movies all you ever saw were the pretty blondes who got anything they wanted. Brunettes actually had to have brains and talent. There are reasons certain statements are clichés.

In 1966, when I was already editor of the first music underground newspaper, *Valley of the Dolls* by Jacqueline Susann was published. I loved it and recognized I might like to write a juicy novel one day for real. I also noticed the extraordinary publicity campaign and made a note of it. As a member of the press, I received the promotional gift of a bottle of "dolls" (pills), which was the brainchild of a woman named Letty Cottin. I didn't now at the time that it was her idea, but of course I ended up meeting her many times with Marlo Thomas and Gloria Steinem. Letty and Gloria founded *Ms.* magazine later on.

In 1971, I was asked to do a guest appearance on *Laugh-In*, the most popular topical comedy/variety series on TV. I was asked because my column was the number one column in *The Hollywood Reporter*. What I wrote was read and absorbed every day by tens of thousands of people, and I had great influence. People love nothing better than seeing their names in print. Being able to do that is a power only understood by those who have had it.

Laugh-In was not taped before an audience. People who were regulars or just guests on it hung out in the empty audience seats.

I had just finished taping my *Laugh-In* bit, and I walked to those seats. I was busy talking to the producer, George Schlatter (yes, the same man who worked for my father at the Las Palmas Theatre), so I didn't see who was in the seat behind me when I sat down. George had to go back to the stage at that point, and I exhaled after completing what I thought was a good job.

Gloria Steinem and I dance the bump at Marlo's 2000 New Year's Eve party.

"You did great," said the voice behind me.

I turned around and was face-to-face with Jacqueline Susann.

"Hi. I'm Jackie Susann. I just love your column."

"And I love your books."

These kinds of surprises never threw me. I am not a "fan" of people. Columnists work in the same business as public personalities, and if your column is good, you become a public personality too. It did not surprise me at all that Jackie and I met. I knew somehow back in 1956 when I read *Peyton Place* and all those other books, that these women would be in my life. I cannot explain how I knew it. I just did. And I never tried to make it so.

"I read your column every day," continued Jackie. "You're going to write books like mine one day. I can tell by reading what you're writing now."

Now THAT knocked me out. I can't be blasé there. I dedicated my first novel to her, and was so upset when she died. I had no idea how sick she was when we met. God bless you, Jackie.

And then...along came Helen. Gurley Brown, that is.

Helen was the one person I pursued. I didn't want to wait for my "inevitable chance meeting." There was no way she didn't know about my column. She read everything about everything. She also kept her eye out for bright young women, because she was always interested in adding to her *Cosmopolitan* writer stable.

I wrote her directly and asked for a meeting. Within days she had answered me and told me to call her secretary to set it up. Right.

At this point I had just received the galleys from my first novel for Warner Books called *Honey Dust*. Did I want Helen to buy an excerpt for *Cosmopolitan*? Obviously. But that would have just been icing on the cake.

I had been to the offices of *Ms.* magazine when it first started, and hung out with Gloria Steinem, Marlo Thomas, and Letty Cottin Pogrebin. They were almost a generation ahead of me, but it still felt like contemporaries when we were sitting there in those practically bare offices.

But this was *Cosmopolitan*. It was established big business, and it was the number one women's magazine at that time. Was I reading it to find out about orgasms or how to wear my hair to please a man? No. However, *Cosmopolitan* and Helen represented, to me, the absolute height of a woman single-handedly producing a monster success. I really respected her.

I was very excited as I walked down the hall to Helen's office holding the book galleys to *Honey Dust*. Her office was so cluttered, I barely could make her out as she walked toward me with a big smile and extended hand. We were friends immediately. She was one of those people who made you feel close and a peer in one second. I'm sure it was a cultivated skill, but it really worked.

Papers were everywhere on her desk, the coffee table, the chairs, the couch...they were tacked to walls. Photos, layouts, stacks of books, scattered pieces of jewelry, scarves, panty hose it was like an explosion in a closet. She even had set up a makeshift makeup mirror and lights in a corner with makeup strewn nearby. I remember seeing lots of pink.

Of all things, she saw me focus in on the makeup area.

Marlo and Dominick.

Helen at my New York book party given for me by Marlo Thomas and Dominick Dunne.

"My life is so crazy. I usually have to get ready here to go out at night," she said.

It was our first bit of conversation. And then we never stopped talking about writing, career "girls," media, books, everything. I was surprised and grateful that she didn't ask me anything about sex. I know that was her favorite topic.

At the end of the meeting I handed her my galleys. She took them and said, "I'm going to read them, but I probably won't buy them."

"I don't care," I replied. "I wrote a book, came to New York, and you are reading my work. That's enough for me."

I received a beautiful note from her about two weeks later, telling me how much she liked the book and the sex scenes. Again, she wrote she wasn't accepting it in *Cosmopolitan*.

Again, I didn't care. I was now friends with Helen Gurley Brown, who respected me as much I respected her. We were official "pen pals."

When *Honey Dust* came out, two different bookstores on Fifth Avenue devoted entire windows to it. It was a stunning experience to stand outside the stores and look at the windows. I remember thinking something like, "Yep, there it is." It wasn't an "Oh my God" moment. It was just a fact to me. Apparently, this reaction wasn't that unusual. Kim Novak told me she had the same reaction when she saw her name on a marquee the first time

I was all over the NY newspaper columns. Joan Rivers had given me a private dinner at her house and invited only New York columnists and CZ Guest. Joan knew they all had to write about it. She invited CZ "for a little color—white."

Marlo Thomas gave me a cocktail party at Mortimer's, the famous Upper East Side society restaurant. I had a great time.

A short time after *Honey Dust* came out, there was a very significant women's March in Washington, D.C. I was standing on a vast lawn near the Washington Monument with California Senator Dianne Feinstein, actress Lynda Carter, and Blaine Trump. I went to the march with Lynda, who grabbed her friend, Blaine, in the crowd. I then spotted my friend Dianne and pulled her in. That was our "little group," waiting for the march to start.

Somewhere in the distance, I saw Helen, all alone, trying to climb over a rope to get into our VIP area. I ran to her, helped her get over, and brought her to the group. Everyone was thrilled to meet her, and she was so happy to be adopted by the group of my friends. It all seemed natural to me, like rounding up your favorite buddies on the playground in kindergarten. I have a picture of all of us from that day framed in my hall.

Me, Lynda Carter, Blaine Trump, Helen Gurley Brown, Senator Dianne Feinstein at the march.

Three years later, I went to New York to give Helen the galleys of my second novel, *Love, Sex and Murder*. She loved that one, too.

For that book, Marlo Thomas and Dominick Dunne gave me a book party at Elaine's on the Upper East Side. It was THE place to have a party, and "everyone who was everyone" was there. It wasn't just a drop-by cocktail party. It was three tables of top press and boldface names who actually stayed for the sit-down dinner.

My first book, Honey Dust, taken at Chasen's Restaurant.

But, the defining moment I remember happened about twenty minutes into the reception part. I was standing holding a bouquet of long-stemmed red roses sent by Carole King. In walked Helen Gurley Brown, with that beautiful smile on her face. THAT was when I lost it. It wasn't on Fifth Avenue. It wasn't seeing half the staff of *Vanity Fair* at the party that got me. I can't explain it. For all the success I had experienced at that point, it was when Helen showed up at the party that I finally connected the dots and truly accepted what I had actually accomplished. I "took that moment," and Helen's and my eyes locked when it was happening. She knew exactly what I was feeling.

Helen was an absolute genius who changed advertising, magazine publishing, and books forever. She also was never paid enough, never recognized enough, and in the end, treated horribly by Hearst. I understand that she was aging out. We all do that, but they didn't handle it well at all. First they put her in charge of "international," and then she just faded away. Shame on them.

I would have established a foundation for her; had a black-tie dinner with all the celebrities; made it a TV special; created HGB scholarships; and HGB Award for a college or charity. I would have tried to give her the world.

Chapter Eighteen

INGRID THULIN—MY OWN PERSONAL INGMAR BERGMAN MOVIE STARRING INGRID THULIN AND ME

Ingmar Bergman was an extraordinary, weird, and sexually-ambiguous famous filmmaker in Sweden. He won every award possible. His stable of stars included Bibi Andersson, Liv Ullman, Max von Sydow, and the most beautiful of all, Ingrid Thulin. Just watch *Wild Strawberries* (1957), *The Magician* (1958), *Winter Light* (1962), and *The Silence* (1963) and you'll see what I mean. She was luminescent—right up there with Garbo.

Without getting too complicated, when a being is startlingly sensual, whether it be Marlon Brando or Monty Clift, or Angelina Jolie or Ingrid Thulin, magical attraction is just magical attraction. It's just a human person, not a gender.

When the Swedish Film Institute was having meetings in Los Angeles, I was invited to have lunch with Ingrid Thulin in the Polo Lounge of the Beverly Hills Hotel. Needless to say, I had seen all her movies, and "God Delivered Unto Thee" another one.

The two of us just got along like fireworks. I have absolutely no idea what we talked about for hours, but when lunch was over she asked me if I'd like to come back to her room after work around six p.m. for cocktails. Seriously. I accepted.

When six p.m. rolled around, I was in the hallway knocking on the door of her suite. It was one of those in the main building that faced Sunset Blvd., but the hotel was so set back you couldn't hear the traffic. She opened the door in what could best be described as a champagne silk dressing gown. It was not an overflowing "Loretta Young number." It was sleek, and moved along her body in all the right places as she walked.

"Please sit down," she said, motioning to the deep green couch with peach and green pillows. Those were and are the colors of the Beverly Hills Hotel. The carpet was also deep green, and the room was filled with flower arrangements welcoming one of Sweden's biggest stars to Hollywood. The shades of the room were drawn, and lights were at a minimum. I have no idea what I had to drink, but guessing from the time period, I presume I had a screwdriver. I do remember she had champagne.

I wish I could remember the words that we exchanged, but all I remember are the feelings. There was something going on that I'd never experienced before. She was clearly coming on to me, but it was in such a chic, European way. I remember the back of my neck starting to sweat. I had never been in this kind of situation before.

And then, suddenly a man entered the living room from the bedroom area.

"This is my husband, Harry Schein, the chairman of the Swedish Film Institute," said Ingrid. Dear Harry was sporting a bad haircut—long where it should be short; short where it should be long, glasses, and an ill-fitting suit. He gave off a vibe like an excited dog about to get a bone.

I tried to relax a bit. Maybe it wasn't what I thought. I mean, here's Harry!

WRONG.

"My husband would like to join us this evening," explained Ingrid. "I've been telling him about you ever since I came back from lunch—your energy, your eyes, that smile. It would be a wonderful evening together."

At that time I didn't know expressions like *Holy F--k!*

The sweat on my neck came back, but this time it was abject fear. Talking about getting in over your head?? Are you kidding me? I've always been the squarest person I'd ever met. I understood what she was asking. I had to get out of there right away.

I jumped up, grabbed my purse, and mumbled something like, "Thanks so much, but I have a dinner interview I have to go to," and I charged out the door.

Am I sorry I did that or not?

Chapter Nineteen

THE SCREEN TEST ONE MOMENT IN TIME

It was the big hair 80s. Three blonde actresses were testing for the lead in an Aaron Spelling one-hour drama for ABC called *Bad Cats*. It was very similar to *Mod Squad*, a show with three detectives—two guys and a pretty blonde.

Screen tests are like the Kentucky Derby. Each horse is groomed and put in a stall. The horse is then let out and runs like hell to win. In this case, obviously, the horses are girls.

The dressing rooms are beautiful. The tests are usually done on a soundstage of another show that's shooting so it's cheaper. You can use existing sets, lights, and cameras. This was an expensive test because they were using film rather than cheap TV video.

All three of the girls were right for the part. One was coming off a big hit movie. Another was a Playboy centerfold winner, and the other was a newcomer with very little experience.

Blonded-out to the nines, each girl did her test. I watched all three. The one coming off of the hit movie was perfectly peppy and her energy just exploded the camera. I thought she was perfect.

The Playboy girl came next. She was totally different from the other two. Her skin was so pale that it was translucent, and her pale blue eyes were rimmed in navy blue. She was ethereal, and on camera it was magic. No other girl could touch that look. In my opinion she was clearly going to be a movie star.

The third girl, the newcomer, was very nice on camera, but, to me, had the least interesting screen test. She just didn't pop, but I DID like her.

Susan Buckner.

Two days later, I found out that the newcomer, the least interesting, got the part. Her name was Michelle Pfeiffer, and *Bad Cats* never sold as a series.

The peppy girl was Susan Buckner, the adorable second-lead in *Grease*, behind Olivia Newton-John. Susan had actually been signed by producer Allan Carr for the part of "Sandy"—(Olivia's eventual part), but when Olivia, the "name," became available, Susan ended up playing the cheerleader, "Patty Simcox."

The third girl, the one who dazzled me with her look, was named Dorothy Stratten. A few weeks later she was murdered by her ex-husband in a brutal Hollywood crime that still horrifies. She was dating the director, Peter Bogdanovich, at the time.

Three girls; three stories; together for one moment in time. And I was there. Yet again. Just another day in my life.

Chapter Twenty

KIM NOVAK GLORIOUS MOVIE STAR
THE ULTIMATE SURVIVOR—AT A VERY HEAVY COST

"No! No! No! Don't kill me," heard unborn baby Marilyn Novak, as she was safe in her mother's womb. "I tell you I heard my parents talking about killing me. They didn't want me, and my mother told me that all the time after I was born. I knew I wouldn't be safe as soon as I was born," said Kim Novak to me one morning as we were having breakfast in my house.

It was not the first time she'd said it. I had heard it many times through the years, and each time she told it she was as upset as the time before.

Right up front I need to explain that there is a Marilyn Novak and a Kim Novak. Marilyn created Kim so she could function in the world. I have been friends with Marilyn/Kim for forty-three years, and, believe me, they are two different people. Keep that in mind as you read on.

Marilyn was born in Chicago to a Czech mother and father who didn't want her. They already had one child, Marilyn's older sister, Arlene, and they didn't want another.

From birth, Marilyn was the pretty one, the golden child with natural blonde hair and hazel eyes. She was an innocent soul who was bullied in school for being so white, so non-Jewish, so sensitive and poetic. She looked like an angel, and bad things happened to angels.

Focus on this: She knew coming out of the womb would not be safe; then, as a child, her father abused her, and then she's raped at 12 by stable boys right after she happily went horseback riding.

KIM AND I ON CARMEL BEACH

It was horrific and devastating, and she told no one. How would you turn out if that happened to you before you were even twelve years old? What kinds of choices would you make? Do you think you could ever trust anyone? She was right the first time about not wanting to come out of the womb into an unsafe world. The womb was a small, safe space. The world was one big, empty, unsafe hell.

You all know the movie magazine version of Kim Novak—the young girl who joined a modeling group called The Fair Teens and learned how to become a model. She ended up doing a tour opening refrigerator doors as "Miss Deep Freeze" across the country. She went to LA as a lark just to accompany a friend who was auditioning for an agent. Kim was sitting in the waiting room and got discovered by a talent scout from Columbia Pictures named Max Arnow. He brought her to Harry Cohn, and "Kim Novak" was born.

However, I'm not writing the fan magazine version. The above paragraph is true, but by the time Kim had come to LA, a trusted priest in Chicago had also sexually attacked her, AND, a male, black, blues singer in a club in Chicago whom she'd fancied had "disappeared and never been found."

"I always felt he was murdered because of me," said Kim.

When a young girl became a movie star in the 50s, she was under contract to a big motion picture studio. That studio did everything for them—I mean everything. They dialed the phone, they did their hair and makeup, they taught them how to talk and walk, they set them up on dates, they made restaurant reservations—they did everything except wipe their bottoms, and if they asked for that too, they would have received it.

Marilyn Novak, the little girl from the Czech ghetto of Chicago, was a frightened, sweet girl whose childhood tragedies and violence kept her from ever really becoming a functioning adult.

The actress "Kim Novak," is a fantasy, a total creation solely done by Marilyn Novak. As she said to me once, referring to her

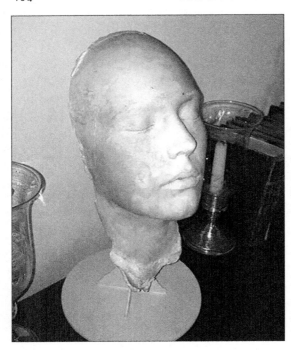

Original Max Factor masque done on Kim in the early 50s. It sits in my house.

creation of "Kim," "And they said I couldn't act!" She laughed the deepest laugh! She'd fooled the entire world.

"I never wanted to be an actress. I wasn't one of THOSE girls," continued Kim. "I wanted to be an artist, a painter. I'd earned three different art scholarships back in Chicago for the Art Institute. That's where I was going right after the refrigerator tour finished. I had no idea about Hollywood. But, I am a strong believer in fate. I think it is so strong that you should just let things happen to you. I never plotted for a part. I never strove for anything. I turned down *Days of Wine and Roses* (1962), *Breakfast at Tiffany's* (1961), and *The Hustler* (1961)."

"Oh my God! How could you turn those down?" I asked. "Let me explain it. I was receiving as many as fifty or more scripts a day. A messenger from William Morris would just leave them on my doorstep. They were all firm offers. It's impossible to read so many scripts and figure out which ones were going to be hits. They were good scripts, but, at that time, they were piled so high I could barely get through them."

The story of Kim refusing to allow the late Columbia President Harry Cohn change her name to Kit Marlowe is well-known. What is not well-known is that when she started making movies and the makeup department slapped all that makeup on her, she went into the ladies room and rubbed as much of it off as she could. She created the look of Kim Novak, that pale face, the "lost in thought, almost vacant eyes," the deeper voice, the slow walk...all by herself in the ladies room!

No one can turn someone into a movie star with hair, clothes, and makeup, Mr. Cohn! The actress becomes a star when she naturally has luminescent, almost see-through skin, and the magic light that comes from within that dazzles a camera. You can't manufacture it. Marilyn Novak turned Kim into a star because she had the real goods. And she knew it. She calculated every nuance of the character of Kim Novak.

Think about *Vertigo* for a second. You have Marilyn playing Kim playing Judy who was playing Madeleine and then playing Judy not as Madeleine. Her performance is one of the most brilliant in cinema.

I have said for years that there are only three truly luminary, mysterious movie stars Garbo, Dietrich, and Novak.

She had to play Kim a lot in real life, too. That was tiring. I remember one time we were shopping at Bullocks in Carmel and no one was recognizing her. She was just wearing jeans and a sweatshirt. "No one knows who you are," I said. "The peace and quiet must be nice for you."

"It is. Now I'm going to show you something so you can have fun. Watch. I'm going to become HER," said Kim, subtly changing her posture, walk, and attitude. There was no change of wardrobe. She wasn't wearing sunglasses that she had to take off. Within seconds, "Kim Novak" was mobbed. She was still wearing jeans and a sweatshirt. She looked at me with a twinkle in her eye and we both laughed.

There are sexy blondes, particularly sexy blonde public personalities, who use seduction for various reasons. And, by the way, the last reason on the list is sex. They use seduction primarily for power and manipulation, and, many times, it is unconscious. The ones who are conscious of its use are evil. The ones who do it in a more innocent manner are not. They are disturbed, but not evil. They use their sexuality to get through life because of what happened to them as children. Their sense of sexuality is altered because of the negative, perverted way they were introduced to it.

Regarding seduction, Kim Novak is the innocent version. Her use of seduction (primarily virtual, not actual) was not particularly conscious. Her behavior was based deeply on childhood incidents. She was more active sexually than perhaps others. Victims of rape frequently are. It is NOT about morals; it's about real damage from childhood.

One time Kim and I were in my kitchen, about to cook sausages. We had gone to Nate 'n' Al's deli in Beverly Hills and bought the really good big ones they sell in their meat department. I placed a sausage on a cutting board to prepare it. As a joke, I took out a very large cutting knife, raised it over my head like a scythe and pretended to bring it down hard, "killing" the sausage by chopping it to bits. I started to sing nonsensical words to a Russian folk song melody—"Romp pah pah," as the knife went down for the kill. Each time I sang "romp," the knife savaged the sausage.

Now that you understand the order of what was happening, by the time I started the second "romp," Kim had grabbed her own long knife and joined in with me. But she joined in, viciously hacking away at the "sausage." I totally understood what was happening. I hope it helped her. Her demons tried to "get her" every day, and she had to constantly fight them off. Can you imagine the pressure?

To truly understand her, you need to understand Rape Treatment Syndrome. Only then can you understand the emotional, mental, and physical terror that Kim lives and loves with. It has affected her every choice and move.

There is something in the medical books called RTS, Rape Treatment Syndrome.

Read this:

When someone has been sexually abused at an early age, how they view sex becomes altered. Instead of the loving bond between a man and a woman that we have been designed for, that physical union becomes marred with painful memories. How an individual reacts and copes to being exposed to a sexual relationship before they were mature enough to understand and handle it will vary from person to person. Having been violated, often repeatedly against their will, teaches a child that sex is not about love; it is about being used and often treated as an object.

Below are just a few symptoms of RTS:
Disorganization
Paralyzing anxiety
Acute Sensitivity
Extreme depression
Panic attacks
Paranoia
Shame

Whether you call her Marilyn or Kim, she suffers from many of these, and none of it is her fault. And, in addition, she is bi-polar, a condition that can also come about because of repeated sexual traumas. Would you like to be in her shoes?

She and I first met in 1973, and, as of this writing, have been friends for forty-three years. I know her whole life, inside and out, and have actually been present next to her for half of it. Kim was my favorite movie star. As a child, when I saw her in *Picnic* (1955), I felt her soul. Whether I really did or not—who knows?— but I thought I did. When I saw her in *Man with the Golden Arm* (1955) and *Eddy Duchin* (1956), I saw the luminescent quality that rang true to her core. When I saw *Vertigo* (1958), I was captivated by the multi-leveled performances. Mind you, I was still so young that my father took me to see it, and I remember saying to him after I saw it, "Daddy, why does she have to die in the end?" He answered, "Retribution. Now you know the meaning of the word."

The first time I saw *Vertigo*, I was so obsessed with the movie that I went to see it repeatedly. A few years later, for my sixteenth birthday, my father asked what I wanted and I said, "I want a private screening of *Vertigo*."

And that's what I got. My father called Paramount and got a print. He then booked the Charles Aidakoff Screening Room on the Sunset Strip. On my birthday, at the appointed time, I sat alone in the darkened room with my "present," and I remember running up to the screen just to be closer to scenes that meant so much to me. I guess every child has some kind of obsession, and mine was Kim Novak and *Vertigo*.

In 1973, Kim had made a TV movie called *Third Girl From the Left* and was going to be in Hollywood to promote it. I was at *The Hollywood Reporter* and called Kim's agent and asked for an interview. I had been waiting fifteen years for it.

The interview was to take place at a ridiculous hotel in the Valley called "Sportsmen's Lodge." It was a glorified motel that had a man-made lake stocked with fish and lots of bridges. It is the least likely place a movie star would ever stay. I couldn't believe Kim was staying there and that's where we would meet. Knowing her as I do now, I know she chose to stay there BECAUSE she knew it was ridiculous. Kim was having a laugh on all of us.

I never wait more than twenty minutes for an interview subject. I give them that leeway, and after twenty minutes I leave. Kim kept me waiting two hours. I probably would have waited two days.

I heard her voice in the lobby, and then into the bar she came, wearing a red turtleneck sweater, jeans, and boots. Her hair and face were perfect. She looked exactly like Kim Novak. She was forty, but looked twenty. She was extremely apologetic and told me that her "people" never told her about the interview. She was quite upset that I'd been kept waiting. And, she has apologized for it repeatedly over the past forty years!

I have no clue what either of us said, but I know we both felt like we had been friends for years, and "got each other." I know now that I was just asking questions and totally showing her how much

I understood "Kim Novak." I handed her the perfect interview, and she handed it right back to me. Upon reflection, we both knew our parts and played them to the hilt.

We started writing letters to each other because we wanted to become friends. Letters! Can you imagine that? This went on for a few years, and then we started talking about my advising her on her career. She sent me an airplane ticket to fly to Carmel to meet with her. By this time, she had sold Gull House, her incredible castle on the rocks above the sea, and married a large-animal veterinarian named Dr. Robert Malloy. They lived on a ranch in the hills of Carmel.

I grew up in Los Angeles in a beautiful Georgian colonial home in the Los Feliz area, about twenty minutes away from Beverly Hills. Los Feliz was the home of Griffith Park, the Griffith Park Observatory (used in *Rebel Without a Cause* (1955)) and the Greek Theatre. As a child, I traveled regularly to San Francisco and Hawaii. But what I NEVER did was pay any attention to nature. I went to school, studied, graduated from USC, and went into journalism. My whole world was Hollywood and the inside of studios and theatres.

Kim Novak's world was all nature—trees, flowers, views, dirt roads, ponds, beaches, mountains, and snow. When I arrived at her ranch, I had to get out and open a wooden gate to get in. There was no intercom or anything fancy. I drove down a dirt road past stables, barns, wagons, huge trees that looked like undecorated Christmas trees, a tiny wooden guest cabin, horse rings, stables, pitchforks, and llamas. I may as well have been on another planet. She taught me her world.

Her house was simply a larger wood cabin with a loft and a huge deck off the living room. Her furniture was made out of carved wood that looked like parts of trees. Indian blankets were hung over the back of couches; a stone fireplace went up to the ceiling.

The view from her deck looked like something out of *Lost Horizon* (1937). Outside her deck were birdbaths, ponds, a statue of St.

We love Carmel Beach.

Francis, circles of flowers, and waterfalls. I had never, ever seen any home setting like this one. Stars' Beverly Hills estates were nothing compared to this, because this nature was NOT manufactured.

She walked me all around the property and introduced me to her horses, llamas, and chickens. They all had names. Her snake, Sincerely, and her goat, Creature, had died a few years before I got there, but I'd remembered them from magazine stories.

We then went for a drive where she showed me Carmel, Pacific Grove, Monterey, the Seventeen Mile Drive with the Lone Cypress, and Big Sur. She was stunned when I'd told her I'd never walked among flowers as we were walking on the path above the water in Pacific Grove. She couldn't believe that I had given up bike riding or roller-skating after I started my career. She couldn't believe that I never took walks, read poetry, or listened to music on a rainy day while looking at starfish under rocks in the ocean.

That wasn't easy to do at Hollywood and Vine!

According to Kim, I wasn't living. She decided she was going to show me a whole new world. For YEARS she sent me plane tickets

Frank Lloyd Bench.

to Carmel for almost every weekend. I went up to her house at least twice a month for my "lessons."

We loved a bench on a cliff at the beach. There is a plaque on it for the architect Frank Lloyd Wright, who designed a house nearby. We called it "Frank Lloyd Bench," and have taken many pictures there through the years.

Here are some examples of adventures that occurred repeatedly over many, many years, and, in some cases, are still happening:

She bought me a bicycle AND roller-skates so we could ride or skate among the piers of Monterey, the paths of Pacific Grove, or the beaches of Carmel. We even kayaked in Monterey Bay. Kim is a great rower. I hated rowing.

She bought me a kite and wrote on it, "Take the time to fly." We took it to Carmel Beach and ran along the sand as it flew up and up, away from life's burdens.

She bought two Walkmans and made two cassette tapes with identical music, so as we rode or skated and listened, we would "be on the same musical trip." All the songs were special, but if one was so moving that we were "overcome," we'd pull over and just gaze out at the sea.

I remember one day we were walking, and "Moonglow" and the Theme from 'Picnic'" came on. She stopped in mid-trail and did the dance for me that she did for Bill Holden. It was an unforgettable moment.

Another time she took me to Gull House to see it for myself. Although she had sold it, it seemed to be unoccupied the day we went. We climbed all over the rocks and around the house as she imbued me with the spirit of her adventures there. We went looking for kelp, and she showed me how you can play it by bending it and making certain sounds.

We had many favorite restaurants in Carmel. We were sitting one night in the Italian one and she ordered a cold asparagus appetizer. I ordered a mozzarella marina. I watched as she picked up the first asparagus in her hands and had the first delicious bite. I had never seen anyone eat asparagus with their hands, although something in my etiquette memory began to trigger.

"Who taught you how to eat asparagus like that?" I said with a slightly disparaging tone.

"Aly Khan," she answered as she deliberately put another one in her mouth and bit with a vigorous crunch.

Oops.

Big Sur was another special favorite, and she took me to the beach with the special caves. You hide in a big circular cave or hoop and, if you position yourself correctly, the water rushes right through and you don't get wet. Wow! That was something! We went to Nepenthe where she danced the way she did in the 60s. We'd go to little dive restaurants hidden under piers where no tourists would go.

Once, early on in our friendship, she invited me to spend my birthday in San Francisco. Per instructions, I was to meet her at the Mark Hopkins Hotel on Nob Hill. I knocked on the door of her room. If you are not familiar with the Mark Hopkins, it sits high on a hill and has a penthouse bar called Top of The Mark. All four sides of that room are glass, and it is breathtaking. What I did NOT know about the Mark (but Kim did) was that there was one suite that was on another part of the roof that had a sunken corner room with skylights that was in the tower section as part of the roof.

The suite was cool enough, and as she led me into it I heard the sounds of jazz pianist George Shearing playing. We walked to the corner area and I saw an amazing sunken room covered with picnic blankets, upon which was an array of caviar, cheese, fruit, baguettes, wine, and vodka. Oh my God. And when I sat down on the blankets, I looked up at the ceiling and saw the sky! Happy Birthday to me!

The next day, she literally took me to the Mission Dolores, the McKittrick Hotel, The Palace of the Legion of Honor, the flower shop, Jimmy Stewart's apartment, her apartment up on Nob Hill, Ernie's, and then we drove down to Mission San Juan Bautista where we saw the old gray horse in the barn and the Bell Tower. All Along the way I was doing Jimmy Stewarts' lines, and she was doing hers. It was totally surreal. She had recreated my favorite movie for me and put me in it! Just jaw-dropping!

She bought us matching foldable bicycles so we could ride around movie lots when she was working. One time we ended up on an Indian set and just hung out in the teepee. No one found us.

Us happy in Oregon.

When Clint Eastwood became mayor of Carmel, Kim moved out of there as fast as she could, to a tiny town in Oregon called Chiloquin. It had only one street. She had to collect her mail at the hardware store because it actually had an address. "Clint called attention to Carmel because of all the publicity. So many tourists were there that I had to leave," she told me.

She moved to Oregon, so I went to Oregon. The Chiloquin house was gigantic compared to the one in Carmel. It was a two-story mountain lodge built right by a rushing river. Again, there was huge deck and tons of "Christmas trees."

Since I was from Los Angeles, I had never seen snow, and on my very first visit, snow fell. It was late at night and Kim ordered me to put on my boots and heavy coat and go out and experience it. We both ran out onto her deck. The moonlight illuminated the flakes. I was in awe. She held out her arms like she was about to do a Wonder Woman spin and started turning around, taking it all in, even letting snow melt on her tongue. I did the same. The river was quiet and there were no sounds at all except for our giggles and delight. It was a freedom and connection to God-created things that I had never experienced. It was yet another gift of magic from Kim.

One time in Oregon, Kim's sister, Arlene, was visiting. She is one of the sweetest people ever. The sisters were reminiscing about the Czech dumplings that their grandmother made, and I suggested that we make them.

"Come with me," whispered Kim, as we left Arlene alone to look up recipes.

We went outside and shared a couple of gigantic martinis. By the time we went back into the house, we were already laughing.

Unaware, Arlene was gathering flour, eggs and water. Kim and I decided to "help her." All I can tell you is Kim and I were laughing so much we were crying. Arlene kept asking, "What's so funny?" and then Kim and I would lose it again. The dumplings sank to the bottom of the pan like bowling balls. They were inedible. It was hilarious. And guess what? The whole thing was videotaped and I still can't watch it without dissolving into tears of laughter.

Eventually, Kim and Bob decided they wanted a bigger place, so they moved to a tiny town in southern Oregon. They bought Lionel Barrymore's old fishing ranch—one hundred twenty acres along the Rogue River that even had three islands within the property. Since it was an old ranch, it had three guest cabins, and a very large main house, which was done over after a fire.

A few years later they bought "half a mountain." I'm not kidding. They wanted their horses to able to experience climbing as well as the flat trails. The entire Oregon spread that they have gives them the most gorgeous, natural playground I've ever seen. They just love living there and having fun.

In that house Kim taught me how to drive an ATV—a dangerous skill I continue to perfect.

Our adventures weren't just confined to California. We have been to New York, Paris, Canada, San Francisco, the Caribbean, London—all over. We have been on planes, trains, and ships.

On our first trip to New York we stayed at the Pierre Hotel on Fifth Ave. at 61st. It's an elegant, classic hotel. We went to see Lily Tomlin on Broadway, and ended up at the Russian Tea Room with a combo of caviar and vodka. We closed the place at 2 a.m. and called for a limo. It had started to snow.

We got in the limo, feeling no pain, and the driver asked where we wanted to go. I thought Kim was going to say, "The Pierre, please." But, no. she said, "I want to go to the edge of New York."

The driver headed down Fifth. Kim and I were in matching fake white fur coats. Suddenly she opened the moon roof and said, "C'mon. Get up here." We ended up standing on the back seat, our upper bodies through the roof of the car, watching all the lights on Fifth Ave. as the wind whipped through us. It was one of the most exhilarating feelings I've ever felt.

"Wait a minute," I shouted to the driver. Let's turn here and see where Katharine Hepburn and Garbo live!"

Kim shrieked with joy.

We let the engine idle in front of Hepburn's apartment in Turtle Bay for a moment and debated ringing the bell. It was almost three a.m. We decided to keep driving.

The snow was making her hair limp and mine frizz. We didn't care. Off we went to the South Street Seaport. We stood up all the way down there, heads up to the sky, and laughed all the way back up Madison. As we neared the Pierre, Kim pointed to the Sherry-Netherland and said, "That's where Columbia always made me stay. I felt like a prisoner there."

Another time we were in New York it was courtesy of CBS. She was going to do some press for them. They gave her the penthouse at the Ritz Carlton on Central Park South that ran the length of the building. It had three fireplaces, two balconies, two bedrooms, and a kitchen—anything you could want. We had a ball.

It seems like we were always in cool hotels. In Paris we stayed at the Hotel de la Tremoille, a tiny hotel behind the Plaza Athenee. We chose it because it was quieter. It was so much fun being in France.

Flying high in the NY limo in the 80s.

I live in Los Angeles, and, many times Kim comes to visit me, sometimes for a month at a time. We found ocean hideaways, walking paths, and trees I never knew existed. Kim hated Hollywood, but she has fond memories regarding food. We went to Chasen's for banana shortcake, Musso and Frank's for everything, Nate 'n' Al's Deli for chopped liver, chubs, and matzo ball soup. Kim loves delis because,

We love Paris.

Kim at my house.

although she was Czech, her family lived in a Jewish neighborhood in Chicago and she loved the food.

I have told you only a few of our incredible adventures that have
gone on all over the world. What's important for you to know is
that over all these years, Kim has told me almost everything about
her life that she never told anyone else. Some of the painful things
you've already heard; some I'll still tell. You've heard some funny
things, too.

I'm going to give you some of her Hollywood stories now, and
keep in mind that, in my opinion, it's a testament to Kim's strength
and faith that she never gave up living. She lives every day with such
severe damage from childhood and adult violence, plus a bipolar

In front of my cabin at Kim's house in Oregon.

condition. She also lives with panic attacks. She fights every day to wake up happy. She lives through her painting and poetry writing, both artistic outlets helping her rid herself of demons within.

When Harry Cohn died, the roles Kim was offered were not as good. Cohn protected her and chose well. It was also the early 60s, and top actresses were suddenly offered stupid things like "beach movies." Kim had no interest in taking her career down that path. She had a wonderful agent at William Morris named Norman Brokaw. He was her agent until the day he died at 89. Norman did his best, but Kim was also impatient. Staying still was uncomfortable for her.

She was friends with Marilyn Monroe and felt sorry for her. Both were blonde sex symbols—Kim rightfully choosing not to identify that way. Both women were sexually damaged and had a form of mental illness. Both were much better actresses than were originally acknowledged. Kim felt some kind of kindred spirit in Marilyn.

At that time, Kim was living in a beautiful home in Bel Air on a street aptly named Tortuoso Way. She'd had a place in Malibu, too, on the Pacific Coast Highway, but she'd sold it after an intruder broke in and tried on all her clothes. She felt it was contaminated and never went back.

One night Kim had been invited to Peter Lawford's beach house to a casual dinner party for Robert Kennedy.

"I got a call from Marilyn saying she'd been invited and she didn't know what to wear. I told her it was casual and I'd probably wear jeans and a sweater. She told me she'd been studying all day, reading everything she could about Bobby, including his speeches. She desperately wanted to sound intelligent and be able to have conversation with him that impressed him. I was so struck by her insecurity," said Kim.

Kim showed up as planned in her jeans.

"Marilyn came in a gown and in full make-up. She sat next to Bobby and enchanted him."

Kim was very upset when Marilyn died. She identified with Marilyn's unhappiness. Kim, unhappy with her roles, thought it was a sign for her to escape. A while later, a mudslide hit Bel Air, and part of the Tortuoso Way house slid down the hill with most of Kim's belongings.

"That was the final sign I needed to just get in my car and get out for good. I remember wanting to get some great dill pickles to eat on the way up the coast to Big Sur. I stopped by a deli in Brentwood and they were out of pickles. That was another sign. I cried when they didn't have those pickles. It may sound crazy, but that was the last straw! I never came back to Hollywood to live. I wanted to be free to live as I wanted, and I was lucky that I had the money to do so."

The good news in this is that her work in *Vertigo* and *Middle of the Night* (1959), and others, has been rediscovered and lauded by film festivals and contemporary critics. I'm very glad about that.

Here are some of her thoughts she's expressed to me through the years:

Tyrone Power—"He didn't like me. He was very dismissive and resentful that I was so new. He only spoke to me in scenes where the camera was rolling. He was ice cold."

Frederic March—"When we made *Middle of the Night* (1959) he kept coming on to me. It was very annoying and difficult to work with him."

Rita Hayworth—"Harry Cohn set us up not to like each other, but the exact opposite happened. We liked each other instantly. She never resented me for being the 'so-called one to take over.' I liked her so much."

Pal Joey (1957)—"I hated that movie, I hated that character. I was embarrassed by having to play that stupid, little showgirl. I don't like my performance."

Richard Quine (Kim's director on so many movies and her fiancé)—"Dick had a drinking problem. I loved him very much, but I just couldn't marry him because of it. That house that was built in the movie *Strangers When We Meet* (1960) was built by Columbia for Dick and me as a wedding present. We never lived in it." Quine later committed suicide and I was the one who had to tell her.

Laurence Harvey—"We shot *Of Human Bondage* (1964) together and I couldn't stand him. He was really rude, and deliberately ate whole cloves of garlic before our love scene. But, I have to say, I think I was quite good in that picture."

Vertigo (1958)—"This was my best performance at all. It was so mysterious, so multi-layered, those are roles that attract me—the duality of things."

Kirk Douglas—"He wasn't very nice to me on *Strangers When We Meet*. He kept trying to direct me. In one dinner scene that took place at a restaurant, during my close up when the camera was only on me, he moved his eyes back and forth in a rhythm trying to get me to say the lines in timing he wanted. I did not enjoy making that movie because of him, but that is all forgiven now."

Jeff Chandler—"He was like my brother. There was never anything between us other than friendship. He was always over at my house fixing lamps or plumbing. I just adored him so much. He was at my house the night before he was to go into the hospital for back surgery. He told me he'd see me as soon as he got out. Those doctors killed him."

Kiss Me, Stupid (1964)—"I signed to do that movie because of Billy Wilder and Peter Sellers. When Peter had a heart attack and had to be replaced with Ray Walston, I was very disappointed. My heart broke and I knew it wouldn't be the movie I wanted. I loved the character of 'Polly,' though."

Harry Cohn—"He may have been the boss of Columbia Pictures, but he never scared me. When I looked at him he was like an old uncle. I stood up to him a lot, and sometimes it worked and sometimes it didn't. Although he really tried to get me to sleep with him, I never did. I remember once I complained that I really needed a vacation from living in the tiny room in the Studio Club. Instead of sending me away, he locked me in a dressing room suite for a week at the studio. At Christmas I baked him cookies myself, and I swear I saw a tear in his eye when I gave them to him. I know everybody was happy when he died, but I wasn't. I liked him."

Frank Sinatra—"When I first met him on *Man with the Golden Arm* (1955), he was so sweet to me. We started dating. I was living at the all-women's Studio Club and he was only allowed on the living room floor. He couldn't come upstairs where our bedrooms were. One time I had the flu and he showed up with chicken soup. The ladies were dying. Another time he had a complete set of first edition classic books of Thomas Wolfe delivered to me. He was also the one who told me my contract at Columbia was unfair because I was becoming a star and the money was too low. He got me Abe Lastfogel, my agent at William Morris. Columbia was furious he interfered. But when we did *Pal Joey* he was a different guy. Maybe he was getting into the role of the character. I don't know. But he was difficult to work with. He refused to show up at rehearsals. Rita and I worked for weeks on a big dance number and he never came to rehearsals. Finally, the day before we were to shoot it, he walked in and we did the number for him. The choreographer, Hermes Pan, danced Frank's part. Rita and I loved the number. After it was over, Frank stood up and wouldn't even look us in the eye. He said, 'I'll do that step; I won't do that.' He cut most of the number and destroyed it. What you see in the film is Frank's version. Rita and I were very disappointed. As the years passed, I forgave Frank."

Alfred Hitchcock—"He treated me with total respect. I don't understand any of these actresses who accuse him of harassment. He was a gentleman to me. I once asked him a question about a scene and he said, 'I hired you for the part because I knew you could do it. Just do it.'"

Jimmy Stewart—"God, how I loved that man. He was in love with me, but that's not the kind of love I felt for him. In *Vertigo* he talked to me and gave me confidence. He showed me a trick about how to not have hand veins show on camera. Before every take, he would raise his arms straight above his head and hold them there for a full minute. Then, just as action was called, he lowered them and started the scene. His hands had no veins showing and they looked like he was a young man.

"Jimmy was like an old shoe. I just felt so comfortable with him. Sometimes we didn't even need to talk. There's a scene in *Bell, Book, and Candle* (1958), where he and I are sitting on a couch, our legs on a coffee table, and we are both barefoot. I just loved his toes. They were so long and sleek. The director called a lunch break and Jimmy and I didn't move. We just sat there for the whole lunch hour just silently being together."

Mike Figgis—"He was the director of the last movie I ever did (to date). It was called *Liebestraum* (1991), and the script was wonderful. I was playing a dying mother with dementia. What a part! I was so excited. Had I known that the part was written by him about his own mother, whom he hated, I might have had second thoughts. I also didn't know that he'd cast his girlfriend in the ingénue lead. He took out all the cruel feelings he had on his mother on me. I have never been treated so viciously by anyone. I rose above it and my performance was really good, so good that it outshone his girlfriend's. He cut my part to shreds to highlight her, and did his best to destroy me as a human while directing me. It was such a horrible experience that I said I'd never go back to make another movie, and I haven't. He's a despicable, sick person."

Sammy Davis, Jr.—Here's the truth. Kim went to a party and Sammy was one of the guests. She had just come from shooting. When they were introduced, they sat down for a drink. They got to know each other. She enjoyed him as a person, and she loved his family. She missed her own family, and Sammy's was warm and friendly. She'd go over for Sunday dinners and it helped her feel a little bit of home in Los Angeles. She also loved that fact that it drove Harry Cohn crazy.

Did she love Sammy? No. He was an adventure that amused her. Did she care that Harry Cohn made her break it off? No. She was done, but she deeply resented the racism.

I knew Sammy, too, from his many TV special and Vegas appearances and all my interviews with him. He and Bobby Darin were the most talented people I'd ever seen. Both could sing, dance, do comedy, drama, do impressions, and play every instrument. When Sammy was dying from throat cancer, he was in Cedars-Sinai Hospital in Los Angeles. Kim happened to come down for one of her visits and we were driving by the hospital.

"You know, Sammy's in there. He's very sick and hardly has any time left. Don't you think it would be a nice surprise if you went up there just to see him before he goes?"

"No, I don't want to go," said Kim.

"But he's going to die and you meant so much to him."

"I just don't know if I want to do it," said Kim.

"It would mean so much to him," I said. Why I was pushing? I have no idea. I guess I'm just a bit of a do-gooder. And, if it happened today, I'd never push her. It was none of my business.

"Oh, all right," she said, very reluctantly.

I parked the car and we went up the elevator to the eighth floor, which is the VIP floor that has suites. Sammy's was at the end of the hall. The main door opened onto the living room. Kim walked in and a roomful of black men stood up in shock.

"We're here to see Sammy," I said.

One of them ran into his room. I could hear him say, "Kim Novak is here!"

Sammy made a loud sound and started to choke. Because it was throat cancer, he could hardly speak. His choking escalated and they had to call a nurse. Kim gave me a look that said—*See, I told you we shouldn't have come.*

In a few minutes Sammy calmed down and we went in. They had taken him out of bed and put him in a chair. There was another chair about four feet away that faced him. Kim just sat in the chair.

"Hi, Sam," said Kim.

He started to cry. Only his tears filled the silence. At that point I knelt down to him. It was my only move. There were no other places to sit. The silence felt very awkward.

"Sammy, you're the greatest entertainer," I said. "Thank you for all the joy you've given me and the world."

Then Kim said something like, "It's been a long time. I came by to say, God bless you."

And then she stood up to go. She was nice to him. She let him see her and gave him that gift.

When we got to the car she said, "Thank you for making me do that."

In 1989, Jimmy Stewart and Kim were asked to present at the Oscars. They hadn't seen each other in years. The Academy put Kim up in the L'Hermitage Hotel in Beverly Hills. Her room faced the street. Even though the Academy offered Kim her own limo to take her to the rehearsals the day before the show, Jimmy insisted that he pick her up in his limo. I was to follow behind in my car.

I had also gotten to know Jimmy a little bit because I interviewed him for *The Reporter*, and I sat next to him a few times at Debbie Reynolds' table when she had her Thalians charity dinner. Jimmy was a sweet angel.

I was looking out the window for the limo and I saw it pull up. I called for Kim to join me at the window. We watched as Jimmy opened his door. We saw a fragile, 81-year-old man, slightly stooped over, have difficulty getting out. But then he did the most amazing thing. He moved a few steps over to a lamppost and straightened himself up with all his might. He folded his arms and crossed one ankle over the other, and posed like a chivalrous young man waiting for a date with a woman he loved. He was making himself presentable for her. Kim and I had tears in our eyes.

A couple of times, Kim has sailed on the elegant Queen Mary and made an appearance in their theatre to do an interview (usually with me) and run one of her movies. I have also had the good fortune to lecture on Hollywood on many ships, and it's really fun when we are together.

What's most important in Kim's life now is her art. She has finally gone back to her first love—painting. I call her "Monet," because of her impressionist style. She is a remarkable, talented artist. Her works have been exhibited at the American Museum of Impressionism in Youngstown, Ohio, one of the most respected museums in the United States. Her work has also been seen at The San Francisco Historical Society, as well as a museum in Prague. Kim is experiencing her greatest joy, and in an environment of total

Kim in one of the many hammocks on her property.

harmony and nature along the Rogue River in Oregon, and nothing could make me happier. She deserves it.

On board the Queen Mary a couple of years ago.

AT SEA EN ROUTE TO SOUTHAMPTON

CUNARD INSIGHTS SPECIAL PRESENTATION
SUE CAMERON INTERVIEWS
KIM NOVAK

Legend... a person who is the centre of stories perpetuated by their telling through history, someone who is timeless in their style and appeal. That was Garbo, that was Dietrich, and that IS Kim Novak. At the height of her fame she had the courage to walk away from fame and fortune in search of her own identity. She is an artist in the worlds of motion pictures, painting, writing, sculpting and photography. Kim Novak possesses a magic that enables her to endure the test of time. She is luminescent both on and offscreen, and is timeless. That is what makes a legend. Join her as she speaks to Hollywood expert Sue Cameron about her life and career. Hosted by your Entertainment Director, Paul O'Loughlin.

At 11.00am in the Royal Court Theatre
Recorded and broadcast on TV Ch 43 from 5.00pm onwards

I took a picture of my feet and sent it to Kim. I had no idea she was going to turn them into a painting. Wow!

Special backstage moment with two of my "Supremes" and TCM's Robert Osborne.

Chapter Twenty-One

LUCIE ARNAZ—WHY I LOVE MY LUCIE

Lucie Arnaz is humble, kind, generous, extremely funny, and an incredible, triple-threat talent. I simply adore her. We are partners in crime.

When Lucie tells a story, she plays all the parts, scores it, and almost does an interpretive dance to enhance it. It's a sight to behold.

For the one person who may have grown up on planet Pluto, yes, her parents were Lucille Ball and Desi Arnaz. I knew them casually. I respect their talent, and I'm so grateful they had children. Other than that, they are not in my consciousness.

My friend is Lucie Whatever-Her-Name-is Luckinbill. In my opinion, Lucie is the most talented person in her family. She's going to write about her own life in her book, and I know it will be incredible.

We met when she was fifteen, doing her first TV series, and I was at *The Hollywood Reporter*. We hit if off nicely, and for the next 30 years, saw each other once in a while—an occasional lunch. Then, one night we had dinner at The Palm in Los Angeles. Something clicked and we really became friends. I even saw her star in *Witches of Eastwick* in London. She introduced me to her family and made me feel as if I were one of them.

I also received a call right after that column was published from Lucille Ball's press agent, Charlie Pomerantz. Lucy invited me to come over to her house for tea. Of course I went, and met the very imposing, strong, Lucille Ball. Her low voice also added to the force of her. I had no idea what she wanted as we started to have tea in her backgammon room.

"I wanted to thank you for writing so nicely about my daughter," said Lucy. "I really appreciated it."

Wow, how nice, I thought.

"The Caper Kids"

The next time I went to the house was in 1971 for Lucie's wedding to Phil Vandervort. It was held in the gorgeous garden.

I had also, in the 60s, spent time with Desi, Jr., and his rock group, Dino, Desi, and Billy. This all was fast becoming a family affair.

Lily Tomlin with Lucie and me at a cool Palm Springs party.

In the Seventies, I even had the extreme pleasure of meeting actor Larry Luckinbill, star of the ABC TV series *The Delphi Bureau*, by interviewing him. I was so impressed with his intelligence and wit. And, lo, and behold, he ended up marrying Lucie!

*   *   *

Lucie and Larry moved to Palm Springs in 2013. I decided to become their semi-permanent houseguest. I'd been thinking of moving to Palm Springs for years, and now I had a place to stay while I "auditioned" the town.

In return, Lucie was my semi-permanent houseguest in Los Angeles whenever she needed a place to stay whether she was in from New York, or after she moved to Palm Springs. We both play Latin percussion, and I'm sure my neighbors were thrilled when we'd improv to a Tito Puente record or Cuba's Benny More. We each played bongos, congas, guiro, claves, shakers—you name it. We had/have "an act."

We attend each other's birthdays; spend holidays together; play with children's toys in the pool. We see each other constantly.

One time she flew in from New York and arrived at my house in L.A. My opening line to her was—
"Did you hear? Suge shot Biggie."
"Why?" said Lucie.
"Because Biggie shot Tupac."
"Who's Tupac?"
"The guy that Biggie shot."
"Who's Biggie?"
"He murdered Tupac."
"What does Suge have to do with it?"
"Tupac was Suge's friend."
It went on and on.

I was actually giving her accurate information, but Lucie had no interest in rap singers. She thought I was starting an Abbott and Costello *Who's on First* routine. It went on and on for days.
As a result, she calls me Suge, after the rapper Suge Knight.
What do I call her? I call her Shecky, after the stand-up comic Shecky Greene. Lucie is, without a doubt, one of the funniest borscht belt stand-up comics you'll ever hear.

A few months later she got the following frantic call from me:
"Shecky! Guess where I am?"
"I have no idea."
"Shecky Greene's old house. I'm serious. I'm in his bathroom right now."
"No way," said Lucie.
"Really!" I said.
"Is he dead?"
"I'm not sure."
Click.

Two weeks later I receive a call from her.
"Suge! Guess where I am?"

"I don't know."

"You won't believe this! I'm at the Palm Springs Post Office and Shecky Greene is ahead of me in line!!!! He's not dead!"

There is a Coffee Bean in Palm Springs, right at the busiest corner of downtown. Directly in front of the store is a bronze statue of Lucille Ball sitting on a bench. It's surrounded by foliage and plantings. The city put it there to honor her. One day when I was on my way to Coffee Bean, I thought the foliage was overgrown and Lucy's face was obscured. I drove to Lucie's house.

"Your mother is overgrown."

"What?"

"I can't see her face on the Coffee Bean statue," I explained.

"I guess the city isn't doing a very good job of gardening," responded Lucie.

"I guess not."

We paused and looked at each other.

"Perhaps it needs trimming,'" said Lucie.

"Do you have gardening shears?" I asked, innocently.

"Yes..."

"I know!" I continued. "Let's find some orange vests and we'll pretend we're prisoners doing clean-up. No one will bother us. It will all look real."

At 10 a.m. the next day, a shiny, BUSY Sunday morning in Palm Springs, we parked the car about a block away and walked toward our target. It was decided that Lucie would prune and I would clean up the branches. There was a line out the door into Coffee Bean.

We started our "jobs" with great precision and attention to detail.

"Hey! Excuse me!" shouted someone in line to Lucie. "Could you move? We want to take a picture with Lucille Ball and you're interfering."

"Of course I'll get out of the way," said Lucie.

I couldn't look at her, and crouched on the ground to collect our trash to take to the garbage can. Then, I couldn't resist it.

The haircut caper.

"Do you think they'll give us time served for our community service work?" I asked Lucie so everyone could hear.

"Oh, definitely," she answered, with a straight face, going back to cutting when the tourists were through.

It was a very sunny spring day in Palm Springs. Lucie was doing an important show in a few days called *One Night Only*, at the McCallum Theatre, a giant performing arts center in Palm Desert. She'd had a break from rehearsals and we were hanging by her pool.

"You know, I haven't seen my parents' house at Thunderbird Country Club in years. I spent a lot of my time growing up there. I wonder if it looks the same?"

"Why don't we go look at it?"

"Well, it's a private club," she said.

"Can we get in?"

"I don't know. There's a code for the main residential gate, but I don't have it," explained Lucie.

I also knew that even if there were a guard there, Lucie would never use her name to get in. Most of the time when meeting new people she never even mentions her last name.

(Which is one of the many reasons I love her.)

"Oh, but now I want to go. It's a cool caper. We've got to do it. We'll just sneak in."

"Okay, but so we don't look suspicious when we're by a gate, just pretend we've been on a jog and you're bending down to tie your shoelaces or something," said Lucie.

She recommended we wait by the gate.

We got out of the car and walked to the gate. Of course, no car was in sight. We'd have to wait until one came along and just follow behind it when the gate opened. It only took a couple of minutes.

We stealthily made our way along the streets she knew so well, as she recounted who lived where. It was really fun.

"Stop! There's my house. There's a car in the driveway."

"Well, I know for sure you're not going to ring the bell and introduce yourself. What do you suggest?"

"I heard that the current resident has made a lot of renovations to the pool area and I'd love to see what she did. Follow me and do as I do," said Lucie.

She walked way wide of the house, slipping herself in-between a couple of houses, and started heading down a sloping lawn. In seconds we were right on the fairway under a row of houses.

"OK. Get down. We're going to crawl," said Lucie.

"What?"

"Down! We can't be seen," said Lucie.

So, down we went, crawling foot by foot as low to the grassy fairway as possible, as we hugged the bottom of the hill.

"Stop. Hang on a second. I think we're right below the house."

"Now what?" I asked.

"We are going to very slowly crawl up the hill until just before our heads see over the top. We won't be seen."

"Unless it's by the people playing this hole, or the folks who live across the fairway," I said. "I truly love our adventures."

Up we went. Inch by inch. We made it to the top. Lucie slowly raised her head so her eyes were about an inch above grass level.

"No one's in the back. Take a look."

Now there were four eyes just above the blades of grass.

"Oh God, it looks *completely* different. I can't even recognize our old yard. That makes me sad. Let's go."

We snuck down the way we got in. When we reached the golf cart gate, we, of course, expected a cart or car to come along any minute. Lucie had a rehearsal she had to get to and wanted to be early—professional that she is.

We waited. No golf cart or car.

And, we waited. And, waited.

Forty-five minutes passed.

Oh, God.

The gate was too high to climb.

We waited some more.

We got out.

The time had come for Lucie to "test drive" living in Palm Springs. She was given a house to stay in. It was in the beautiful, exclusive gated community called Morningside in Rancho Mirage. It was a gorgeous property surrounded by lemon trees with the largest, most luscious lemons I've ever seen.

"I love it here. Morningside is so beautiful," I said.

"Me, too," said Lucie. "By the way, did you now that Barbara Sinatra lives directly across the street?"

"No kidding. That's cool."

The next day we decided we had to harvest those lemons and make fresh lemonade. It was our momentary passion. I'm short, so Lucie had to pick them. We raced into the house and squeezed to our heart's content.

"Ok. It's time to add the sugar," I said.

Lucie went rummaging around the cabinets in the kitchen we'd never seen until the day before.

"That's one of those things about being in a new property that's someone else's house," said Lucie, opening and closing cabinets and drawers. "You never know where anything is."

There was no sugar anywhere.

"Oh, no," I said. "We can't stop now. Look at all that gorgeous juice."

"Well, we can always drink it unsweetened," said Lucie.

I thought for a second and then spoke.

"I have an idea! We'll go borrow a cup of sugar from our neighbor, Barbara Sinatra."

"No!"

"Why not? I know her," I said.

"Well, I do, too. We used to play doubles together," said Lucie.

"Perfect! What could go wrong? Let's go."

Lucie grabbed an empty cup and we marched across the street and knocked on the door. After a few minutes, the door was opened by a woman butler dressed in an all-white uniform of slacks, jacket, shirt, and bow tie. Yes, I'm serious.

"May I help you? she said in a very proper, suspicious way.

"Hi, I'm Sue Cameron, and I know Barbara."

"And I'm Lucie Arnaz. We used to play tennis together. Sue and I are in the house across the street and we're making lemonade and we don't have any sugar. Do you think you could spare a cup of sugar?"

"One moment please."

And then the door was shut in our faces.

We waited, wondering what on earth was going to happen next.

After a long time, the door opened.

"Mrs. Sinatra will be happy to give you a cup of sugar, and she'd like to see you in the living room."

Lucie handed the cup to the butler and in we walked.

There, on the white couch in the living room was Barbara, wearing a seafoam green velour leisure/track suit, watching a tennis match. Her lunch was laid out on the coffee table. She had on no makeup and looked beautiful. Her blonde hair was perfectly coiffed. She couldn't have been more friendly or happier to see us. She showed us all around the house, and thought it was very funny that we needed sugar.

Soon after, the butler returned with the cup full of sugar. As Barbara walked us to the door, it seemed like she wanted to go with us for some lemonade.

"Would you like to join us for some lemonade?" asked Lucie.

"Only if you add vodka," answered Barbara.

Lucie and I have a mutual friend named Valarie Pettiford. She's a Tony-nominated incredible singer and "Fosse" dancer. When the three of us get together, something is bound to happen. At one of our after-show celebrations, we ended up talking about Disneyland and how much it meant to us as children.

"Why don't we just go there right away?" asked Lucie.

"Yes!!!!!" Valarie and I screamed in unison.

"I'll call Disneyland and the Disneyland Hotel and get us the room and passes," said Lucie. "Let's go this weekend."

"I'm in!" I said.

"Me, too," said Valarie.

Without any incident, we all showed up at Lucie's, got in her car and drove down on that next Saturday.

"I'm so excited," said Lucie. "We don't have any parents to watch us. We can do whatever we want. We can stay as late as we want and go on any ride over and over again."

"And, we can drink!" said Valarie.

"We're going to stay up all night! We finally have no restrictions on us. OMG!" I said.

We arrived at the entrance and noticed that the "s" was missing from the Disneyland sign. Valarie got out and we took a video of her saying, "We goin' ta Dineyland." It was hilarious. You had to be there to get her inflection.

The three of us stayed in one room at the hotel. Valarie and Lucie took the twin beds and I ended up on the couch. I didn't care. I love couches. We put on really comfortable shoes and ventured into the park. It was about one p.m.

Disneyland kids again! Valarie, Lucie and me.

"I want to go on the teacups! I want Pirates of the Caribbean! It's a Small World!" we all shouted.

"Well, I'll tell you what I don't want," said Lucie. "I don't want Space Mountain. I shot a TV special years ago with Tommy Tune and they shot a number of us singing while riding Space Mountain. It was all I could do not to throw up."

"Oh, Lord. I hate that ride," I responded. "I'm claustrophobic, and that ride freaked me out. I'll never go again."

We started out on the teacups in Fantasyland. It was fabulous. We went everywhere we wanted.

At five p.m., I reluctantly admitted I was getting really tired. I was afraid to say that because we all were so excited about staying up all night. I was embarrassed.

"Thank God you said something," said Valarie. "I'm exhausted."

"I have to lie down," said Lucie.

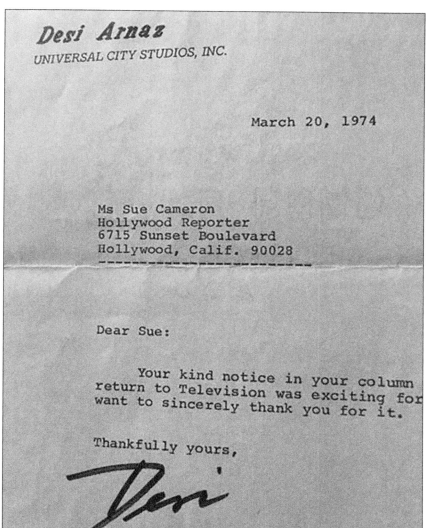

Desi Arnaz
UNIVERSAL CITY STUDIOS, INC.

March 20, 1974

Ms Sue Cameron
Hollywood Reporter
6715 Sunset Boulevard
Hollywood, Calif. 90028

Dear Sue:

Your kind notice in your column
return to Television was exciting for
want to sincerely thank you for it.

Thankfully yours,

DESI ARNAZ

From Desi to me.

Our vigorous threesome of determined adventurers barely lasted six hours. When we went back to the hotel we went directly to the restaurant so we could have dinner early and then go right to bed for the night.

We never went back to the park the next day.

Oh, well.

In 2017, Lucie and Larry and I were having dinner at Indian Wells Country Club. It was for a celebration of the Club's 60th Anniversary. Desi Arnaz was a co-creator and founder of the Indian Wells Hotel and Club, and Lucie and Larry were celebrating all that by hosting an evening in his honor. It also just *happened* to fall on March 2nd, 2017, the 100th anniversary of his birth, and they had hired a terrific Latin band to play Desi's music.

After the dinner and program were over, the band struck up his Latin tunes.

"Let's go!" said Lucie. "We're going to sit in with the band!"

"Do THEY know that?"

"No. C'mon!"

The percussion section didn't know what hit 'em.

Suge and Shecky strike again. I wonder what's next?

Chapter Twenty-Two

THE SLEAZY ABC-TV ADVENTURES AND THE JOY OF SUZANNE SOMERS

It was 1978, and the head of CBS programming had been wooing me for about a year to come work at CBS as head of children's programming. His name was Fred Silverman, and he'd been reading my column for years. I was very outspoken in it, constantly taking networks to task for putting shows in wrong timeslots, hiring wrong actors, approving stupid scripts. I guess Fred was impressed, because at one point he told me he wanted to have lunch with me. He flew me to New York first class, put me up at the Plaza Hotel, and took me to La Caravelle for lunch. I actually didn't think that was very unusual! I was "wooed" a lot in my position as a columnist for one of the two most powerful trade papers in Hollywood.

While we were having lunch he said, "I want you to come to CBS and be head of children's programming."

"Oh, I'd hate that. I don't know anything about children, and I really don't like them very much."

He almost choked on his soup. Nobody talked to Fred Silverman that way—well, almost no one. But I just answered honestly. I had absolutely no interest in that area.

Over the next couple of years he asked me to lunch every time he was in LA. We loved to talk the TV game and had really fun times together. I didn't need him for anything and said exactly what I believed on every subject. We laughed a lot, and I think he found our relationship very refreshing.

One night I was hostessing a Saturday night dinner party given by the TV producer of *Dynasty* and *Love Boat*, Doug Cramer. I loved doing that. Doug's very private parties always were sit-down dinners with heads of networks, stars, and TV heavyweights. I was the only reporter there, and I got tons of news.

I was standing at the fireplace when Fred came over and said, "I need you to meet me at the Beverly Hills Hotel for brunch tomorrow at exactly ten o'clock. It's really important."

He had never spoken this strongly or surreptitiously before. There was no real need for that. I would have met him anyway, but I was intrigued.

The next morning he was seated in his favorite booth and we ordered breakfast quickly. He was making small talk and looking at his watch.

"What is going on?" I asked.

"I'm leaving CBS and going to ABC to head their programming. No one knows this but you. A press release will go out tomorrow, but I'm giving you the story right now."

This was an extraordinary scoop—the biggest of my career. "Oh my God, I've got to go right now!"

The Hollywood Reporter's presses were actually in their big complex where my office was, and I knew that the paper would literally be put on the presses by noon. All the issues would be printed out by three p.m. to be distributed by six a.m. across the country. I had around ninety minutes to act.

I jumped up out of my seat. "Thank you! Thank you!" I said.

Fred grabbed my arm as I got up. "I know you turned me down at CBS, but you're going to say yes to me at ABC!"

Just like in the movies, I raced to my car and drove madly to get to the presses. I literally walked in and screamed, "Stop the presses!" The giant metal machines screeched to a halt. I had no time to revel in what I had just done. I went right over to the plant manager and said, "We have to redo the front page. I'll have the lead story for you in twenty minutes. Get ready to reset."

I didn't call the publisher. There was no time. As I reflect back now, I'm flattered that the print guys took my word for it immediately and just let me pull the plug. How cool.

Needless to say, I, and *The Hollywood Reporter*, scooped every single news outlet with our new front page. The news was delivered everywhere in the industry even before ABC sent out their press release. In today's 24-hour news cycle this story may sound silly, but, believe me, this was the equivalent of walking on air at CNN and stopping a live show in its tracks.

A few months later, Fred offered me director of daytime development. It was the job where he first started, and it was well-known that starting in that job was the precursor to being groomed to take over the network one day. This time I said yes. My reporter's curiosity compelled me to go on the inside and sit in on those closed boardrooms.

The contract negotiations were dragging on, so I called one of my closest friends, Marlo Thomas, a powerhouse woman in every area, who also happened to be a very big ABC star, and voice my concern.

"I'll take care of this," she said.

She called me back a few minutes later. "I just spoke with Michael (Eisner, president of the network), and I told him that if he didn't finish your contract by the end of the day, I would picket in front of the network and call ABC news to cover it."

My contract was closed by the end of the day.

I love Marlo Thomas and her family for so many reasons. She really understands the idea of mutual friendship. We have supported each other unconditionally for over 40 years.

And, guess what? Going to ABC was the dumbest move I'd ever made in my career.

Yes, Fred wanted me and believed in me, but also, by hiring me—a very public hire—the first TV critic EVER to be a network executive—and a woman, he was satisfying the FCC's requirement to hire more women. It took the heat off of ABC; and I had no clue. I should have known when my first call was from *The Wall Street Journal* wanting to interview me. I was such a babe in the woods in the corporate world.

There were two other women working at ABC at that time. One was Marcy Carsey, a comedy executive who went on to produce *The Cosby Show*, and a woman named Pam Dixon, who was head of casting. I reached out to both of them to see if they would have lunch with me. I knew immediately that I was in a men's club and would have loved support. Neither one of them ever would set a lunch date, although Marcy would always give me a friendly hello. Pam Dixon, in particular, was rude and cut me off like ice even when I just said hello. Pam was the worst example of women in business—so desperate and frightened to hold on to the "women's spot" that they wanted to kill any other woman in that path.

I was miserable and sitting in a spectacular office overlooking Century City. I had an unlimited expense account. I had a secretary I didn't know what to do with. And, every six weeks, I was flown first class to New York and put up at the St. Regis Hotel and went to meetings in the New York office. If I'd wanted a car and driver in New York, all I had to do was ask. It was insane. I remember the first morning there. I'd decided to walk to work. I was wearing a proper suit and carrying a briefcase. I swear to you that I heard the title music from the movie *The Best of Everything* as I walked to yet another office in the sky.

My job was to listen to pitches for game shows and soap operas. I had the power to give money to game show producers to do "run-throughs" of their shows at the network to see if we wanted to give them money for a pilot. Only if they made a pilot and we liked it, did a show get on the air.

As far as soaps were concerned, the only one that shot in LA was *General Hospital,* and it was my job to meet with the producers and writers to go over future storylines, as well as approve casting of actors. I was the one who discovered an unknown exercise teacher named Richard Simmons and put him on *General Hospital.*

I remember my first executive board meeting. I was seated at a long marble table, seemingly half the size of a football field, surrounded by all men. An executive would present a show, and then the president, Michael Eisner, would ask what we thought of it. No one would answer. No one ever wanted to be on record as having an opinion. I, of course, answered exactly whether it should go on the air or not. I learned quickly that if you do that and if the show failed, you'd be responsible. Quick lesson.

So here are some of the terrible things that happened:

I created *Family Feud*, and didn't earn a dime! Yes. There it is. I was in my office and thought that a good game idea would be to have families competing against each other to match an audience answer. I walked down the hall and told the idea to Brandon Stoddard, my immediate superior. He loved it. I watched him pick up the phone and call the game show producer Mark Goodson. Brandon said, "I have an idea, and then pitched it." Brandon never told Mark it was my idea. He stole it from me as I was standing there. Later on, when Mark Goodson told the story, it was all HIS idea. When you work at a network, any idea you have is something they own. Executives don't make any money if they come up with it. The damn show is still running. I could have purchased several countries right now if I'd been able to legally own MY idea.

ABC wanted to a cancel *Let's Make a Deal*, starring Monty Hall, a show that had made them millions for decades. I was the one who had to tell Monty Hall. It was horrible because it should have been done by the president of the network out of respect for all his success and what he brought to ABC. Naturally, he took it very badly and blamed me.

I saw how network executives and producers "fixed" screen tests so certain actors would get the part. They would like one actor better than another; they'd switch the order of the tests so a bad actor would precede the one they wanted to get the role, or some executive was just sleeping with someone and ordered us to give them the part. No questions asked.

I saw how game show prize money was lessened by crooked producers that switched game boards right in the middle of tapings. I personally saw Jack Barry, who had already been convicted of fixing the game show *21*, moving cards on a game board from behind to make sure the contestant didn't win the bonus round. I pointed it out immediately to another executive from the network that was there, and he said, "Just forget about what you saw."

I was taken to lunch by a top game show producer who tried to bribe me. He offered me x number of dollars for a pilot commitment; x number for a series commitment; x number for every week the show stayed on the air. I tried to be really cool and seem interested, but I was horrified. The producer went on to say, "Don't worry about this. Everybody does it," and then he proceeded to name every executive at ABC who was on the take!!!

The minute I got back to the office I ran to Brandon Stoddard, the executive I reported to, and told him the story. His name was NOT on the list of the dirty ABC executives. Brandon turned into steel and said, "You are not to talk to anyone. Go back to your office right now and write down what you told me. Do not make a copy, and bring it right back."

I did as I was told and was back in twenty minutes. I handed him my paper. He read it, and then locked it in a safe that was literally hidden behind a painting in his office.

"Brandon, this is a crime. I think we should call the police and set up a sting. I'll pretend to take their offer and accept one check and then you can arrest them." I was so naïve; so inexperienced in the corporate world.

He raised his voice. "I told you, you are to say nothing to anyone. We never had this conversation. Do you understand me?"

I kept my mouth shut. To Brandon's credit, over a period of the next sixteen months, each executive on the take was quietly let go. There was no pattern to it, and nothing could be traced. I learned that if ABC, or any company that wanted to go public, had a scandal attached it would affect the deal. It's always all about the money.

Regarding me, ABC was now terrified. I was a reporter and I'd seen too much, even though I was working for them, and not a newspaper. So, one day I was asked to report to the office of the president of the network, Michael Eisner. I like Michael. I always have, and we had a great rapport when I was a reporter. Michael was sitting there with Fred and Brandon.

"We have a great idea for you," said Michael. "We want to do a daily talk/variety show from Honolulu starring Don Ho. What do you think of that?"

"It's a terrible idea. He's old-school and very offensive to women. He sticks his tongue down their throats when he kisses them during his nightclub act. The show will never last." Yes, people, I still hadn't fully learned my lesson of keeping my mouth shut.

"Well, we've bought it, and you're going to Honolulu to supervise the show, " said Michael. "You leave in three weeks."

I was stunned.

Three weeks later, I found myself in a corner suite of the Royal Hawaiian Hotel overlooking Waikiki Beach. Again, I had an unlimited expense account. Anything I wanted I could charge. Without getting into the technical business stuff in too much detail, ABC had favorite producers they liked to work with. Many of these producers had the same lawyer/business manager, and this business manager had all of his former employees hired by ABC to make up their business affairs department. It was a big money game where shows were given budgets higher than they needed to produce a show. It was ABC's way of keeping the producers happy by giving them extra fees. The lawyer/business manager got a cut of the producers' profits, and everybody was happy. *The Don Ho Show* was just another money-moving scheme for different entities. The budget they were given was much higher than it needed to be. I knew where all that extra money went, but I'm not going into it here.

I realized very quickly that I was "sent away" to Hawaii to hush-up the payola scandal I'd brought to Brandon. ABC didn't care how much they had to pay to keep me away. When I realized that, I bought first class airline tickets for my parents and friends and flew them over and back. I had my celebrity friends flown over as guests on the show so I could play with them. They all had rooms at the Royal Hawaiian. I chartered boats. I went to work in a bikini because the show was shot on the beach. If this was my payoff, I was going to have a VERY good time.

Another thing I found out when I was there was that Don was a member of the Hawaiian mafia. That's right. One day I just needed a break and I drove a rental car to the town of Kailua. I sat on the beach for a while and then went to McDonald's—something I would never eat today. I enjoyed my break, drove back to the Royal Hawaiian and then went to the set where they were shooting. The first person I saw was Don.

"How was McDonald's? he asked.

"How did you know I was at McDonald's?

"I had you followed. There's a threat on your life from some people who don't like me, and I'm protecting you."

Did I even need to tell you what I felt?

I left the set and went back to my hotel and called ABC.

"Get me out of here. I've had it," I said to Brandon. "The show's a mess. There's a mob hit out on me. Don's in the mafia. This is insane, I'm coming back."

I knew that this "indefinite Hawaiian vacation" was my pay-off, and that the minute I was back on the mainland ABC would "no longer need my services," and that's exactly what happened. And, by the way, *The Don Ho Show* tanked. And, another "by-the-way," Fred Silverman let me hang after all that wooing for years.

NOTE: Fred tried to make it up to me later by going into business with me. We had a partnership where he would put my actor-friends in the shows he would develop and produce. I was to get producer credit for providing them to him. Our sweet partnership was killed by an over-year-long writers' strike that paralyzed the business.

The one bright light in all of this ABC horror was an unknown young blonde girl named Suzanne Somers. A fellow named Alan Hamel came in one day and pitched a game show. I liked it and we ordered a run-through. I don't even remember the game, but I know we needed a model to display the prizes. Alan introduced us to his girl-

WE ALL LIVE IN PALM SPRINGS—LARRY LUCKINBILL, LUCIE, ALAN HAMEL, AND SUZANNE.

friend, Suzanne Somers, who had done absolutely nothing yet in her career. I liked her the instant we met. She may have looked like a cliché blonde, and acted like one for the show, but she was certainly not that. She was sweet, wise, unpretentious, and very funny. Since none of the other women at ABC wanted anything to do with me, Suzanne was the first woman who did. The show didn't sell, but we became friends.

A few years later, she ended up being cast in a little show called *Three's Company* for ABC. Some of those executives actually remembered her from the game show. Within weeks, Suzanne exploded into TV's newest star commodity. Her career was on fire, and I was so happy for her.

Suzanne hired a publicist named Jay Bernstein. Jay is the guy who thought of the Farrah Fawcett poster. He was bright, but quite sleazy. He was not interested in quality or any longevity for his clients. He was about the fast buck. Suzanne's hiring of Jay was a big mistake, I thought.

One day I ran into Suzanne at the Farmer's Market right next to CBS. When she saw me she jumped up and down.

"Guess what!" she said excitedly. "I just came from CBS and they offered me a million dollars if I signed with them to do TV movies just for them. Can you believe it? A million dollars! I've never had money in my life!!!

"You can't take it," I said.

"What?"

"You can't take that deal."

Suzanne stopped jumping and looked incredulous.

"ABC put you in *Three's Company* and made you a star. They do their own movies of the week and will absolutely put you in them. If you take that CBS deal, ABC will end up firing you from *Three's Company* and you'll lose everything. You have no idea how angry a network can get if they think a star is ungrateful and screws them over, whether you mean to do it or not."

Suzanne just looked at me. I know I got through to her for a second because I saw her eyes get the message. But it was only fleeting.

"I just can't turn down that money."

And then she hugged me and went on her way.

In a recent conversation, Suzanne told me that she DID call ABC to talk over the situation, and the president, Steve Gentry, never returned her call.

We all know what happened. All I can tell you is that several years later, when she was ice cold and couldn't get a TV show to save her life, she came to me for help. I'd heard of a new sitcom at ABC that they were casting called *Step by Step*, starring Patrick Duffy. They were looking for an actress to play his wife. I told her she was perfect.

"ABC? They'll never hire me," said Suzanne.

"Yes, they will. They want to make you come in and read for the entire network for the part. They want to embarrass you by asking you to do that and make you grovel. If you want the part, that's what you have to do."

And here's why I love Suzanne Somers. She went to ABC and did just that, and they gave her the part. She threw away her ego and knew that it was just business. I know of almost no actor who could or would have done that. She holds a special place in my heart.

Chapter Twenty-Three

RICHARD SIMMONS ONCE UPON A TUTU

Once upon a time there was an exercise teacher with classes in a small studio in Beverly Hills. I had begun hearing about this "crazy guy" from different friends. Apparently he was a former waiter, and then maitre'd at a restaurant called Derrick's in Los Angeles. He had gotten financing from some of Derrick's' customers to open his own business. His gym/studio was open for lunch, and his healthy buffet and personality were attracting diners. I went over to check it out myself.

That day I met a curly-haired tutu-wearing dynamo named Richard Simmons. He'd heard of me from *The Reporter*, and he knew I had just become an executive at ABC. He was ALL OVER ME to help his career. I think it was the heaviest onslaught of energy and pressure I'd ever experienced. But I liked him. I put him on *General Hospital* for such splashy guest shots as an exercise/diet guru. And, he was a smash. Richard was on his way.

The queeny, flashy Richard, was, of course, a total creation of former fat kid Milton Simmons, from New Orleans. When Richard wasn't being "Richard," he was a frightened, sweet child. He was also a very smart businessman and extremely empathetic to people in pain.

After he was a hit on *General Hospital*, he begged me to help him get his own show. He wanted a five-day-a-week talk exercise show that was national, not local. I told him I'd do it, but he had to give me 15% of his income, and sign a contract. He did. That was a standard figure for someone who acted as a "manager" or "advisor" to a star/actor/product—whatever you wanted to call it.

I took Richard to an agency called ICM. It was and is a very successful, powerful agency. An "agent," unlike a manager, is an

My birthday party at Richard's studio in 1975. (l-r) Lesley Gore, My Sister Sam, producer Karyl Miller, Jackie DeShannon, Lynda Carter with her hands on my head, Liz Torres, Dusty Springfield, Jessica Walter, and Marlo Thomas.

authorized procurer of employment. They are licensed, and they receive a standard 10% for each job or deal they get.

In order to get a show on the air, it's important to pair the star with a successful producer who has a track record. ICM had producer clients like that, and they paired Richard up with one of them. He was someone I knew, and I was very happy about it. With this guy's history of producing hit shows, and Richard's star potential, I was fairly certain he'd get his show.

Once the producer and the star are partnered, they come up with ideas for a "pilot," which is a kind of demonstration tape of a possible episode that will never air. Once they have their ideas together, the agency pitches the ideas to TV stations, both networks and syndicated, to get them to finance the pilot. Once the pilot is financed, it is shot and then whoever finances it decides if they want to buy it permanently and make it a series.

Things went very well. They got the money for the pilot and shot it. I was next to Richard all the way, putting my two cents in at every turn. I had been a network executive in charge of many pilots. Richard and I were side-by-side, as I did my job and got him the series he wanted. The show sold to hundreds of syndicated stations across the country. Richard and I were ecstatic.

Well, I was ecstatic for one day.

The day after the show sold, I received a call from Richard at my office.

"This is Richard. I'm letting you go as my manager. This isn't going to work."

"What? I just got you the show you wanted. I did my job perfectly," I replied.

"I have to go," said Richard.

And then he hung up on me. I sat on my couch in a state of shock. And then I called my lawyer and filed a suit.

The show went on to make millions for Richard. I got a $25,000 settlement.

I have never been angrier with a person in my life.

A few years later, Richard and I ended up in the first class section of a plane flying to New York. I looked at him and felt total rage. The anger that was coming out of my eyes and body would have fried an elephant, but I said nothing and went to my seat. Richard rushed to me and started crying. I asked the stewardess to remove him, forcibly, if need be, from my sight. He kept saying, "I have to talk to you, I have to talk to you." He was removed.

At that time in my career, I was back on television doing Hollywood reporting segments every week on a live local show in Los Angeles. It was the same kind of gig I had done for Dick Clark on ABC's *Happening*, only this was a local show like *Live with Regis and Kelly*.

About two years after the plane incident, I was in my dressing room in the TV studio about to go on live. I heard a commotion outside my door. It was Richard, who, much to my shock, was also doing the show. He'd found out I was on and was insisting he be let into my room. Filled with rage again, and how he screwed me over financially and lied to my face, I wouldn't let him in. It was also horrendous, because I was upset and had to go on live TV in about fifteen minutes and look like nothing was wrong—AND HE'D BE ON THE SET LIVE WITH ME. I called out for a producer.

One came in and I said, "Keep him away from me. He harasses me every time he sees me. I'm doing my segment and then leaving at the commercial break. I need someone from your staff to walk me to the set and back to my dressing room."

Richard was still crying and screaming outside my dressing room. It was five minutes till we were live. The producer left and I heard him taking Richard away. I had 30 seconds to calm down before going on. I pulled it off, and it was NOT easy.

The third time he "attacked" me was when I was having lunch at Mr. Chow's restaurant in Beverly Hills. I had just finished paying and was walking to the door to leave. Unfortunately, he was walking in and we were face-to-face. I was totally trapped with no one around to wrangle him away. He started sobbing and dropped to his knees before me (and everyone else at the restaurant).

"Please, I am begging you! You've got to let me talk to you. I've been trying to tell you what really happened for years. Please, please. I never wanted to hurt you," cried Richard.

By this time he was grabbing my ankles.

"Get up! This is ridiculous!"

He got up and tried to get it together. He took my hands and spoke in a calmer voice. "Please, just give me five minutes and I'll never bother you again. You have to know the truth."

Something told me to let him talk.

"The day after the talk show sold, the producer (and you'll notice I've never named him here because the bastard, who should have died years ago, is still alive) called me into his office and locked the door. He yelled at me and told me that he had the power to put the show on or kill it. And he did, because he had the track record. If he walked away my show would die. He told me that I had to sign a contract with him right then and there giving him 50% of my income or he'd kill the show. The contract was on the desk. I was locked in the room. He said he wouldn't let me out until I signed it.

It was my dream ever since I was a kid to have my own show. I had to sign it. I couldn't lose the show. I was sick inside. I hated making that call to you. I hated lying to you. It was the most horrible thing that has ever happened to me."

I didn't cave. I didn't say "There, there, sweet boy." But, I believed him. I knew the producer was a sleaze, despite his track record. Just because you do successful talk shows doesn't mean you are a nice person. The whole thing was just disgusting.

"I believe you, Richard."

He started to cry again and fell to his knees. I patted him on the top of his head and left.

That vile producer is still working, but the end must be near, although evil people seem to live longer. Richard is a recluse hiding in his house. He has lots of money, but his career is on hold. I live on a golf course and smile every day. I wish him well and hope he's all right.

Chapter Twenty-Four

PHOEBE SNOW PORTRAIT OF COURAGE AND TRAGEDY

Oh, God
Fix me
Put me back
Together
Cause I came
Here to sing
　　　　-Phoebe Snow

On July 17th, 2009, I was sitting at a table near the front of the stage in Birdland, a jazz club in New York City. It was Lucie Arnaz's birthday, and I am always with her to celebrate it. Tonight she'd decided to have her party at Birdland, where she would sing and do her act, but it was a more casual version, where other singer-friends sitting in the audience would come up and either duet with her or sing a solo. Lucie is always such a happy, positive person, and her energy permeated the room.

I noticed the singer, Phoebe Snow, sitting alone at a table in the front row. Phoebe's biggest hit record was "Poetry Man," which she wrote, along with most of her other successful songs. She was enormous in the mid-seventies, appearing on the cover of *Rolling Stone*, and in numerous episodes of *Saturday Night Live*. Critics were constantly raving about her extraordinary vocal instrument that ranged from deep bass to operatic soprano. I remembered something about a daughter she had that was disabled, and that she dropped out of sight to care for her. Looking at her table, she had a very quiet, contemplative aura surrounding her that signaled "I'm in my own zone. Don't approach." It was a very spiritual feeling coming from her, and I watched her for a long time.

Her hair was still that crazy, curly, almost black mass, and she still wore thick glasses and was a little overweight. I'd been an admirer of her voice in the seventies, but, truthfully, I'd paid very little attention. I'd seen act after act, interviewed one singer after another. I was busy on my own career trajectory.

About a half-hour into Lucie's show, she looked at Phoebe and said, "Would you like to come up and sing something?"

Phoebe looked at her and hesitated.

The audience started to scream for her. A "sighting" of Phoebe Snow was very rare, and they knew it.

Phoebe lumbered up on stage, looking quite shy and embarrassed by the cheers. She walked over to Lucie's very talented music director, arranger, and accompanist, Ron Abel, and said, "You Send Me." They discussed the key, and off she went to center stage. Ron's sensual, soulful piano notes started up and Phoebe opened her mouth to sing.

Her rendition of "You Send Me" was one of the most memorable moments I've ever experienced from a live singer. Her voice was in peak form, caressing and teasing when she felt like it, soaring in runs when the moment was right. The audience was absolutely silent, some members with mouths agape, as I think was mine. I can't tell you how long the song went on, because I'd left my conscious body to go on a trip with Phoebe that was completely unexpected. Extraordinary talent like that is the most exciting thing to me in the world.

The song was over and she got a hollering, standing ovation and shouts of more. She humbly bowed her head, mouthing thank you, and then almost ran off the stage. I was propelled from where I was standing to simply run after her, pushed by an unseen force. There was no thought process behind it. I just aimed right for her.

I found her hiding in the back, using a wall to hold herself up. She was sweating and shaky and appeared traumatized. I remembered that Dusty Springfield was one of her idols, so I said, "I want you to know that Dusty Springfield just loved you. She thought your voice was extraordinary."

Phoebe grabbed me and started crying. It was astonishing. Through her tears she said, "Oh, God. Did she really say that? My dream for my whole career was to do a duet with her. And now you're telling me this? Thank you! Thank you."

"I should introduce myself. My name is Sue Cameron."

"The writer?"

"Yes," I answered.

"I've read all your stuff on the music business. I've been following you for years. "I bet we know so many people in common. Here's my phone number. Let's talk some time. Right now I need to just be back here by myself for a while."

Well, that started it. Phoebe called me and called me. I loved talking to her because we would exchange music business stories. A typical phone call would last one hour. Eventually, she came to LA for a visit and we had lunch at a Thai restaurant in Hollywood. It was there that I discovered how much Phoebe and I loved great food. If someone doesn't LOVE food, they can't be trusted.

"I've been thinking about your music," I said. "I think you need tracks behind you that are very R&B, and you need producers like Babyface or Nile Rodgers."

"You're a Funketeer," said Phoebe, a smirk on her face.

"Yes I am. How cool."

"You've just said the words I've been looking for. I haven't found anyone in years who understands the music I want to do," continued Phoebe. "Would you be interested in working with me?"

Uh oh, was my first thought. I was afraid that might happen if I expressed my opinion about music. At the time of our lunch, I was not very interested in doing anything. I was taking a break from writing columns and books. But, the one thing that could always get my attention was working in music and live acts, as long as it was with an extraordinary talent. It was where my heart was.

"I'll think about it, Phoebe. I'm very flattered. You have one of the greatest vocal instruments I've ever heard."

To cut through all of it, after lots of calls, I said I'd do it.

"Phoebe, here's exactly what you need–a new band, a new agent, a new act, a new recording deal, a new record producer, a new

Friends forever.

website, and a make-over." I figured I'd just get it all over with right up front. If she didn't agree, then we wouldn't work together.

"Yes to all of it, but can I ask you for three extra things?" asked Phoebe.

"Sure," I said.

"I want to have dinner with Steven Spielberg. I want to meet with George Schlatter, the producer of *Laugh-In* (a 70s hit TV show), and I want to have coffee or a meal with Angie Dickinson."

"Done."

What might seem an impossible list to most people was an easy one for me. I'd been friends with Steven, George, and Angie for years.

Some time went by before we actually started working, and during that time her daughter, Valerie, aged thirty-one, died from a brain hemorrhage as a result of damage that happened when she was born. I never met Valerie. She was the result of a love affair with a handsome guitar player in Phoebe's band named Phil Kearns, and Phil married her.

During the birth, according to Phoebe, the actual obstetrician stepped out and left Phoebe hanging while Valerie struggled to breathe, stuck in the birth canal. As a result, she was born with brain damage that was not there prior to the time the birth process started. Phoebe sued the hospital and was given a large sum of money. She never spent that money, by the way, always referring to it as "Valerie's money."

She divorced Kearns after he turned out to be gay and have substance abuse problems, but Phil was always concerned about Valerie and didn't desert her. He simply followed Phoebe's wishes.

"The doctors took one look at Valerie and told me to put her in an institution immediately. They said she'd never live, and if she did, neither one of us would have a quality life. I told them that I don't abandon my child, and I took her home. She lived for 31 years," said Phoebe defiantly.

But all of Phoebe's attention and money had to go to Valerie's care—constant supervision and nurses and doctors. Eventually, recording labels and producers and managers became fed up with Phoebe because she refused to go into the studio or tour.

"I had a big manager who forbade me to bring Valerie even to my hotel room while I was in the studio. I wouldn't follow her orders, and she was so angry that she called other labels and blackballed me in the industry," said Phoebe. "Her name is.......................and don't you forget it. She really hurt me."

I won't forget the name, Phoebe. I promise.

She took occasional gigs for money, but her focus on Valerie stopped all her momentum. There were no more magazine covers or TV shows.

"I only did gigs for money to support Valerie's care. I knew I hit rock bottom when my opening act turned out to be a woman with gigantic breasts the size of Cleveland, who played the piano with them," said Phoebe dryly.

Fortunately, with her original big money, Phoebe bought a three-bedroom, three-bath condo over-looking all of New York in Fort Lee, New Jersey. She'd had to have a third bed and bath for the twenty-four hour nursing care. It was decorated in black leather furniture with dark wood everywhere. Even though it had huge picture windows and a pool below, it felt like a dungeon to me. I think that's what Phoebe intended. Her life was dark; her insides were dark.

Once, when I was in a rented apartment in New York, staying there for a while to work on the business of Phoebe, she picked up a guitar that was there and did her whole, original nightclub folk act for me—an audience of one. It was beyond magical.

At another time, Howard Stern called and asked if she would sing at his wedding to Beth, and Phoebe said yes. Darlene Love called and asked Phoebe to do her Christmas show and she said no. I ever knew what the yeses or nos would be.

Valerie's condition and her death totally turned Phoebe against conventional western medicine. She was constantly searching for new therapies she thought she needed, whether it was "bat juice" or thyme pills, or whatever gimmick there was around. She went to no western doctors. Instead, she went to a dubious clinic in Mexico that charged her for "sheep serum" treatments and took tens of thousands of dollars from her.

She had high blood pressure and cholesterol problems, and refused to take the right western medications to help her. I tried to be gentle, but I did warn her on more than one occasion that she could die because her numbers were dangerously high from lack of proper care.

"If I have a stroke, then I have a stroke," said Phoebe.

I should have noticed then that she was slowly committing suicide by eating wrong and not treating herself for her medical problems. She didn't want to live after Valerie died.

"The only reason I'm hanging on is because of the music. I want to sing. Valerie would want me to sing," said Phoebe.

I just wanted to help her achieve that.

Before we met, she also became hooked on a cult religion that I will not name. There are certain cult religions that prey on misfits and take their money. I knew from the moment I met these people surrounding her that they were trouble. They didn't like me immediately, because the leaders knew that I saw right through them and might take away their "Phoebe bank."

Please conclude that Phoebe was a personal and career mess when I stepped in.

There were two more things about Phoebe that you should know. The first is that she was fascinated with forensic medicine and murders. She befriended famed forensic expert Dr. Michael Baden and his lawyer-wife Linda, as well as Dr. Cyril Wecht. She spent hours on the phone with them going over evidence of cases they'd handled. I began to figure out why. It was the second thing you should know.

Phoebe thought that aliens were taking over her body and turning her into one of them. Yes. You read that correctly. She talked about it all the time and kept coming up with examples that proved to her she was right. I just placated her and tried to direct her attention back to her career.

When she had a hysterectomy, she'd kept her uterus in a jar in the closet of her apartment in Fort Lee. I saw it. She insisted that I look at it. It was covered with bumps and spots. I took a picture of it and sent it to my gynecologist. He diagnosed a typical condition. It had nothing to do with aliens. Phoebe pooh-poohed my doctor and continued to believe she was "being taken over." She had a cardboard mailing box prepared with Dr. Cyril Wecht's address on it so she could send it and have him analyze it. She never mailed it.

The alien part is where Steven Spielberg came in. In his movie Close Encounters of the Third Kind, one shot featured a train going by with the name PHOEBE SNOW on it. Phoebe felt it was a sign. She also felt she'd had encounters and wanted to talk to him.

For the next year and a half, I spoke with everyone from Q-Tip to Babyface, to Steely Dan, to Darlene Love to Gospel Pastor Donnie McClurkin to Greg Phillinganes (Michael Jackson's keyboard player and noted arranger). Everybody wanted to work with Phoebe. She was the rock/pop world's "singer's singer." Every time I mentioned her name to another singer or music industry person, I would hear a gasp and their remark that she was the best ever. She was so beloved and appreciated by all. It was like a religious experience each time.

Along the way on this journey, I learned that Phoebe did vocal exercises two to four hours a day, whether she was working or not. She also worked with an opera coach twice a week. That's the kind of discipline one needs to be respectful and care for one's instrument. She didn't smoke or drink.

She recounted stories to me of her difficult childhood in school, her grandfather who worked for the mob, and regaled me with stories of a very dysfunctional middle-class Jewish family in New Jersey. I heard about her financial struggles as she tried to make it. She told me the names of the famous rockers she'd slept with. She told me everything.

The story of the mother-daughter, rock music, and her legendary interactions with major music figures was in the process of being turned into a stage play or a movie. The incredible writer, Don Scardino, (Emmy-winning 30 Rock, Tracy Ullman), was committed to produce it, and we were interviewing writers.

Debbie and Phoebe at the Carlyle in New York.

We recorded with the wonderful Greg Phillinganes in Los Angeles. Phoebe footed the bill for two songs that were incredible. We
also met with Babyface and were awaiting that result. We'd interviewed musicians and put a band together. I changed Phoebe's
clothes, hair and make-up, and done a photo session. We had a
new agency that was excited about booking her. She had Yoko
Ono's lawyer. We were "killing it."

When Phoebe came to LA for the Greg Phillinganes sessions, we
had coffee with Angie Dickinson at Starbucks on Santa Monica in
West Hollywood. Both Angie and Phoebe had lost their daughters.

Phoebe wanted to meet with Angie to thank her for the time, years before, when Phoebe and her husband, Phil, were having dinner at Imperial Gardens, a restaurant in Hollywood. Baby Valerie was with them. Angie and Burt Bacharach were also in the restaurant, and Phoebe knew their daughter, Nikki, was also challenged. (Nikki later committed suicide at age forty-one.)

I watched these two women, as Angie reached across the table for Phoebe's hand. That touch shared their deep sorrow, and few words were necessary. Once again, I was witness to an extraordinary moment.

"I just wanted to thank you in person for the time you came by our table at Imperial Gardens," said Phoebe. "You looked at my baby and said to her, 'You're going to have a tough time, little one.' I've never forgotten your kindness."

All three of us teared up.

Next on the LA agenda was George Schlatter. I had no idea why she wanted to see George, but, because I asked him, he agreed to meet. We went to his office on Beverly Blvd. where we were surrounded by autographed photos on his walls of Sammy Davis, Goldie Hawn, Bob Hope, Richard Nixon, Lily Tomlin, George Burns, Milton Berle, Lucille Ball—a complete history of show business.

We were seated in his office when his secretary said Joy Behar was calling. From the conversation I heard, it was clear that Joy was asking his opinion on Whoopi Goldberg being offered a seat on the panel of *The View*. No one knew that yet.

George then joined us in his chair by the coffee table and couch. Phoebe brought up a story written by George's brother in one of the *Chicken Soup for the Soul* books about George's difficult childhood physical injuries that he had to overcome. I had absolutely no knowledge of anything she was talking about. I suddenly saw George, a former nightclub bouncer, turn into a little boy, fighting back tears.

"I just wanted to tell you how much reading that chapter helped me get the courage to go on after my daughter died," said Phoebe.

More tears. Another remarkable happening from her "original list."

There was another person who was important to Phoebe named Tony Melfa. He'd been her road manager for many years and was like her brother. He is a wonderful guy who really cared for her, and the feeling was mutual. At one point very casually, Phoebe mentioned way late in our relationship that she had a sister named Julie. I had absolutely no idea she'd had a sister. I thought she was an only child.

"My sister and I don't really talk. She's done some things to me that I don't like. She's a strange character," said Phoebe.

In December of 2009, Phoebe and I met with Ron Delsener, the most famous concert promoter in the business, who was chairman of Live Nation. He was a huge admirer of Phoebe's. We told him about all the changes and that we were now ready to go. Ron picked up the phone and called City Winery, a very chic-yet-hip music space in New York that attracted top entertainers. He proposed that Phoebe do a "residency" there to try out all her new things and start building again. (By the way, whenever Phoebe did a show anywhere, it was sold out. Her fans were diehards and they never failed to support her.)

Phoebe and I took a cab over to City Winery and met with the owner. I struck a deal where she would sing every Tuesday night for a five-figure amount, and get all of the door money or 50%. I can't remember the actual door deal. It doesn't matter at this juncture. We had an opening night set for March of 2010, and every single thing that I wanted to set for her to make her ready was done. It had taken a year-and-a-half of my solid work.

In early January, I flew to New York for the first rehearsal with the new band. It was terrific beyond our wildest dreams. We both were so happy. I was going to return at the beginning of March to go over final rehearsals, set the lights and sound, meet with the PR people, invite opening night guests, etc.

On January 15th, 2010, I was at a screening at the Director's Guild, a private theatre for members of the Director's Guild and their guests. Studios used it to preview movies or hold panel discussion events. I don't even remember why I was there, but in walked Steven Spielberg. My eyes lit up. He was the last thing on Phoebe's list that I had promised to do. Steven and I had known each other since we both started out in the business. We were kids together eating at Universal Pictures Commissary pretending to be grown-ups. At that time he had his first job, directing Joan Crawford in a TV show called *Night Gallery*, and I was *The Hollywood Reporter* columnist and TV editor. We clicked from the moment we met.

"Steven. Hi!" I said as we hugged.

"Sue! It's so great to see you!"

"I have a bizarre question for you, Steven. Would you like to have dinner with Phoebe Snow?" I asked.

"I LOVE Phoebe Snow," he answered. "Of course I'll have dinner."

I was filled with excitement when I got home. I'd just pulled off the triple play of Dickinson-Schlatter-Spielberg. I called Phoebe immediately. It was already after midnight in New Jersey.

"Phoebe! Guess what!"

"What?"

"I just saw Steven Spielberg and he said he'd like to have dinner with you!"

"Are you fucking kidding me?" she shouted.

"No," I said. "He loves you. The next time you're in Los Angeles or he's in New York, we're going to do it!"

"I can't believe it!" she exclaimed. "I can't believe it! You actually did what you said you'd do. No one has ever done that for me before! I love you. Sue. I really do. Wow! Thank you so much!"

"Ok, Phoebe. Now that I've made you happy, get some sleep and I'll talk to you tomorrow."

"Get some sleep? I'll never sleep. Who cares? I love you. Bye."

"Bye, Phoebe."

January 16th, 2010
Three p.m. L.A time. My phone rings.

"Is this Sue? I'm Adam, the son of Phoebe Snow's friend Mattie.
We've been trying to get you"
"My phone hasn't been on for a while. You don't sound good," I
said, my heart racing.
"Phoebe had a stroke this morning. It doesn't look good."
My living room started to spin.
"What are you saying? Is she going to die?"
"I don't know. We don't know anything. Call this number and ask
for Jay."

I fell to the floor, crying.

In a few moments, when I could get up off the floor, I spoke to
her friend Jay, who said that Phoebe called him saying she was
losing consciousness and to come over. He said he told her to call
an ambulance, but she refused. (Naturally.) When he got there she
was weak, but answered the door. He wanted to call 911 again, but
she refused. She finally agreed to go to a doctor. She told him she
was going to take a shower. He didn't want her to do that. He just
wanted to get her to the doctor, but it had to be Phoebe's way.
Too much time had passed and Jay was concerned. Finally, he
went to her bathroom and found her on the floor, totally unconscious. She had suffered a massive brain bleed and was rushed to
Hackensack Hospital in Hackensack, New Jersey. Jay could get no
one on the phone, and there was no order for him to be her health
power of attorney. A doctor finally told him that if they didn't operate, she'd surely die, and even if they did, he didn't know what the
outcome would be. They operated and she was in a coma.

I got on the first plane for New Jersey that I could take, and
spent five hours not knowing if she was dead or alive. I don't wish
that kind of trip on anyone.
When I got to the hospital, there was chaos in the corridor outside Phoebe's room from friends—people she liked and those she

didn't. Phoebe had told me everything about whom she really cared for and whom she didn't. It put me in a terrible position of being the policeman. No one was in charge before I arrived. I heard that Phoebe's sister had been there earlier.

Oh, God, I thought. Her sister, the one she doesn't like and refuses to speak to, is now the closest living relative with the medical power. Good Lord.

I was very apprehensive as I walked in the room to see Phoebe. When I saw her, I was so happy that she was alive (or so I thought), that my heart soared. Sure there were tubes all over. Sure there was a machine breathing for her, sure her head was covered in a rubber ice cloth—but she was there! I could touch her, talk to her, feel her warm skin. I was determined then and there that she was going to wake up. If anyone could make her wake up, I'd be the one. We had so many plans!

How arrogant and ignorant I was.

"Phoebe! Phoebe! It's Sue. Wake up!"

If I uttered those words once, I uttered them thousands of times over the next year and a half that she was in a coma.

A head nurse came in and I liked her right away. She stayed for a while and sensed I knew what I was doing and was grateful someone could handle things.

"You need to know something," said the nurse, "and I'm telling you because you can handle it. I've seen many of these cases, and I know who's going to make it or not most of the time. Listen carefully to me, there is a window where, if you understand that she's never going wake up, we can let her go gently. If you miss that window, it's going to be thousands of dollars and months and months of false hope, and the end will be the same. I'm telling you that this case right now is one where you're going to lose that window fast. Do you understand me?"

"I do."

I wanted to throw up.

I did understand her, and I refused to believe it. Let me tell any of you reading this, that if you're ever faced with that situation, believe the nurse and act on it.

It turned out that Tony Melfa had the power of attorney, not Phoebe's sister, Julie. Because Phoebe hated western medicine and anything to do with health business, she'd also let all her union insurance lapse. She had no coverage and was building up tens of thousands of dollars a day.

I moved into the Courtyard by Marriott in Hackensack. I wouldn't wish that on my worst enemy. I would sit by Phoebe's side from morning to night, talking to her, playing her favorite music, singing to her. I would literally lift her eyelids so I could look into her eyes and talk in a loud voice to her. Sometimes she looked focused; sometimes not.

I grabbed an "on-call" priest (Chinese man who barely spoke English) in the hospital and had him duet with me on Dusty Spring-field's "I Only Wanna be with You." I was going to do anything to try to get through to her.

Weeks went by. Her sister, Julie, turned out to be a very nice person who was doing her best to help. We got along well. I eventually had to put a security list together of people who could see Phoebe. Phoebe looked terrible and I knew she wouldn't want to be seen. People who were not on the list called me every name in the book. Too bad, people. I was only doing what Phoebe wanted, and she told me she never liked you, you just didn't know that. It was just awful everywhere.

Every coma patient has a "shelf-life" at a regular hospital. If you're not coming out of it, you need to be moved to a different hospital. The next hospital, for lack of better description, is the "waking up hospital." It is there that they try to get her to wake up using various techniques. Because Phoebe had no insurance, things were a disaster. She had Valerie's money—about $1.5 million in an account. Tony Melfa had to get a lawyer and go to court to get any of it to pay for her expenses, but the court order took time, and this was an emergency. Hackensack was literally evicting her. She already owed them hundreds of thousands of dollars.

I was standing at Hackensack Hospital and Phoebe needed to be moved the very next day to a new hospital. The new facility needed $20,000 cash to let her in. It was all up to me. *Oh, God.*

I called Joan Rivers and Howard Stern, and, God bless them, they each gave me $10,000. Howard's was a gift, and Joan's was a loan which Phoebe's estate paid back. Because of them, I was able to get Phoebe to the new hospital.

One day, at that hospital, I left her for about 15 minutes to get some lunch. When I came back, Phoebe was sitting up in bed, eyes open, watching TV.

"Phoebe!" I screamed. "You're awake!"

I rushed over to her, kissing her on both cheeks and talking a mile a minute. She just looked at me and didn't speak. So excited, I rushed to a CD player and put on her *Phoebe Snow Live* album and cranked up the volume. I looked over at her and saw her face screw up in tears. She was inconsolable, and, within seconds, went right back into the coma.

The doctor told me that these incidents are common, and that she wasn't really awake, even though she was sitting up and her eyes were open. He said that they had done everything they could, and that it was time to take her to a long-term facility.

By this time, I'd flown from Los Angeles to New Jersey seven times, and lived in three different motels. It was absolute hell. I was completely alone, with no one to help me.

The next hospital was in Edison, New Jersey. It was where Luther Vandross went after his stroke, and we all know how that turned out...

And, as it happened, Phoebe's doctor and nurses were Luther's exact team. You know what? God bless them. They were angels.

You need to have this picture of Phoebe, totally helpless. If they wanted to put her in a chair, they'd have to bring in a forklift with a three-pronged hammock attached to lift her out of bed like a horse from the river, and place her in a chair. She could do nothing by herself. She had a plastic helmet on her head, and her head listed to one side. The machines went along with her to the chair. Her eyes were either closed, or she stared out into space. It was a horrible way to live, and a horrific thing to see constantly. I tried to put the picture of a happy, singing Phoebe on stage having a ball, out of my head.

Experiencing this terrible scene hour by hour, day-by-day was unspeakably painful, but I couldn't leave her. I was the only one willing to be there on a constant basis, and, before her stroke, she had literally turned her life over to me. I had to see it through.

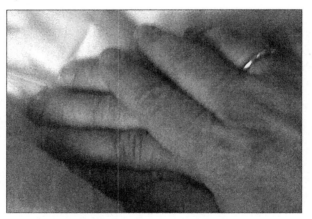

Even though phoebe was in a coma, I never let go.

They'd given her a tracheotomy, and one day a nurse said, "I'm going to try something. I'm going to take out the plug in the tube and put my thumb over the trach. When I do that, if she can talk at all, she may be able to make a sound. Let's see."

She took out the tube, placed her thumb over the trach and I said, "Phoebe. Say hello."

"Hello," was heard by both the nurse and me. It was guttural and faint, but it absolutely was hello. That sent me off on another round of hope. Of course it didn't last. Doctor after doctor came in a repeatedly and said she'd never wake up.

At this point I was now desperate. Phoebe's own aunt and uncle didn't want to visit. Her sister did whatever she could, and Tony was taking care of the business. I was the hands-on person at the hospital.

I called Helen Reddy, one of Phoebe's favorite singers and dear friend to both Phoebe and me. Helen was in New York at the time. Phoebe's favorite song was Helen's "You and Me Against the World." It was Phoebe's song with Valerie. During a few days when I was in Los Angles, Helen took a taxi for two hours to get to the hospital, and she spent another two hours singing every song she knew to Phoebe. Phoebe never moved. Helen was heartsick.

I called Greg Phillinganes and arranged for him to make a visit. She'd loved the songs they'd recorded a few months earlier. Greg left in tears.

I called Joan Rivers and said, "If anybody's voice could wake Phoebe up, it's yours. I'm standing by her bedside right now. I'm going to put the phone up to her ear. In three seconds, say something wonderful."

I heard, "Hey, Phoebe, This is Joan Rivers. Wake up, you stupid bitch!"

I thought it was hilarious. No reaction from Phoebe.

By this time, I'd made eleven cross-country trips. I was a wreck. One day Phoebe's doctor came to see me in the room.

"You have to go home. I've been watching you for months. If you keep staying here, you're going to end up in the bed next to her. I'm not making a suggestion. I'm telling you to go home and not come back. It's time to let her go and save you."

I lost it. Months and months of unspoken hope and stress exploded. I really was hysterical. I called my dear, sweet friend, Lucie Arnaz, who was in New York at her apartment. I told her what happened and she said, "Get over here NOW."

I arrived and collapsed. I couldn't eat. I couldn't stop crying. Ron Abel, Lucie's conductor, came over. The two of them held me and just let me do whatever I had to do. I'll never forget their love and how they took care of me. They helped me make arrangements to go home.

I did go to the hospital to see Phoebe one more time. Her sister was there and saw exactly what happened.

I walked over to the bed and took her hand.

"Phoebe, I told you I'd take care of you and get you whatever you wanted for your career. I did that. So now I want you to tell me again what you want. Do you want this all to end?"

Phoebe opened her eyes with a bang and they were as clear and focused as if she were taking a law review test or something. It absolutely told me that she'd heard me, was so grateful someone finally asked the question, and that she was done. Julie witnessed it. We called Tony, who still held the power of attorney.

Phoebe went to be with Valerie on May 26th, 2011.

I know she's so happy to be with her daughter again.

I flew back to arrange the funeral. I wanted her band to play "Poetry Man" with no lead singer. They did. I asked Bill Clinton

Bill Clinton and Phoebe.

to write a letter that I could read for him. He and Phoebe adored each other. I showed Phoebe's interview from CBS Sunday Morning. Howard Stern, Darlene Love, Gloria Steinem, Paul Schaeffer, Lesley Gore, Blue Note's Bruce Lundvall, Valerie Harper so many friends filled the chapel of the funeral home. It was in the same room where she'd held Valerie's funeral. Jimmy Webb called me in tears, and Robert Lamm, the lead singer of Chicago, called as well. It's still a blur for me.

I arrived the day before, and sat holding Phoebe's hand next to the open casket for hours. In my purse, I had two bracelets given to her by Valerie that she always wore. I put them on her cold, stiff wrist. No one saw me do it.

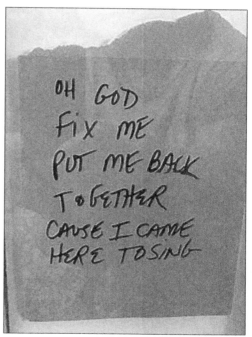

A year later, I was seeing a very authentic, professional medium by the name of Marla Frees, and she channeled someone who was obviously Phoebe. She said, "Oh, there's someone here who's so happy to see you. She's just lighting up. She's talking about how you kept yelling at her and she heard you the whole time. She said you never shut up."

I started to laugh.

"Wait, she's saying something else. She's saying, 'Thank you for remembering the bracelets.'"

This note that I found written by phoebe says it all.

Chapter Twenty-Five

DYNASTY, ROCK HUDSON, THAT KISS, THOSE QUAALUDES

Dynasty, starring Linda Evans, John Forsythe, and Joan Collins, represented the glorious excesses of the Reagan Era 80s. If you were involved with the show at all, you became part of the Carringtons yourself. Aaron Spelling and Doug Cramer gave so many parties for the cast, that you were smothered literally in caviar and diamonds.

I remember one New Year's Eve they took over Chasen's Restaurant, the most famous Hollywood one of all, and held a black-tie dinner party. I was *Dynasty* Executive Producer Doug Cramer's date. There was a red-carpet entrance, and as each couple walked in, a live orchestra played the *Dynasty* theme. You felt like royalty.

While most of the stars wore real jewelry, there was a *Dynasty* jewelry line with copies of all of Joan and Linda's necklaces, earrings, bracelets, and rings. They all were styled alike, available in sapphires, rubies, or emeralds. Doug gave me all three sets. I think I was wearing the sapphires that night. Around 11:30 p.m., John Forsythe asked me to dance. It was at the height of the *Dynasty* frenzy, and there I was, dancing with "Blake Carrington," the current most wanted man in the world by millions of TV viewers. John was such a gentleman.

Linda Evans is one of the kindest, nicest people you would ever hope to meet. She WAS Krystle Carrington. We first met at a dinner party in the 70s at the beach house of Bridget and David Hedison. Again, I was Doug's date. I remembered Linda from *Bachelor Father* days, her first TV series, and then *The Big Valley.* I realized that because of *The Hollywood Reporter* that almost anyone I would meet in the business knew who I was, so I wasn't surprised Linda did too. But we really didn't know each other.

Dynasty Executive Producer Doug Cramer, Linda Evans, Craig Johnson, and myself at a more casual party.

One thing I always loved about her was her hair. It was perfect, and I loved her style. I asked her that night who cut her hair. She told me it was Gene Shacove in Beverly Hills. I told her I was going to make an appointment.

"Tell me when your appointment is for and I'll go with you," she said.

I couldn't believe it. I'd only known her two hours, told her I loved her hair, and now she was taking me to get it cut?????

Well, that's exactly what she did.

I love Linda Evans. Everyone on *Dynasty* or wherever Linda worked loved her.

One person didn't love her...Joan Collins.

Joan was a "man's woman," and she had absolutely no interest in even being friendly with another woman. She viewed every woman as competition to be slaughtered. When Joan joined *Dynasty*, it was in the second season, and Linda was the big female star. Joan was jealous and tried to make Linda's life miserable in many ways. Linda rose above it and kept her dignity. And, I must say, Joan was sensational on the show.

The only time Joan ever even acknowledged that I existed was when I was Doug's date and we were out to dinner in a foursome. There were only three other people at the table, and she would have to at least make eye contact with me for a second. I used to direct questions at her, forcing her to talk to me. I made a game of it. If we were at a function seated at a round table of eight, I'd be wallpaper. She never spent one second of her time being nice to someone who wasn't useful. But, to be fair, Joan was a very entertaining, witty, dinner companion to all the men.

NOTE: LINDA EVANS AND THE ROCK HUDSON AIDS KISS

Way before Dynasty, *I had met Rock a few times. He'd invited me on more than one occasion to Sunday parties he gave almost every week. I only went twice because the parties were populated with young, hunky boys, barely over 18, in various stages of undress. I was uncomfortable.*

But, Rock was also always very gracious and respectful to me. He was a nice man who was not very bright.

I went on the set and said hello. I was totally shocked by how he looked. I went right from the set to executive producer Doug Cramer's office.

"He has AIDS. He looks really sick," I said to Doug.

"No, he doesn't have AIDS. He's lost some weight. He's fine."

"He has AIDS," I repeated. "I don't care what he or his agent has told you. You can just see it by looking at him."

"No. He's fine!"

Well, he wasn't fine.

There was great concern in Hollywood during the early days of AIDS as to how it was transmitted. Many, many actresses privately expressed their concerns to producers and agents about having to kiss gay men. I can't tell you the number of actresses who called me for advice on the situation. It didn't matter whether they were on half-hour comedies, feature films, dramatic TV shows, daytime soaps—it was a huge deal. In MANY cases, scripts were re-written, taking the kissing out. The actresses simply did not want to kiss

Linda and I still see each other occasionally.

any actor they thought might be gay. That seemed to be the best way to resolve it at the time. We have to remember that in the 80s the disease was just being discovered. There was no credible scientific information that said AIDS could NOT be transmitted by kissing. All we heard about was "exchanging of bodily fluids by any means might be a way to catch it."

Linda did not want to kiss Rock, either. I found out later that Rock didn't want to kiss her as well. Rock tried to get the script rewritten, and the producers said no.

The producers assured her he didn't have AIDS and said it was ok to kiss him.

Linda did it, and tried to keep her mouth as shut as she could. Rock also did the same. She was a trouper, and didn't want to cause waves. I am not saying here that any of the Dynasty producers lied to her. Rock was the one who was lying. But, I reiterate, it was so obvious when you looked at him.

When it was announced he had AIDS, Linda immediately took an HIV test and was negative. I would have been so angry with the Dynasty executives, I probably would have gone into their office with an Uzi. Linda, as usual, was a lovely lady.

I was not. I ripped Doug apart.

Not everybody remembers that Ali MacGraw was in *Dynasty* for about ten episodes. I do.

When I was a teen and started reading *Mademoiselle* magazine, I noticed that every August they asked a guest editor to edit the August Back to College issue.

One August there appeared a young woman wearing a rust mock turtle sweater with a matching rust headband, a grey skirt with matching tights, grey suede ankle boots, sitting on a fence with her bicycle resting against it. The bicycle had a basket full of textbooks.

It was Ali MacGraw, and I wanted to be just like her, immediately. Even though going to an Eastern all girls college like Vassar, Radcliffe, Smith, or Sarah Lawrence was not a new thought for me, this solidified it. From that moment on, I begged my mother to let me go back East. She said no every time. She was very controlling and didn't want me out of her sight. I ended up going to USC and was very happy, but my dream never died.

Back to Ali. Not only was she on that cover, but everything about her was perfect. I especially wanted her eyebrows. I loved that slightly crooked front tooth; I loved her brain and that fact that she was intelligent, but artistic and not necessarily driven. I was driven enough for both of us.

She went on to act in *Goodbye, Columbus*, a role that Lesley Ann Warren was signed for, but had to withdraw from because she found out she was pregnant. When *Love Story* came out, and Ali played the exact type of girl who was on that *Mademoiselle* cover, my Ali admiration was sky high. I also loved her in the Alan King movie, *Just Tell Me What You Want*.

After I joined *The Hollywood Reporter*, it was surprising to me that I never ran into her, but I didn't pursue it. I could have easily called Ali's press agent and asked for an interview. When I saw her on the *The Tonight Show* come out wearing jeans, a white t-shirt, a tux jacket and black loafers, I didn't know what to do with myself. She invented that look, and everyone else has been copying her ever since.

I just got on with my life.

Now let's go to the 80s, and *Dynasty* is the number one show on TV. Douglas Cramer was the executive producer. He, more than anyone, was responsible for the "look" of *Dynasty*. He didn't create the show, but he made it what it was.

Then Ali got cast in the show. Uh oh.

I was on the set all the time because of my friendship with Doug, Linda Evans, and a number of the cast members. I chose to still keep my mouth shut about what Ali meant to me in terms of style and my college fantasy.

"Hi, it's Douglas," said the voice on the other end of the phone. "I need a favor."

"Of course. I'm here to help," I replied.

"I need you to come over to the set right away. It's Ali MacGraw's first day and she's terrified once she gets in front of the camera. She's great and fun and happy when she's hanging around the set, but the minute that camera turns on she's stiff as a board. I want you to walk on the set and spend the day with her. She knows who you are. She doesn't know you're coming. I just want a friendly person around her who can talk to her before each scene. Try to relax her and make her comfortable."

There are no words here. I simply couldn't believe what I was about to do.

In less than an hour, I was on the set saying hello. I quickly forgot about that *Mademoiselle* girl, and saw a fantastic person who was just simply scared of a camera—NOT a still camera, obviously, but one for movies. Even though she had done a number of movies prior to *Dynasty*, as the years went by, and she worked less, her fear grew.

She was very happy to meet me, and I immediately started telling her stories about Linda Evans and Joan Collins to put her at ease. They were really funny stories, but she didn't laugh. She was as sweet as could be, but so scared that I couldn't get her focus away from the terror. I tried for almost three hours and couldn't make a breakthrough. My heart really went out to her. I knew that if she'd done well on the show, she could have been on a long time and made a ton of money.

At the end of her contract, and everybody else's on the show, *Dynasty*'s finale was the "Moldavian Massacre." The entire cast was at a black tie wedding in the fictional country of Moldavia. Gunmen were going to interrupt the wedding and start shooting people down. Some would only be wounded; some would be dead. The stars of the show had no idea whether they'd be shot and killed, just wounded, or totally fine. The tension on the set was extraordinary. Some of the stars had scripts that told them when they heard gunshots they should act wounded and fall down. Some didn't, but they could have been shot standing up. No one knew.

They were shooting it in Beverly Hills at the Doheny Mansion, a real mansion where the oil-rich Dohenys had lived for years. It was still the same in present day and was quite extraordinary.

I was also friends with *Dynasty*'s wonderful producer, Elaine Rich. She was the line producer, which meant she was always on the set and ran the nuts and bolts of getting the show done. She had a special job that day.

Here's what happened:

The director shouted ACTION. The scene began. Catherine Oxenberg and her prince groom were saying vows. I was hidden behind the camera on the side. The gunmen rushed into the room and opened fire. The actors who were supposed to fall did so on cue, and remained still on the floor (as they were told to do).

The director yelled "CUT" and "EVERYBODY FREEZE."

The floor of the ballroom was covered with "bodies."

Elaine Rich entered the room holding a vial of fake blood and a sponge. She walked over to Ali, threw blood on her and said, "You're dead." (i.e. "You're fired.")

Ali didn't know it was going to happen, and I was watching. She couldn't move because she was "dead." Elaine continued on walking around the floor "killing people."

"NOBODY MOVE," shouted the director. "THOSE OF YOU WHO ARE DEAD, STAY DEAD. IF YOU ARE JUST WOUNDED, SLOWLY REACT TO YOUR WOUND AND BE IN PAIN. IF YOU ARE DAZED, TRY TO STAND UP." He got his last shots, and then the scenes were over.

I watched Ali get up and look at the person next to her. She was a little embarrassed that she'd been killed, and she had a look on her face where I knew she just wanted to get back to her dressing room and get home as soon as possible. I didn't go after her. It would have been an invasion of privacy.

It's many years later now, and she has moved to Santa Fe.

I still want her eyebrows.

* * *

THE QUAALUDES OVERDOSE:

Helmut Berger was an extremely handsome German actor who was the director Luchino Visconti's lover. Take a look at him in *The Damned*, and you'll see how gorgeous he was. When I saw that movie, I thought he was one of the most exciting, sexy men I'd ever seen right up there with Alain Delon.

The actress, Pamela Bellwood, was a regular on *Dynasty* from the start. She was a very bright, sophisticated, worldly person, and she and Helmut hit it off. The rest of the cast really didn't "get him." Helmut was quite eccentric and liked drugs and alcohol. He hid out a lot in Pamela's dressing room because they had bonded.

Helmut almost always showed up "compromised" when he reported for work. It was very difficult to shoot scenes with him because he couldn't remember lines or stage movements.

I had the misfortune to show up one day about thirty minutes before they were going to fire him.

I heard the roar/wail from him emanate from the soundstage when they told him. I was visiting with Pamela in her upstairs dressing room. *Dynasty* producer, Elaine Rich, who delivered the news, made a BIG mistake. She did it BEFORE he had finished his scenes for the day. He had one scene left to shoot. Shows are very expensive to produce. The budget for just ONE *Dynasty* episode was at least $2–3 million. If anything went wrong and they had to go into union overtime, it would cost tens of thousands of dollars.

Suddenly thundering footsteps came toward Pamela's dressing room. Helmut opened the door and slammed it shut. He hurled himself on the couch. I was sitting on the floor and Pamela was in her makeup chair.

He was muttering and snarling in German, and then said, "What's in your refrigerator?"

Before Pamela could answer, he opened it and discovered two bottles of champagne. He popped them open one right after the other and starting drinking bottle No. 1 as if it were water. Then he took a large bottle of pills from his jacket, removed the top, tilted his head back, and dumped them all into his mouth. He washed it down with the remains in the first bottle and then started on the second.

Pamela and I looked at each other with great alarm in our eyes.

In about fifteen minutes, Helmut began to slur his words. I do remember making out things like, "Now let them try and get me to shoot that scene." He was deliberately rendering himself impossible to shoot, knowing he would cost them tons of money.

Ten more minutes passed, and the slurring became totally unintelligible and he was beginning to sink into the couch. Fighting it, (why?) he tried to stand up. He got part way up and then passed out cold, face down on the floor.

Pamela and I found the empty bottle of pills in his jacket. They were Quaaludes that had expired at least two years prior.

"Keep checking his breathing," I shouted to Pamela. "I'm going to get help."

I ran down the dressing room area stairs and ran into Elaine Rich. "Quick! Helmut is passed out on the floor in Pamela's dressing room I think he ODed! We need an ambulance."

Elaine ran to the room and saw him on the floor.

"Is he breathing? she asked Pamela.

"Yes," she answered.

"Hurry, you've got to call an ambulance," I implored.

"Both of you stay right here, and nobody make any calls. Do you understand? " ordered Elaine in an ice cold tone.

Pamela and I didn't move.

Five minutes later, which seemed more like a half-hour, Elaine returned with a "doctor" holding a black bag.

"Shoot 'em up," she said. "That bastard is going to shoot that scene." And then she walked out.

The doctor bent over Helmut and gave him a shot that must have been some form of liquid speed. Within two or three minutes, Helmut was conscious and back on the couch.

He shot the scene, left the studio, and was on a plane to Italy the next day. No extra expenses for Dynasty except for whatever that doctor charged.

Good Lord.

Chapter Twenty-Six

LANA TURNER—A BROAD WHO GOT THE JOKE

For decades and decades there have been beautiful women movie stars in Hollywood. Most come from a small hometown and they're the "prom queen," or the pretty waitress at the diner, or they're a beauty contestant/small-time model. I believe this was a little more prevalent in the 30s, 40s, and 50s, but it still goes on.

If any of these women become really big stars, either they take their new personas seriously, or they get the joke that they are really and still "Julia Jean Turner from Wallace, Idaho." Those who get the joke really usually enjoy being stars and they get the game. They know that when they are home with no makeup eating a chicken pie, that's who they really are. When they go out, they are playing a part.

I personally have never cared for those women who brought that star image inside their house and played the part, like a Joan Crawford, for instance.

Lana got the joke.

At some point in the 90s, I was introduced to her daughter, Cheryl Crane. For those of you who have been living on Mars with no media ever, Cheryl murdered her mother's boyfriend, Johnny Stompanato, to protect her mother. Stompanato was a pretty boy and a petty gangster who hung around Hollywood. He was very violent, and Cheryl heard him hitting and threatening her mother. According to Cheryl, he told Lana he was going to destroy her face because she refused to take him as her date to the Oscars. Cheryl believed that would happen, and in a panic, took a knife from the kitchen. She had no intention of using it. She just wanted to scare him away. When she ran into the bedroom, Johnny charged at her, unaware she had a knife pointed at him. He ran into the knife and died from his wound.

For years in Hollywood, people thought Lana did the killing, and fifteen-year-old Cheryl took the blame so her mother wouldn't lose her career. It was a gigantic scandal.

I ended up having dinner with Cheryl and some friends on more than one occasion. We also had a few lunches. I liked, and still like her tremendously. She's confident, forthright, and truly "real." Of course, the murder came up at one point, and she looked me in the eye and said, "My mother did not kill him. I did."

I hadn't even asked the question, but the incident had been brought up.

"Would you like to have dinner with my mother and me tomorrow night. We're going to a nightclub and I think you'd enjoy meeting her," said Cheryl.

"I'd love to."

I drove to Lana's condo in Century City, a development between Beverly Hills and Westwood. Lana walked out in sequins and fur and her hair done to the "nines." Cheryl and I looked very nice in our conservative black suits.

Lana sat next to me in the passenger seat and we shook hands. I smiled at her and she smiled back, and then we started laughing. It was totally spontaneous. We just "knew" we were on the same page. I continued to laugh a bit as I saw her primping in the mirror, making sure that "Lana Turner" was ready for her entrance into the club.

We arrived and the doorman opened her car door. She got out like there were 100 close-up cameras and Clark Gable was waiting for her. In truth, there were very few cameras because it was just dinner. She didn't mind. She always believed that a star should be "on" in public. It was her job.

The maitre'd was waiting for her, and when he escorted us to our booth, right in the middle of the front row, you could feel all eyes. I sat across from Lana, and Cheryl sat in-between us.

"Well, that's done," I said to Lana, with a slight smirk on my face.

"You bet, honey. Now I need a drink!"

Drinks were brought to the table. Even though Lana knew she was continuously on display, no one could hear what we were saying. She sat straight up, looking very proper and fashionable, but the bawdy stories coming out of her mouth were worthy of a truck stop diner.

Lana was one cool, "chick," and I really liked her.

"Marlene never wanted plastic surgery. The person that you saw was unrecognizable because gravity simply pulls down the face, neck, and cheekbones. In Marlene's case, she has really thin, Germanic skin, and it wrinkles badly and has no elasticity. What she does when she's on stage or on camera is a special technique. First you take the real hair and pull it back in a high ponytail with a rubber band. You put it on top of the head, but try to make it very flat. Then your makeup artist takes almost what looks like a spider web—rubber strings individually attached to tape, and tapes each band or string around your full hairline with the tape at the hairline and the bands aiming back. Once the tapes are secure, he pulls as hard as he can and the bands pull and lift the skin so there are no wrinkles or sagging anywhere. He then ties a knot in the back securing all the bands. A little nude-colored wig cap is put over the knot and the ponytail, and then a gorgeous blonde wig goes on.

Voila! Marlene Dietrich!

I want to be very clear here and say that I am not criticizing or shaming Marlene Dietrich in any way. I'm glad she didn't have plastic surgery. I hate stars that have constantly changing faces and end up looking like freaks. Marlene was magic. She spent her retirement years in an apartment in Paris, rarely going out or seeing anyone. I understand that she liked to talk on the phone a lot to people, and that's what kept her company. She had a family and grandchildren, and I have a feeling she did not have a bad time toward the end. She chose the life she wanted.

NOTE:
Of course we know Marlene and Garbo had a little "tete a tete" in the 30s. When Kim Novak became famous in 1955, Marlene went gaga over her. Much to Kim's shock, dismay, and disinterest, she received an unsolicited gift from Marlene consisting of custom-made lace brassieres. Marlene had gone to the trouble of obtaining Kim's measurements from someone at Columbia Pictures, ordering the bras, and having them delivered. I wish Kim had saved the card. I know she would have given it to me.

Lizabeth Scott was another very special classic film noir blonde with a husky voice and a very sexy lisp. She was hugely popular in the 40s, and if Lauren Bacall had not come along and overshadowed her, she would have been an even bigger star. Her career was damaged in the mid-50s by a story in a disgusting magazine called *Confidential* that said Lizabeth preferred women. She denied it, fought back, but after her co-starring role with Elvis Presley in *Loving You* (1957), her roles were few and far between. And then she disappeared.

I always want to know why someone disappears. It fascinates me. I was so curious about Lizabeth, yet I never made an attempt to find her. Deep down, I knew we'd meet some time.

Every year since 1970, I had gone to Debbie Reynolds' charity, The Thalians Ball. And, every year, Debbie would have a very private party in her hotel suite after the party was over. Some years there would only be three of us. Sometimes it was fifty. It just depended on Debbie's mood. This particular year, she wanted it to be very small. I think there were eight of us. Then came a knock at the door and I heard the words, "This is Lizabeth Scott." First I thought I was going to die. Then I said, "Thank you, God." It was happening.

Lizabeth was in her mid-late 70s, and she entered wearing black leather pants, a white silk collared shirt, and a black sequined jacket. She was wearing black leather high-heeled boots, and she looked about forty! It was simply jaw-dropping. Her hair was still in that classic blunt cut bob. She was with a very nice casting director named Marvin Paige, with whom she felt comfortable and protected as an escort.

I must say that even Debbie was shocked Lizabeth was there.

Lizabeth sat on an ottoman near Debbie, who was on the couch. I was sitting on the floor between the two of them. When I was introduced to Lizabeth, she immediately knew me from my column and complimented me. I was thrilled.

She and Debbie and I were having a great conversation, and then some drunken woman, who was an uninvited guest of another uninvited guest, rushed over to Lizabeth, got on her knees, grabbed Lizabeth's hand and kissed it saying, "Oh my God, you are my goddess." It was mortifying. Lizabeth snatched her hand away as fast as she could and coldly said, "Please get up. This is not necessary."

I was prepared to throw her out bodily.

"Come get your friend and please leave," said Debbie very strongly to the crashers. "Now!"

I waited a few days after that evening and then called Marvin Paige to ask him if he'd set up a lunch for the three of us for me to get to know Lizabeth better. He did, and she accepted. We met at Caffe Roma, a Beverly Hills old-school outdoor café in a court-yard. It was not hip and trendy, but rather filled with people from the 50s and 60s who still lunched there. I understood why she felt comfortable.

This time she was in jeans, boots, and a sweater. She had on the classic Tiffany watch, their gold signet ring, and heavy gold brace-lets. She and Ali MacGraw were the chicest, most classic style icons I've ever known.

After some small talk, I asked her why she'd stayed in LA. She looked a little bit shocked by the question because I'd prefaced it by talking a little about actresses who left to go live in the country or by the sea.

"I like it here," she said simply. "I like the weather. I came here from the cold east coast and I like to be warm. My friends are here and this is home to me."

She was very smart. She knew I was trying to figure out how, finan-cially, since she'd not worked for a long time, how this was possible. I would never ask that of course, but she continued talking.

"I've always known what to do with my money. Every dime I had I put into many companies like Coca Cola or Phillip Morris in the 40s. I also kept buying property. I'm quite fine."

"What do you have for breakfast every morning. Whatever it is, it sure is working for you," I said next.

"Fruit, toast, and coffee. That's it," she replied.

At that point I toasted her with my iced tea and we laughed. Lizabeth got "the game" and outplayed Hollywood. Whatever she did here, she did for her own joy. I am happy to say that we had many more lunches through the years, into her eighties. She still drove. She went everywhere during the day by herself. She was a real lady, an independent original, and a pistol. I adored her and was so blessed to have her in my life.

I'm going to end with Garbo, simply because it was a short moment. I don't know anyone who has met Garbo, Dietrich, Scott, and Novak other than myself. There must be somebody else, but I have yet to meet him or her.

One day in the mid-80s I was walking along Fifth Avenue in New York. It was a brisk day, but not freezing. I was walking south, on the east side of the street. Ahead of me was a tall woman wearing a trench coat, British schoolgirls' brown shoes, and a fedora hat. I had never felt such magnetism coming from behind a person. I was compelled to follow her.

This went on for three blocks and then she stopped to look in a Saks Fifth Ave. window. I walked ahead to the next window so I could look back and see her face.

Yes, it was Garbo. I felt light-headed. It's not about stars. I really want to make that point. I've had stars coming out of every pore of my skin. But there are a few of God's creatures who almost transcend reality. Garbo was one.

She caught me looking at her and acknowledged it with the tiniest beginnings of a smile.

I actually said to her, "Great hat."

She did a quick nod and said, "Thank you."

"Nice to see you," I said."

She nodded and then looked back at the window. It was time for me to move on.

Chapter Twenty-Eight

REBECCA SCHAEFFER—THE MURDER OF AN ANGEL AND TO ALL MY MURDERED FRIENDS

How many of you actually knew someone who was murdered? For your sake, I hope most of you haven't experienced it. I HAVE ACTUALLY KNOWN FIVE, and if you add in others that I just met and spent only a short time with, the total would go to NINE.

That's because my environment was all celebrity-all the time. Sharon Tate, Nicole Brown Simpson, Bobby Fuller (of the Bobby Fuller Four who was shot on a drug deal), and the publicist, Ronnie Chasen (who was supposedly the victim of a smash and grab robbery. Yeah, right). The others were Dorothy Stratten, Sal Mineo, and John Lennon. Whew! Try dealing with all of that.

I left one name out of that paragraph—Rebecca Schaeffer. That was the hardest of all.

If you don't know her name, I assure you that you'll never forget it when I'm through. Rebecca Schaeffer was the twenty-year-old actress who was murdered by a fan on July 18th, 1989.

On July 16th, 1989, Rebecca and I had just finished a fun lunch at the Beverly Hills Hotel. I walked her to her car and we made plans to get together the next week. I never saw her alive again.

When I first met Rebecca Schaeffer, she had been cast as the teenage younger sister in Pam Dawber's CBS sitcom, *My Sister Sam*. I knew her because a friend of her parents had sent her to me for advice. Rebecca was 19 at the time. She was born in Oregon, and had very intelligent parents. Her father was a therapist. Rebecca got involved in modeling and ended up in New York. She was so pretty, so bubbly, that she quickly ended up in Hollywood and on a sitcom. Rebecca looked like "Miss Teen USA," with masses of light brown

Rebecca with her parents, Benson and Danna.

curls framing her beautiful face. She had big, round, brown eyes, a turned-up nose, and winning smile.

She shone so brightly on that show that she got some movie roles and TV movies roles almost immediately. She was the "pick to click." I adored her on sight because she was bright and funny and uncorrupted. In fact, she was the smartest young star I'd ever met. Her parents came to visit her at one of the tapings and I remember I said to them, "Your daughter is so smart and aware. Nothing's going to happen to her." Her parents were very worried that something could happen in crazy Hollywood. I still see her parents' faces smiling at me and looking relieved.

My Sister Sam shot on a lot called the Warner Ranch in Burbank. *High Noon* was shot on its western street. *Fantasy Island* was shot in its jungle area. Many famous movies and TV shows were shot there, and still are. I went to the set of *My Sister Sam* every Friday afternoon and stayed until around ten or eleven p.m., when they finished shooting. Rebecca had a very large trailer/dressing room that could have slept a family of six or eight very comfortably.

The show was shot in front of a live audience, so it was more like a play with "re-takes." They started shooting around five or six, and the hours prior were a combination of last-minute rehearsals,

memorizing last-minute line changes, and hair and makeup appli-
cations. While it was very busy, there were also gaps of sometimes more than two hours at a time where Rebecca would sit
in her dressing room. A good portion of that time was when she
answered her fan mail. I remember her being so excited that she
even HAD fan mail. Her eyes lit up that people she didn't know
wrote to her and cared about her. She told me she felt a strong
obligation to personally answer every letter. Some of her fans mis-
took that an answer from her was an invitation to become a pen
pal, and more and more fans were writing reciprocal letters thinking she was a friend. She loved it and continued to write back to
some of them.

"Rebecca, it's not always a good idea to write back to fans at
all. I'm particularly concerned that they think you're friends with
them and are now writing back and forth," I said. "That can cause
problems."

"A lot of them are girls my age and I can help them," said the
happy Rebecca.

"I know this is new to you, but not all of them you think are girls
are even girls. A lot of crazy people write fan mail. It's best never
to answer personally. The only thing you should ever do is send
back an autographed picture, and even that's not so great."

She looked disappointed, and I hated to see that. I also wasn't
sure that I'd gotten through to her.

One Friday afternoon we got a call in the dressing room from
the guard at the main gate saying a young man was there with
flowers, insisting that he deliver them in person and that he's a
friend.

"What's his name? I asked.

"Robert Bardo," answered the guard.

"Do you know anyone named Robert Bardo? I asked Rebecca.

"No," she answered.

A couple weeks later we'd heard that a young man had broken
into the lot trying to get a hold of Rebecca. The show was not
in production that week. Incidents like that from fans were not

unusual. And we NEVER put two and two together to think it was the guy with the flowers. Once that first incident was over, we forgot about it. It meant nothing. I've seen fans try to get on lots to deliver flowers tons of times.

July 18th, 1989
My home phone rang.
"Hello?"
"Rebecca's dead."
"What?"
"Rebecca's dead. It's Karyl. She was shot by some crazy guy. He rang the bell of her apartment house. Rebecca's intercom buzzer was broken so she didn't know who it was. She just went out to the gate and he shot her point blank. I don't know any more yet."

Karyl Miller was an executive producer of the show and a friend. "We were just at the Hollywood Bowl last night. I can't believe it," continued Karyl.

The room was spinning and I felt like I was submerged in water. I couldn't hear Karyl anymore. I started crying. And crying. Shooting Rebecca was like someone killing an innocent baby. It was snuffing out a career that was about to explode. It was killing a truly rare human being for no reason at all. It was unfathomable.

Oh my God. Her parents, I thought. *Oh, no. No. No.*

We found out fairly soon that the guy who shot her was the same one with the flowers and the same one who broke into the studio. He had gone to the DMV and simply had someone look up Rebecca's home address. Why did he shoot her?

Because she had answered his letters and then stopped answering them as she was told to do to protect herself. He was furious. He was "in love" with her and hated the rejection. He was NUTS.

I wanted him dead. I would have gladly pulled the switch or administered the lethal shot.

Instead, the prosecuting attorney was Marcia Clark, the same attorney who, years later, would contribute to blowing the OJ Simpson trial. Rebecca's parents, Danna and Benson, wanted her to go for the death penalty. Marcia told them it was "hard to get" and talked them into allowing life without parole. She said she wanted to spare them any more hurt in case she couldn't get the death penalty. She didn't want him to go for an insanity plea because she wanted him in jail, not a more comfy hospital jail. All I know is, Robert Bardo is still alive and breathing, and sweet, 20-year-old Rebecca is in the ground.

The only good thing to come out of this is that the law was changed and now the DMV won't give out addresses. Whoopee.

Rebecca's funeral was held on a grassy area of the Warner Ranch lot. We all spoke about this beautiful girl as her parents watched and tried to make it through. At the close of the ceremony, a string quartet played Schubert's "Death and the Maiden."

The pain was indescribable. It still is.

Chapter Twenty-Nine

LYNDA CARTER—BABE IN THE WOODS—A MAGNIFICENT WONDER

"I have just found the most incredible girl," said producer Douglas Cramer on the phone. "I have finally found Wonder Woman."

He had a new TV show called *Wonder Woman*, and he'd been trying for months to cast it. He'd literally seen hundreds of audition tapes and had as many meetings in person with aspiring actresses, and he didn't like any of them. He'd actually confided in me that if he couldn't find the right girl, he wouldn't do the show. It was almost impossible to find a truly beautiful brunette, close to six feet tall, who had the beauty, brains, stature, and sense of humor to play the character correctly. Doug had nearly given up.

Douglas Cramer was one of the "Kings of Television." He had worked at ABC and also been head of 20th Century Fox TV and Paramount TV. As president of both of those companies, he was responsible for selling and supervising *Bridget Loves Bernie*, *Love, American Style*, *Star Trek*, *The Odd Couple*, *The Brady Bunch*, and *Mission Impossible*—just to name a few. He left to start his own production company. And its first two shows were going to be *The Love Boat* and *Wonder Woman*. He later partnered with Aaron Spelling and executive produced *Dynasty*.

"What's her name?" I asked.

"Lynda Carter," he answered.

"Where'd you find her?"

"A producer friend of mine named Larry Gordon sent me her audition tape for another project he was doing, and the minute I saw it I knew I had our Wonder Woman. I'm giving the scoop to you!"

I was thrilled, because the Wonder Woman search was big news in Hollywood. For me to break the story in my column in *The Hollywood Reporter* was great for me, and great for Doug. He and I worked in tandem a lot. He had a nose for news and reporting, and I knew a good show or actor when I saw it. He gave me stories and exclusive access to his stars and shows before ANY other reporter. And, I always wrote glowingly about his projects. BUT, let me say right now, this was no "deal." If he did a show I didn't like I would tell him, and print the review accordingly.

Doug, a very dapper dresser, was also known for his dinner parties, which he cast as if he were doing an episode of *The Tonight Show*. He would have me, of course, the columnist, cover the party and his hostess, plus one or two stars, maybe an artist or two like David Hockney, and network executives. His house was like a modern art museum, with walls covered in Schnabels, Kellys, Jim Dine, Jasper Johns, Lichtenstein, Agnes Martin, etc. It was jaw-dropping.

A typical dinner party night went as follows—I would arrive at the house around four or five and have a massage. He would have one after me. We relaxed, played soft music, and discussed the guests, seating charts, and the goals for the party. It was always all business. There were other nights for pure fun. Doug did all the menus. I was in charge of music, and I always had Barry White "Love's Theme" playing as guests walked in. It was like Roy Scheider in *All that Jazz* (1979). "It's showtime, folks!" After the party was over, we'd both go over what we'd learned and see what was "column-worthy."

"I have a favor to ask of you," continued Doug. "Lynda just got here from Arizona. She doesn't know anyone. She doesn't know how the business works. She's very vulnerable. I need you to guide her. Tonight is the ABC affiliates dinner. I'm having her picked up in a limo and then I'd like to send the car to you with her in it so you can accompany her all night. I'll be around as much as I can, but I've got to talk to the affiliates. You know what to do to protect her and who she should and shouldn't speak to."

"Of course, I'd be happy to handle it, and I was going anyway, as you knew I would be."

FYI—"affiliates" are the local stations in each city that are affiliated with the network. Any network had to have outlets in each

3/24/75

Sue,

   A note to tell you how v_e_ry much I appreciate the column you wrote on "Wonder Woman." It was super fanastic!! —or maybe I should say "W_onder_-ful"! You are a very special talented lady. The light of life shines upon you. Thank-you again!

Love
Lynda Carter

Lynda's original thank you note to me.

city on which to broadcast their programs. They'd be dead without them, and each affiliate had the option to run or not run the product. It was very important for ABC to keep the affiliates happy with expensive hotel rooms, rich buffets, and show them a parade of stars. It looks glamorous, but it's a shark pond.

And, Lynda Carter, with zero experience, was about to be thrown in headfirst.

The affiliates evenings were "dressy business" attire, so I put on a pretty black suit and a powder blue silk blouse, complemented by superb jewelry. I was only in my 20s, like Lynda—I was older by a few years, of course! But, I was born in Hollywood, was aware of my power, and knew the game cold. Nothing bad was going to happen to Lynda on MY watch.

The limo pulled up and the driver came out and opened the door to the backseat. There sat Lynda Carter, a girl plucked from obscurity, who was about to be one of my closest friends.

Yes, Lynda was one of the most beautiful girls I'd ever seen, but there was something about her that transcended that. There was a sweetness, an innocence, and an inner dignity that shone through. I could certainly see she was really vulnerable to the explosion that was about to happen to her, but I knew her heart would always be in the right place.

I can't really remember what she had on that night. I think she was wearing a dressy black dress with a v or scoop neck. She showed off her assets, but it was not vulgar or intentionally salacious. She was just built that way, and her neckline was not inappropriate.

"Hi, I'm Sue. It's a pleasure to meet you."

"It's very nice to meet you, too. Thank you so much for your column. It was very exciting for me to see it," said Lynda.

"How are you feeling right now?"

"It's just a whirlwind. Three days ago I was worrying about paying my rent this month, and suddenly I'm on my way to an ABC party. I just can't believe it!"

"You have nothing to worry about. That's why Doug is sending you with me. Tonight is 'show and tell' for you. You will be on display all night. Your job is to smile and just talk to all these station bosses. Just thank them for running *Wonder Woman*. You're not hustling. This isn't anything cheap. It's just the business of promoting a new series. Believe me, all of ABC is on your side. They want you to be a success. I'll be right with you. If you have any questions, just tap me or say you need to go to the ladies' room. You're going to be just fine. I can tell."

"Thanks. This is all just so fast," she said.

"Where did you come from?" I asked.

"I was born in Arizona and I've been singing with a band all over the country. I've even played lounges in Las Vegas. I know what it's like to be in crowds," she answered. "I also was in a beauty pageant. I won Miss USA for the Miss World Pageant."

She was not bragging in any way. Nor was she shy. She just humbly stated the facts.

"I came to Hollywood and haven't had much luck until now. I live in an old house on Hollywood Blvd. with four other actresses," she continued.

"You may be moving soon," I countered.

When we got out of the car, she turned out to be six feet tall in heels. She looked at me and laughed and said, "Mutt and Jeff." It was very cute. It still is.

Doug Cramer was waiting for us when we entered the ballroom of the Century Plaza Hotel in Beverly Hills. He smiled at us with great delight and approval. He took Lynda's arm and I stood on her other side. We entered the room, ready to work. God knows, Lynda provided great ammunition, and we had control of the trigger. Moments like that are extremely memorable. It's very rare when you can watch a star being born.

Lynda entered that room filled with men in grey or navy suits, and lit it up like there was a lightning storm overhead. I could see that she understood her mission; that it was a necessary business exercise. She walked around and either Doug or I would introduce her, or, sometimes, she'd introduce herself. She appeared to be very comfortable in her own skin, and radiated confidence and humility which is very hard to do. The only reason she could do that was because it was the truth. She radiated from within and it lit up the room. Talk about a hit! *Wonder Woman* went to number one that very night. It was simply extraordinary to watch. I'll never forget it.

Within a week, Lynda was in costume shooting the two-hour movie series opening special episode. She was at The Arboretum, a beautiful public garden area in a suburb of Los Angeles called Pasadena. Her co-star in the scenes was Cloris Leachman of *Mary Tyler Moore Show* fame. Cloris was her mother and the scenes were taking place in Wonder Woman's fictional homeland. At that time, Lynda was represented by an agent, Merritt Blake. She did not have a personal manager, press agent, personal hair and makeup people, masseuses, manicurists, and all those entourage people. It really was just Lynda going to work alone and talking to

Doug and me if she had any questions. She was really happy I was there. I could tell my presence made her feel good.

When the show aired and became a hit almost immediately, Lynda became a public personality. That's very different from just being known in the business as an actress who got a good job. A hit turns your world into a cyclone. Hangers-on start to circle you to literally find out how to make money off of you. Whoever that star is, in this case, Lynda, that star had better be able to have good instinct, and/or have good, honest, strong people around to keep them safe.

Another thing that the public doesn't know is that shooting a one-hour film show is the most exhausting thing an actor can do. A typical start to the day for Lynda would be to be picked up by a car and driver at four or five a.m. (depending upon her call time when she needed to be in the studio). She might have gotten home at ten or eleven at night from work the day before. She'd still be in her pajamas and robe in the car at four or five a.m. (or maybe sweats), arrive at the studio and then sit two hours for hair and makeup.

Note: She also, when she got home the night before, had to memorize lines for the next day. Sleeping? Eating? Any relaxation? Very hard to do. The lead character is in almost every scene. Instead of a half-hour sitcom, which is shot in one day in front of an audience, a one-hour film show shoots like a movie...no audience, take after take, angle after angle—close-up long, shot, etc. It is absolutely grueling.

But that's not all.

Lynda was working for ABC and Warner Bros, and they needed her to be available for interviews, photo sessions, TV talk show appearances, and maybe even visiting affiliate cities to promote the show. And, when was she supposed to fit that in?

There simply are not enough hours in the day. And, this is ALL NEW to her!

That's the world that faces actors who become successful. Good Lord.

I visited Lynda regularly. Sometimes I would come at lunch; other times I'd come early and we'd have a chance to talk while she was in makeup. Sometimes I'd come at the end of the day so we'd be able to have a longer visit.

Lynda's dressing room was a typical "star trailer"—a motor home with a living room and full kitchen, TV dining area, a bathroom and bedroom. These kinds of accommodations were not luxuries; they were necessities in order to be ready to function.

Lynda and I talked a lot about the different people who were approaching her. I would tell her which press agents were honorable and did their jobs, which journalists could be trusted—I was available for all guidance. I remember one particular night where she was so exhausted she was almost in tears. She was extremely vulnerable. I suggested she cut our visit short, go home, and just sleep as long as she could. We talked about maybe driving to Santa Barbara for a one-night getaway—just anything to give her a break. I was very, very concerned when I left her that night.

I spoke with her the next afternoon and she was happy and excited. She told me that right after I left, a man knocked on her dressing room door (uninvited and on a supposedly secure studio lot), and introduced himself. I will not mention his name. He said he was a personal manager and he wanted to meet her and tell her about services he would provide for her career. This is the classic example of what I kept trying to tell her about people "preying" on her. It was a vulnerable night. I wasn't there, and she was a sitting duck.

Let me say that many actors DO need personal managers, particularly when they are stars of series where they don't have a lot of time to devote to business. Lynda DID need a personal manager, but there are those who put the client's interest above their own, and those who put themselves first. The one who "cold-called" at her door was an opportunist. As soon as she told me who it was I was horrified. But I could also tell by her voice that she was already intrigued by his pitch.

A personal manager is like a team captain overseeing the agent and publicist; interacting with producers and network executives;

creating career advice and planning. It's much like a campaign manager if you're running for president. A number of personal managers try to get successful clients so they can become producers of the client's product, like TV specials, movies, or nightclub acts. They get money off the top in the budget. These kinds of managers use their clients to get more power for themselves. In Lynda's case, that's exactly what happened. And along the way, the ideal thing happened for the manager. She fell for him. Now he had total control.

In order to maintain control, the first thing they do is try to keep their client away from old friends and family. They want to sequester them because they are the golden goose financing the show.

I was in a terrible position. I was very much against this guy and knew what he was up to. I had two opportunities to try and stop the marriage, and I did the wrong thing each time. The first time was when Lynda and I had lunch and she told me that her manager/boyfriend had set up his mother as her money manager. And, worse, they had bought a house together. She asked me if they should really get married because she had concerns. I told her that I wished she hadn't given financial control to his mother, and that she was now in a bad position because his name was on her deed. I thought she was trapped and I said that she might as well marry him because she'd handed over her money. It was terrible, terrible advice. I thought if she was legally married, it would protect her property better. Then she could get a divorce. I should have told her to get a lawyer and back out of everything. I did have a gut feeling, though, that she wasn't able to emotionally break away at that time.

"I need to talk to you right now. You have to come over to my house." It was Lynda calling me in the middle of the night before her wedding day. She was in a rented house that was the destination for the wedding. It was next door to the Playboy Mansion. I drove over right away and found her in the kitchen sautéing a tortilla and putting it around a hot dog.

"I don't think I should marry him," she said.

"Uh oh. You're running out of time," I responded. Again, I did not say, "Get out. Just get in my car and I'll call the wedding coordinator and cancel." I wish I had. I don't know If she would have actually done it or not, but I should have spoken up. I have regretted it forever, and told her so on many occasions.

The wedding took place. I "smiled" as she walked down the aisle. She left on her honeymoon, and I only saw her two or three times until the marriage ended. He did exactly what I thought he'd do—separate her from anyone who might tell her the truth.

If a magazine or a TV show wanted an interview, her "manager" insisted that he be on the cover with her, or the TV show with her. It was one of the most blatant uses of a star that I'd ever seen. And, she didn't know those were his demands. She was too busy working. There was only time to just adhere to the schedule. Their marriage lasted five years, and her "manager's" demands hurt her in the industry. People began blaming her, thinking she was aware of what he was doing, but she never knew it. People in the industry were ecstatic when she filed for divorce. He'd made so any enemies.

Note: It was my great pleasure, several years later, to be interviewed by Vanity Fair about Lynda, her life, her career, and our friendship. My favorite part of the interview was when I was asked about her first husband. I said, "If I had known that night I left her in her dressing room trailer that he was going to show up, I would have hidden on the roof and dropped an anvil on his head."

On the day of the announcement of the filing for divorce, I walked into Lynda's dressing room where she was getting ready to shoot one of her TV specials. He had "blocked me" out of her life, but that was all over.

Lynda was sitting in a makeup chair when I walked in. She saw me, jumped up, screamed with joy, and we both hugged and hugged. The nightmare was over. We were back. From that moment until this very day, we celebrate our glorious friendship.

At that time in her life, in addition to her TV movies and specials, Lynda's life was filled with live performing. It was the 80s, and all the big stars from TV were playing the circuit of Vegas Hotels

Friends on the road again.

like Caesar's Palace or Harrah's Tahoe and Reno, or the resorts in Atlantic City. It was a great time in the United States because people had money—they were making it, and they were spending it. The motto was, the more sequins, the better. Life was a party!

For me, I was away all the time with Lynda, or Joan Rivers, or Debbie Reynolds, or Connie Stevens or the list goes on. What's important to know is that the first concern of all performers is the quality of their work. They rehearsed, they knew their lighting and sound, and they wrote a lot of their own "patter" (the stuff they say in between song and dance numbers). They went to work around five p.m. to do hair and make-up. Then they did two shows, at eight p.m. and eleven p.m., and work ended around one a.m.

All performers are "high" when they get off the stage because of the energy they get back from the audience, as well as they joy of performing. You can't just go right to bed. You need to "come down." Sometimes you hang out with the band or the dancers. Many times friends are there to see you, so you sit with them and talk. Whatever you are doing, it is fun.

When you are there with the performer, you get access to the codes to get in the secret doors that lead to and from the stage. You get tips on "hot tables" for gambling, and you spend a lot of time in kitchens. Yes, kitchens. You probably don't know this, but most hotel showrooms are attached to the banquet kitchen. The only way to get to the stage is by walking by smelly garbage. It happens every time, in every hotel. So, the next time you see a performer in Vegas like Cher or Celine, just know that they walked through garbage to get to you.

Another perk is the stars' suites. Many of them are two-story "palaces" with Jacuzzis, overlooking the strip. They have butlers, their own kitchen and dining room, and many even have pianos so the star can rehearse. You can get anything you want from room service twenty-four hours a day. When a hotel makes good gambling money because a certain star is playing there and drawing customers, that star can get the moon brought down from the sky if she wants.

But when everybody's gone, and it just you and your buddy, it's the greatest playground in the world. I remember one night in Tahoe, Lynda was given a house on the lake to stay in instead of a suite at the hotel. (Joan Rivers was given a boat and captain at her disposal when she and I were there together.) Picture that the night's shows are over, and there we are in a house with a gigantic indoor swimming pool with the lake illuminated by the moon. And, we, "the kids" are loose. We were doing cannonballs and somersaults and laughing our heads off.

Meanwhile, back in Los Angeles, to celebrate being free again, Lynda had bought a ranch in the hills of Malibu. It had stables, a pool, a tennis court, and a main house. It was a serene escape from Hollywood, and she enjoyed having friends over for barbeques and tennis. But, I think one of Lynda's favorite activities was just quietly sitting down and reading a book under the trees. No matter how much "Hollywood" is in your life, people usually end up

*At Lynda's recording session
several years ago.*

Us today.

being who they really are, and Lynda is just a "nice girl." That may sound boring, but it shouldn't. She's a real person. Maybe running lines with her while we both are in the pool isn't an everyday activity for most people. But it's just life.

Yes, it's just life when you're standing on the set of the infamous Maybelline commercial when Lynda comes up out of the water in close-up for the mascara. Or you're in the dressing room when Angie Dickinson comes to discuss a scene they're about to shoot together. When you are a Hollywood columnist, these things are normal. If your job is to interview celebrities and spend time with them, it is only natural that friendships develop and you go through the journey together.

One time, after Lynda returned from a Maybelline appearance and dinner in Memphis, she told me about a wonderful man she'd met named Robert Altman. He was the lawyer representing Schering-Plough, the parent company that owned Maybelline. She seemed to be very impressed with him and I was happy to hear that. You can imagine the number of "Hollywood Hounds" who were after Wonder Woman! Lynda was a great escape artist!

A few months went by and Lynda and Robert decided to get married. I was thrilled for her, but sad that she was going to move to Washington, D.C. I understood that that's where Robert's law practice was, and she promised she'd keep the ranch and stay there for work. The good times did not stop. Robert just joined the party.

Lynda became the "Toast of Washington," and she and Robert ended up on the cover of *The Washingtonian* magazine. They were sought-after guests and were, and continue to be, very involved with the Democratic Party. They had two children, James and Jessica, and both are following their father into law.

Being a mother was of paramount importance to Lynda, and she eventually sold the ranch and turned her attention to family. Fortunately, she could work whenever she felt like it, and she was able to design a life that fit her.

Artistically, music has always been Lynda's greatest passion, and for years now she has been performing in clubs and concert halls with her own band, and writing songs and making albums. We still try to meet on the road when we can.

It's rare to have happy endings in Hollywood, but this is one of them. And she and I are still the two kids who keep laughing together.

Chapter Thirty

VALERIE HARPER YESTERDAY, TODAY, AND HOPEFULLY TOMORROW AND THE MARY, VALERIE, BETTY, CLORIS, AND GEORGIA REUNION ON HOT IN CLEVELAND

I loved the *Mary Tyler Moore Show*. I gave it a rave review in *The Hollywood Reporter* and couldn't wait to visit the set. In fact, I visited the second week the show aired.

Here's what happened in ONE visit:

I arrived at lunchtime, and Mary was wearing a leotard. She had an area where she did dance routines every day as her form of exercise. She couldn't have been nicer, but she wanted to get back to her routine.

Valerie was having lunch in her dressing room, and from the moment we met we were instant best friends. She was so warm, open, and optimistic.

Ed Asner and I clicked and he asked me out. He was married at the time. I didn't know that, so I agreed to a lunch. That lunch led to more lunches. I adored him, but I wouldn't cross the line with a married man.

My love for Valerie put me in a pattern of visiting the show a lot. Of course, there were also was a lot of good items for my column, but she and I just wanted to hang out. The more I showed up to see Val, the friendliness of Mary toward me faded. I understood. I was playing favorites.

Valerie eventually left the *Mary* show for her own show, *Rhoda*, and it was a success, too. When that ended, Valerie had various series, some good, some merely ok. That's not what this chapter is about.

One day, Valerie and I were just hanging out at her house and we got to talking about sex and hookers. It was just "casual lunch talk." Since we were into equality, Valerie brought up male escorts and wondered whether they were paid more or less than women.

"Go get the phonebook," I said.

"Why?" she asked.

"We're going to book a male escort for the evening."

"No...."

"Oh, yes," I replied.

Valerie came back with the phone book and we looked up escort services in Beverly Hills.

"Here's what you do," I said to Valerie. "You become a different character and just call each service and ask the prices. Use different voices, accents, whatever."

Now she was "into it."

"Should I ask for hourly prices? The whole night?"

She picked up the phone, and suddenly she was a Chinese woman. Then she was from Texas; the Bronx; France. It was amazing, and we got tons of information. We deduced that woman were paid more than men. Good to know.

Another time I was at my desk at *The Reporter* (yet again) and the phone rang.

"We have to help Linda Lovelace." The voice on the phone was Valerie's. The "Linda Lovelace" she was referring to was the porn star of *Deep Throat*. Linda had been brutally manipulated by the producer of that and was truly a battered woman.

"What's up with Linda?" I asked. I'd also met her a few times and been horrified by what had happened to her.

"She needs a kidney," continued Valerie. "Meet me at Diane Ladd's house."

I picked up my purse and drove to Diane Ladd's house without asking any questions.

But, I ask you, how many of you would ever get a call from Valerie Harper telling you a porn star needs a kidney and you have to go to Diane Ladd's house? This was just a typical day for me. As I

Dinner at my house with Valerie, Phoebe, and Lesley Ann Warren.

drove over to Diane's, I did ask myself, exactly whose kidney were we talking about removing!

Linda got a kidney, by the way. And, I had actually met her the night of the *Deep Throat* premiere. As a promotion, the distributors actually placed a small towel on each of the seats that said *Deep Throat* on it. I remember watching Linda and then meeting her. She was totally dazed like a robot. She had no idea what was happening. I felt very sorry for her.

Then there was the night we went to the Tina Turner concert at the Hollywood Bowl, and when Tina did "Proud Mary," Valerie and I stood up and did the entire dance in the aisle. We knew ALL the moves!

At some point, ABC wanted to make a TV-movie based on the Mary and Rhoda characters. It sounded like a fun idea. Please keep in mind that many years had passed since *The Mary Tyler Moore Show*. Both Mary and Val had starred in movies, Broadway shows, and other series. Valerie was not the little newcomer who was paid about $750 a show for the first year of *Mary*.

When ABC offered the project to the two women, Mary refused to do it if she and Valerie were paid the same salary. She wanted to keep Valerie "in her place." Valerie refused to do it for less—rightfully so. The movie was called *Mary and Rhoda*, after all.

The fight dragged on for weeks. Valerie stood her ground. Mary finally agreed to equal money.

When the movie started shooting, it was clear to Valerie and everyone on the set that Mary had carried her anger about the negotiations on to the set. She was nasty to Val. She held up the crew constantly. An example of that was when a wardrobe girl brought her slippers that she had previously approved to wear in a scene. When Mary saw them she refused to wear them, claiming they were hideous. She wanted a different pair of slippers, a pair that could only be purchased in a specific store in New York. She would not shoot unless she had those slippers. Do you know what it costs to hold up an entire crew and cast per hour? The answer is thousands and thousands of dollars.

"But Mary, we won't even see your feet in the shot," implored the director.

It didn't matter. The set was shut down for hours.

At a press conference to promote the movie, Mary didn't even say hello to Valerie, and she refused to be in any pictures with her.

Mary and Rhoda aired and got good ratings. They were so good that normally ABC, or any network, would want to make another one. But Mary had caused so much trouble on the set and cost them so much overage on the budget, that the ABC executive in charge said, "ABC will never work with Mary Tyler Moore again." And they never did.

There was tremendous damage done to the friendship between Valerie and Mary. But, what the public never knew is that their friendship always was tenuous because of Mary's jealousy.

After a long time went by, Valerie picked up the phone and called Mary. Valerie NEVER had any bad feelings toward Mary, but it's true that it was difficult working on *Mary and Rhoda*. Valerie always cut Mary some slack because of her diabetes. Mary has had a severe case. Valerie had always tried to continue that phone relationship. She is a kind soul who has forgiven Mary for everything. And, she checked in repeatedly with Mary's nurses to see how she was doing right up until the day Mary died.

* * *

"I want you to know that I had lung cancer, but the doctor operated on it and it's gone," said Valerie in a phone call to me years ago.

I instantly started to cry.

"No. No, No," said Valerie. "This is why I didn't tell you before the surgery. I didn't want to upset you. I knew you'd react like this. I'm fine! The doctor cut it out and got it all. Relax."

Ok. I relaxed.

Then, in 2013, I got a call from Valerie's husband, Tony Cacciotti, that she'd had some kind of "incident" while rehearsing a play in New York. It was a play I'd already seen her in about Tallulah Bankhead that she'd done in Pasadena, California.

"We don't know what's wrong. It's like some kind of stroke. She fainted and was slurring her words. She's stable now and I'm going to bring her home. We're closing the play."

Within forty-eight hours, Valerie was home and I was on the phone with her.

"I just don't know what happened. It's some kind of brain problem. I feel fine right now, but Tony's not telling me much. I'm still a little confused."

I called Tony.

"Are you in a room where you can talk and Val can't hear you?"

"Yes," said Tony.

"What's happening?"

"It's bad. It's really bad. It's brain cancer and the doctors at the hospital in New York told me she only has six weeks to live. I won't accept that!"

"Tony! Oh my God! Does she know?" I asked.

"No, but we're seeing the doctors at Cedars today and she'll know then."

"What time is your appointment? I'll meet you both in the waiting room after."

I couldn't really register anything in my being at that moment. I just cried.

A couple of hours later I was in the corridor outside the doctors' office. Waiting. Waiting. I was determined not to cry there. Then Val and Tony came out. There was no one else in the corridor at that moment. I hugged Valerie.

"Sweet Sue. God love you. You're always there for me," said Val, grabbing my hands. "Listen to me. I'm ok. I promise you I'm ok. If God wants me to go, if this is my time, so be it. I've had a great life."

I wanted to vomit. I couldn't speak.

Finally, I said, "I'm NOT ok with this."

"But you have to be, darling."

It turned out that the lung cancer that supposedly was "totally removed" a few years earlier had metastasized to the brain. But it wasn't a malignant growth that could be cut out. It was something called leptomeningeal carcinomatosis—floating malignant cells in the lining of the brain and spine. You couldn't operate on floating targets. There was no cure. The doctors were going to prescribe massive amounts of chemo in pill form. Valerie was to take ten or twenty pills each Friday. That was it. That was all they had to help.

But now, since Valerie was a celebrity, the media had to be dealt with. There had to be a single announcement and then well-placed and well-scheduled interviews. It kind of leaked to the press, so for at least the first week of the news, TV and radio crews and tabloid reporters crammed the street in front of Valerie's house. She couldn't leave. For her doctors' appointments she had to put on a scarf and go to her garage behind the house and lie down in the back seat while Tony drove away as fast as he could.

The story was on every TV and radio station, plus the covers of magazines around the world.

The first TV show she did was *The Doctors*, and both she and Tony were on. Valerie again was cheerful and said she wanted to go public to help other people who might be facing the same journey. Her bravery and grace made America fall in love with her even more than they had before. The waves of good energy and love filled her, and, for me, I think that's what has pulled her through so far.

Then. If you can imagine, Valerie got an offer to do *Dancing with the Stars*. Most people who were told they had three months or less to live might turn that offer down. Not Valerie. She wanted to

At Dancing with the Stars.

show everyone that you can't stop living and you must go on. I was with her on that set almost every day. It was so inspiring, for me, and the rest of the world.

Valerie, by the way, was a trained Broadway dancer. With all the chemo she was taking, it affected her short-term memory and it was very hard for her to remember the steps. As a true professional dancer, it was very hard for her to accept that she couldn't dance up to her ability. But she smiled through it and loved every second.

Within about three weeks after *Dancing*, Valerie received an offer from the TV show, *Hot in Cleveland*. It starred her old friend from *Mary* days, Betty White. The writers had written a special episode in which Valerie would star, with other roles written for Mary and Cloris Leachman. Georgia Engel, also of *Mary*, was already a regular on *Hot*, so she'd be in it, too. It was to be a reunion of *The Mary Tyler Moore Show* and Valerie's great goodbye. What an astonishing idea.

I told Valerie that she needed someone on the set with her at all times, and that I wanted to do it. She said yes.

I was the only reporter present for five days and nights straight during the historic taping of *Hot in Cleveland* for the "Valerie Good-Bye."

As I may have mentioned, these kinds of sitcoms are taped in front of a live audience, usually on a Friday night. The actors report for work on the Monday before. Monday is a short day with just a table read (they all sit around a table and read the script aloud). There are also wardrobe meetings. The rest of the week—Tuesday, Wednesday, and Thursday are like school days. You show up wearing your own clothes and just keep rehearsing the scenes—memorizing your lines, and learning the blocking (where to stand and move).

Let's get this cast of characters straight:

Betty White:
The boss of the show and one of the greatest dames on the planet. Betty is in her 90s and experiences some natural forgetfulness, so she has difficulty with her lines.

Mary Tyler Moore:
Mary and Valerie have hardly seen each other since *Mary and Rhoda*. Because Valerie tried, out of politeness and genuine caring, to keep up a relationship with Mary, despite what had been done to her, they were on good speaking terms. Mary didn't hesitate for a second to say yes to doing the show and was very loving all week. I forgave her immediately.

When Mary showed up on the first day, we were all in a state of shock at her appearance. She was ravaged by the diabetes. Her eyesight was almost gone. She was so fragile that she could barely walk. Her husband, Dr. Robert Levine, was by her side every second. And yet she smiled that big *Mary* smile. She was valiant and our hearts went out to her.

Cloris Leachman:

Cloris is one of the biggest wacka-doodles of all time. She is outrageous, eccentric, insane, and, most of the time she's aware of it, and uses it to get her way.

I remember the first time I came in contact with her "antics." She had just won an Emmy for *Mary*, and I was at a post-Emmy dinner given by Doug Cramer at The Bistro, the fanciest restaurant in Beverly Hills. We were at the right corner table at the end of a wall-long set of tables. Cloris and her party came in and sat at the left corner table, the farthest table away from us. Everybody was out for a good time.

In the middle of our dinner, we all felt something move under our table. I felt someone grab my ankle. Another guest felt teeth on a thigh. What?

We lifted up the tablecloth and found Cloris Leachman, who had crawled on all fours under ALL the tables along the wall in order to reach us.

I told this story to Valerie at one point and she said, "You have no idea how many times I've been asked to calm Cloris down through the years."

Cloris has a wonderful daughter named Dinah, who is her "mother's keeper." Cloris was driven to work every morning by her daughter. Cloris got directly out of bed, did not brush her teeth, and arrived at the set every day in pajamas and a bathrobe. One morning, Cloris was over an hour late. We were panicked and called Dinah. Dinah couldn't find her mother either. Just as we were thinking of calling the police, Cloris ambled in in her usual outfit.

"Where were you?" asked Valerie.

"I hitchhiked."

At that point the producer pulled me aside and said, "Dinah's not here. No one can control Cloris and we have to get some work done. Would you please ask Valerie if she'd do it?" (Mind you, Valerie is the one with six weeks to live!)

I went to Valerie and told her what the producer needed.

"Was it ever thus," she said, assuming her usual position of controlling Cloris, just like she did for years on *Mary*.

Another time on the set I was drinking a coke, and Cloris walked by and, without saying a word or breaking stride, she pulled the can out of my hand and threw it in the trash.

She turned back to me and said, "Don't drink that again. It will kill you."

During a rehearsal on Thursday, very close to tape day, Cloris just decided that instead of her lines, she was going to do a monologue—and she did it, while all the other stars stood by, mouths open.

Georgia Engel:
Georgia played the ditz who was married to the Ted Baxter character on *Mary*. She played a similar role on *Hot*. She is not a ditz. She is extremely bright, observes everything, and is way ahead of most people.

The entire week was made up of very special moments. Just to be standing on the set and watching the rehearsals was like a dream. No one ever thought the *Mary* cast would ever work together again. It was also complicated because Betty was very unhappy with Cloris' unprofessional behavior and didn't want to be anywhere near her.

Mary couldn't rehearse her lines with people because she couldn't see them to read them. She spent most of her time in her dressing room with an aide who helped her memorize the lines from hearing them over and over.

Georgia, Valerie, and I were frequently meeting in Georgia's room going—How can we help Mary? How can we make Betty feel better about Cloris? How can we make Cloris stick to the script?

Macabre sense of humor, but "death's door Valerie" was the healthiest of them all!

The First Magical Moment:
The ladies were rehearsing a scene around a restaurant table. Almost everyone was having trouble remembering lines. The pro-

ducer called a union crew break. By law, a certain number of crew breaks must be called based on how many hours of work. They usually last fifteen minutes.

This time, the ladies didn't get up and go back to their dressing rooms. They were at that comfortable table and just started to talk and reminisce. After about five minutes, many of us pulled out iPhones to record it. It was a moment in time that needed to be saved. I can't even describe to you what happened among them. It was private and beautiful.

Then, on another day, Katie Couric arrived on the set to do an interview. She had her one-hour long daytime talk show an ABC at the time. She was the only reporter allowed on the set on a day that was a rehearsal day. Each one of the ladies was excited Katie was coming.

When Katie arrived, Valerie asked me, "Should I go over and say hello?"

"Yes, she's primarily here for you!"

I walked with Valerie to the corner where Katie was having her microphone put on before the interview. Valerie said hello, and Katie barely gave her the time of day. I had heard from others that Katie was a rude bitch, but I saw it firsthand. Valerie was surprised, slightly hurt, and taken aback. We just walked away and looked at each other.

"Wow," I said.

"Yeah," said Valerie.

Then all the ladies sat down on the set and Katie joined them to start the interview. The red light on the camera went on, meaning it was taping, and that perky, little Katie just flashed that phony smile and did a great interview.

The day of the taping is a long day. The actresses get in makeup early, and most scenes are pre-taped without an audience to make sure that there will be a completed show "in the can." This way, without an audience, you can do stop and start or feed someone a line. When they finished the show, there's a long meal break, a makeup touch up and then the show before the live audience is taped.

They reminisced while we all stood by.

The Second Magical Moment:

There was a tiny office near the makeup and hair area backstage. All the women were there, and one by one, as they finished their touch-ups, they entered the tiny office. It was about twenty minutes before the final taping and I was sitting with Valerie, Mary, Cloris, Betty, and Georgia in this postage-stamp-sized office. The lights were kind of dim, the energy very heavy.

You could feel that all of them knew this would be the last time they'd ever be together. There was silence. One or two might glance up occasionally, make eye contact and look down.

Valerie started to cry. "I love all of you so much. Your being here with me is such a gift. I can't believe all this is happening."

Now, Mary and I were crying.

"I love you, Val," said Mary.

That was it for me. I was gone. Everyone was crying and trying to save their makeup. I know Betty and Cloris and Georgia each said something. My heart was too heavy to remember. I had known each of them for years, but this was the private moment for the record books. I never lost site of the moment I was experiencing, and was so grateful to, once again, be the only person there as the blessed observer and chronicler. God put me there and continues to do so throughout my life. That's why these stories need to be told.

The show that night was extraordinary. When these women walked out together to be introduced to the live audience before taping there was a standing ovation that lasted about ten minutes. The applause and the tears filled the air. We all were witnessing a miracle.

God bless all of those remarkable women.

As for me, it was one of the most jaw-dropping weeks in my life.

Note:

As I write this, three years have passed since they shot that show. Valerie is now in medical journals as one of the most successful miracles. Her doctors came up with a pill combo to keep her cancer from spreading. She takes many pills a week, ten of which are heavy-duty chemo pills—and, sometimes they put her on a different pill and dosage. They knock her out for two or three days, but she gets up and lives her life. She walks two miles every day. She has shot more movies and TV shows. She has helped and inspired millions of people. My admiration for her courage and spirit knows no bounds. Her husband, Tony Cacciotti, a former personal trainer, should be commended as the architect and cheerleader of her heath regime. I believe that Valerie's will, Tony's close attention, and all the prayers from the public have made a tremendous difference in her journey.

And, with Mary's passing, it did, indeed, turn out to be the last time all of them were together.

Chapter Thirty-One

DEBBIE REYNOLDS—UNCENSORED, AND TRULY LOVED

(Written many months prior to December, 2016)

I never liked Debbie Reynolds when I was a child. I thought she was so "Goody Two Shoes." I remember when Eddie Fisher left her for Elizabeth Taylor, I totally understood why Eddie would dump her. The world was furious. I was on Eddie's side.

The summer when that happened, I was spending every day playing bridge on the beach in front of the Balboa Bay Club, a very exclusive private club on the water in Newport Beach, California. Truthfully, my parents had been members since 1953, so I'd spent EVERY summer of my life there. At that time, the club had a few private rooms for rent for members-only. They were right behind the beach, separated by a lawn. As I was about to bid two no trump, my mother said, "Look! There's Debbie Reynolds. She must be hiding out here because of the scandal."

I looked, and there was Debbie, wearing a cloth turban on her head, sunglasses, a bathing suit, and a cover up. She looked really sad. I felt bad for her.

Let's zip from 1959 to 1970. I am a daily columnist at *The Hollywood Reporter* and I have a rare evening at home. I'm thrilled I don't have to cover anything and can just rest. I turn on *The Dick Cavett Show* and hear him say, "Ladies and gentlemen, Debbie Reynolds." I decide to watch. And what I see is the funniest, hippest, brightest conversationalist I've ever seen in my life. There's no girl scout here. There's a bawdy, saucy explosion.

The first thing I did when I got to the office the next morning was call Debbie's publicist, Rick Ingersoll, and request an interview with her. No one says no to *The Hollywood Reporter*, and Rick and I had worked together on many of his clients like Carol Burnett and Rita Hayworth.

Rick called me back in an hour and told me that Debbie can see me at her house at three p.m. on the coming Thursday. I was really looking forward to it.

On that Thursday, I pulled up in front of Debbie's house on Greenway Drive in Beverly Hills. I hated her house on sight. It was a cold, ugly white modern mausoleum-looking building that was totally soulless and depressing.

Ding Dong. I was let in by Mary, Debbie's long-time housekeeper and cook who was destined to be one of my favorite people in the world. Mary walked me through the white marble entryway into a large living room. Everything was white—floors, walls, furniture—it was hideous. One wall of the living room was all windows and I could see a pool and a children's playhouse. Debbie was not home. That did not sit well with me.

About twenty minutes later I heard a ruckus at the front door. Debbie never enters a room quietly. She rushed in saying how sorry she was that her luncheon ran late, etc. She was wearing a stupid little royal-blue hat with a feather in it that matched her blue suit. She looked like a total PTA lady. My heart sank.

She asked me to follow her into the den where she placed me in a chair directly opposite hers. We were not on comfortable couches. It felt like we were on a Sunday news program facing each other for questions and answers. I took out my green lined notepad and pen, and she removed her hat. As I was about to ask the first question, the phone rang. Mary entered in the room and said, "Miss Debbie, President Lyndon Johnson is on the phone for you." Debbie gave me a kind of "look how important I am face I'm not just some silly movie star," and went to the phone. I tried really hard to hear the conversation, but I couldn't.

She returned to the room looking self-satisfied and said nothing. I started to ask questions. Famous movie stars have been interviewed thousands of times. They get used to the questions and pretty much know what's going to be asked. When doing an interview, both interviewer and interviewee have a job to do. I try to have good questions, and the interviewee must have good answers. As a reporter, I'm used to kind of cleaning up what the stars answer. Although they answer the questions, sometimes thoughts get unfocused, and I just edit things to make them more clear. It's no big deal. But Debbie was a different story.

"Excuse me, but I just have to say something," I said, stopping the interview in its tracks. "I have been listening to your answers and I am watching you edit as you speak. I have never seen anyone do that in an interview. Every answer you give is completely clear."

"Well, of course, dear. I was trained by MGM, the greatest studio in the world," responded Debbie, her back becoming even straighter. "It's what one is supposed to do in an interview."

"It's just amazing. I've never seen it before," I replied.

There was a pause and silence entered the room.

"You don't like me, do you? asked Debbie.

"Actually, when I was growing up that was true. I thought you were boring. But then I saw you on *Dick Cavett* and realized you're not like that at all. You're really funny and bright. I'm the one who ASKED for this interview because of it."

"Look at you there with your perfect pants and boots and striped sweater. Miss USC Journalism School in person," continued Debbie. "You think you're qualified to write about us stars? You don't know anything. You can't graduate from college and think you know the entertainment industry. You know what I'm going to do for you? I'm going to teach you how everything works so you can be a real reporter with the understanding of what it's like to be a performer in show business. I'm on the road with my nightclub act almost every week. I'm going to send you a plane ticket to fly to me each week so you can learn what this business is really about."

What on earth is happening here? I thought. Who is this person?

"Come with me," she said as she stood up and walked out of the room.

"I bet you hate this outfit I'm wearing, don't you?'

"Yes. It looks like the PTA."

"I hate it, too, said Debbie. "And look at this house. I don't like it either. I hate modern. Do you remember a Tudor house on the corner of Sunset at Hillcrest?"

"I do. It's fantastic," I answered.

"That was Harry Karl's house when we first married. I loved that house. Then all of a sudden, he insisted upon going modern, and here I am hating every minute of being in this house. Now follow me."

We walked away from the formal living quarters into the master bedroom. "Here's where Harry and I sleep. I hate having sex with him and try to never do it. Now let me show you another room."

I guarantee you, I have NEVER had an interview experience like this in my life or ever again.

"You see this room. It's Harry's den and dressing room. You see that barber chair? This is where Harry gets his haircuts and manicures. But the manicurists are hookers. Blowjobs come with the deal. I'm happy about it. It takes the pressure off me."

Keep in mind, I had only known Debbie Reynolds for about an hour before this "tour" started.

We ended up back in the living room.

"You have enough from those original questions to write a decent piece on me. That's good for now. Your real education is about to begin next week. Now I want you to meet Carrie."

I followed her outside to the large playhouse that looked like one of today's tiny houses for adults.

"Carrie, dear, would you come outside to meet my new friend?" asked Debbie.

"No."

Debbie paused for a second.

"Well, that's Carrie. She's only eleven, but she's going to do what she wants to do. Let's go into the kitchen instead. I want you to meet Mary. I pay her. She HAS to talk to me."

I saw Mary working busily at the stove.

"Mary this is Sue, Sue this is Mary. Sue is going to be around a lot, so I wanted you to get to meet each other. Are you making your wonderful Swiss steak for dinner?"

"Yes, I am," answered Mary.

"I want Sue to go home with some. She needs to taste your cooking. Sue, I'm going to leave you now. It's time to play with Carrie, but my office will be calling you tomorrow with your flight information. See you soon."

NOTE: Mary worked for Debbie until the day she was just too old to continue. Mary's sister, Gloria, worked for Carrie. All four of them ended up at the Coldwater Canyon property.

Thirty seconds later I was standing at my car, holding a container of Swiss steak and wondering about the amazing buzz saw/hurricane being I had just met. Debbie Reynolds was thirty-eight years old, and she was about to become my mentor and friend for my entire life.

Sure enough, Debbie's office called me the next day and sent me a plane ticket to her opening at the Desert Inn in Las Vegas for the next week.

My going to see Debbie in Las Vegas was only the beginning of a zillion trips to Las Vegas, sometimes even weekly, because during the 70s, all the TV and movie headliners like Lynda Carter, Helen Reddy, Ann-Margret, Connie Stevens, Joan Rivers, and many more, played the big rooms in all the best hotels. There were nights where I'd see two and three shows a night and hang with the star afterward. Stars are always "up" or very energized after a show, and they always want to talk, have a drink, and be with friends to "come down."

Once, I ended up driving at three a.m. in a van into the desert to look at stars with Connie Stevens; I went with Helen Reddy to Don Rickles' one a.m. show; I went swimming with Lynda Carter in the middle of the night in the gigantic pool at her rented house provided by the hotel. The adventures were endless and fabulous.

Coconut Grove nightclub with me, and unnamed Thalians supporter, Debbie, and Carrie in 1970.

Betty Grable, Eddie Fisher, and me at the Coconut Grove.

Being with Debbie Reynolds for hours and hours and days and days, stretching into decades, was an adventure like no other.

That first time I went to the Desert Inn, I arrived around three p.m. and went to the show room. At that time, she was doing a gigantic act. For her opening number, she had the DEBBIE letters of her name thirty feet tall in lights come down from the roof of the stage as she sat on the bottom of a "B." She had twelve male dancers. During *Singing in the Rain* (1952), she had an actual rain curtain with real water come down on the stage. There were four-teen different numbers, over 350 light cues, at least ten costume changes in ninety minutes—and it all had to run smoothly.

It's important to mention here that Debbie's opening number cos-tume in 1970 was a black or red hot-pants tuxedo. Her little satin hot pants were over black or red fishnet stockings and black or red dancers' "character" shoes. On top was a white pique tuxedo shirt sewn to a matching black or red vest, with a sequined white bow tie. She also had a vaudevillian straw hat if she wished to wear it. That "Girl Scout" was the cutest, hottest thing you could ever see.

The Desert Inn Crystal Room showroom could play to 5000 people a week, and that's what Debbie did. Every show was sold out. It was one of the largest on the Vegas Strip. Long tables seat-ing at least twenty people were placed perpendicular to the stage. In the center of the room were the prized booths where "high roll-ers" (gamblers) sat, or other VIPs. Behind the row of booths were more perpendicular tables.

Debbie "produced and directed" every one of her acts. Yes, she had choreographers and set designers, but it was all Debbie. She had every step and every cue memorized.

Before I even let her know I was there, I sat in the empty audi-ence area and watched her work. She was always pleasant and respectful to the people who worked for her, but she was like General Patton reviewing the troops. No one worked harder than Debbie.

They went through each number from top to bottom with Deb-bie occasionally stopping the action to talk to the sound or light person in the booth in the back of the theatre, or her conductor if a tempo wasn't right. I could see that she not only had to be a performer, but also a director, producer, choreographer, lighting and sound director, wardrobe designer, liaison to the management of the Desert Inn, hostess to guests, and available for interviews. I was astonished.

At one point she said on mic, so everyone could hear, "Cameron, are you out there?"

"Yes," I answered.

"Good. Keep watching," said Debbie.

On the first opening night that I saw, she worked from three p.m. to six p.m. rehearsing everything. At six p.m. she went to her dressing room to start putting on her makeup to be ready for the show at eight p.m. I think she may have only had fifteen minutes rest! By the time she went on at eight p.m, the audience had no idea that she had already been working five hours straight.

Anyone who thinks a live performer just walks in, puts on a costume and makeup and cruises on stage to sing, is woefully uneducated.

When you work in a Las Vegas showroom, your show is not allowed to go over its allotted time by even one minute. For the hotel, it's all about getting the audience out of the showroom and into the casino. When Debbie played the Desert Inn for then-owner, Howard Hughes, she made more gambling money for the hotel than any entertainer.

As soon as her first show was over, she had only about a forty-five-minute break before she had to start getting ready for the second show. Mind you, she'd been working since three p.m., and she had yet to EAT.

And, by the way, after every show, friends and fans want to come back to the dressing room area to greet her, and that takes up most of her break between shows. It also, of course, happens after the last show.

I might mention here that Debbie's mother, Maxene, was the head wardrobe mistress for all of Debbie's shows, and could be found in the wardrobe room sewing away to fix last minute problems. Maxene was a killer force. I could see where Debbie got her strength.

Maxene Reynolds was a real ball-buster. She scared a lot of people. I don't think she scared Debbie, but, through the years, I could see they had a "prickly" relationship. Debbie was always respectful and supported her mother financially almost from the day she became famous. Debbie's father, Ray, was a quiet man—so quiet I think I only ever heard him say about three words. He was a skinny, bespectacled Texan without the boots. He was extremely meek, almost as if he were a ghost. Debbie never told me one story about him or mentioned him, even if I was sitting across from him at the dinner table. But he seemed very nice.

The lack of what I perceived to be a "warm" mother is the reason why Debbie picked out two specific older women to take that role. The first was actress Agnes Moorhead. It was a little before my time, but I remember Debbie telling me that they tried to eat dinner together almost every night.

I saw that devotion on the set of a movie called *What's the Matter with Helen* (1971). Debbie's movie offers were beginning to wane, and she felt it was important to give herself a boost. She had a production company called Raymax, after her parents. Raymax produced *What's the Matter with Helen?* That's a fancy way of saying that Debbie put a lot of her own money up to get the movie made.

Debbie had seen the success of Bette Davis and Joan Crawford in *Whatever Happened to Baby Jane?* (1962), and she thought doing *Helen* might work. She hired Shelly Winters to play opposite her (as the crazy person) and Agnes to play the very important role of an evangelist.

Debbie was always in Agnes' trailer, seeking advice and encouragement. One time I knocked on the door, opened it after I heard the "come in," and Debbie was literally kneeling before Agnes, her head on Agnes' lap, and Agnes was patting her head. It almost looked like Madonna and Child. Debbie needed mother figures in her life that didn't scare her and were nurturing. Agnes filled that role. The other who did that was Lillian Burns Sidney, the drama coach at MGM. More on her later.

I went to the set a lot. The movie took place in the 20s, and the sets just took me away to another time. Debbie looked incredible in the costumes, and there were even some musical numbers. It got good reviews, but wasn't a box office hit. That hurt Debbie very much, both personally AND financially.

"I missed Agnes terribly after she died," Debbie told me in a conversation shortly after. "She had no family. I was it. Near the end she got a really unscrupulous lawyer who stole Agnes' house from me. She left it to me (big, beautiful Tudor in Beverly Hills on Roxbury Drive). He falsified the papers. I didn't fight him. I just didn't have the energy. So many things were going wrong in my life at that time, but every time I drive by the house I want to kill him."

The set of *What's the Matter with Helen* was surreal. Shelley Winters was from the Strasberg Acting School and she practiced "The Method." It was all about mood lighting, music, staying in character. Debbie practiced the method of hitting your mark and just "doing it."

Shelley insisted on having an old record player playing mournful songs of the 20s before her scenes.

"She is driving me insane," said Debbie. "I want to take that record player and shove it up her ass."

* * *

After the last show at the Desert Inn, which was about 12:30 a.m. or so, and the crowds of well-wishers would leave, Debbie would do one of two things—first, she would sit with friends (like me), open her favorite wine, Bernkasteler Doktor, and relax and tell funny stories until about six a.m. That was how she relaxed. She also finally ate. The order was always a grilled cheese and tomato sandwich on white bread.

The second thing she might do, which she did several times during a long engagement, would be to invite all her dancers, musicians, and friends up to a private penthouse in the Desert Inn, and she'd run an old Hollywood black and white movie. There was an open bar, buffet tables filled with food, and we'd all sit on pillows on the floor. One entire wall of the penthouse was floor to ceiling windows, and it was extraordinary to see all the Vegas lights behind us as the movie played in front. Believe, me, we saw plenty of sunrises too!

The first time I was there when she had movie night, I remember eleven-year-old Carrie sound asleep on the floor, oblivious to the movie. She was curled up in her robe, with a throw pillow from one of the couches under her head.

"Will you help me carry her to her room? Get her feet," said Debbie to me.

We carried Carrie in an elevator full of strangers, down one floor to Debbie's suite.

"She doesn't like to miss any of the action," whispered Debbie, smiling to her "audience."

It was not the last time we carried Carrie.

As Carrie got older, and we were still in Vegas, Debbie would force her to sing in the show. Carrie, very reluctantly, sang "Bridge Over Troubled Water," and really could sing. She'd inherited her father, Eddie's, perfect, strong voice.

"I wanted her to be a singer so badly," said Debbie, years later, "but she just refused to do it after a while. What a voice."

Eventually Debbie went to bed at six a.m., and she got up around one p.m. and had breakfast. Debbie stayed either in a two or three-bedroom suite within the hotel, or, the Desert Inn had houses along a golf course that was in the back of the hotel. It was Debbie's choice where she stayed. I always stayed in one of the rooms they provided for her. Frequently, in her early years of playing Vegas, her parents stayed with her in the golf course house.

Every time I think of the house she stayed in, I remember back to the many times we (she) staggered back as we giggled together walking all over the golf course, missing holes and poles, all the way to the house in the dark, just before dawn, or, in the blinding morning light.

I also remember when she broke three toes during a show and had to keep working. We had a bucket that I filled with ice in her dressing room and I shoved her foot in it in-between shows because there's no such thing as missing a show just because you have broken toes. We took that bucket back to the house after the second show and iced most of the night.

Debbie's dressing room at the Desert Inn was disgusting. She was the highest paid entertainer on the Vegas Strip, but Howard

Hughes (and most all of the hotel owners) didn't really care about the human aspect of things. They just cared about the money. The furniture in Debbie's room consisted of a couch covered in ripped brown plastic that was supposed to look like leather, and it had the stuffing coming out. There were a couple of mismatched wooden chairs, and a wooden coffee table that was a different color wood than the chairs. There was also one wooden end table with a lamp on it. None of the fabrics matched. It looked worse than a skid-row waiting room. Tape held up one leg of her dressing table.

For four years, Debbie had been asking management to please replace her dressing room furniture with something decent. God knows, hotels always have storage rooms full of furniture they put in their hotel rooms. And for four years, no one paid any attention to Debbie's request.

One night around four a.m., Debbie and I were alone in the dressing room. All the staff and stagehands had gone home. We were totally alone, and feeling "no pain." Debbie started commenting again on the terrible furniture.

"I have an idea. Just follow me."

I picked up a chair and started to walk out of the room.

"What are you doing?" asked Debbie.

"I'm throwing all your furniture away. We're putting every piece into the dumpster right now."

"Mr. Hughes is going to kill me," said Debbie.

"No he's not. You're too powerful. I guarantee you that if we empty out this room, tomorrow night when you walk in at six to get ready for your show, all this furniture will be replaced with the good stuff. C'mon!"

"I'm going to be fired."

Debbie and I took every piece of furniture, one at a time, carried it down the long hall and into the parking lot and tossed it in the dumpster. We even managed to throw that couch up and over. When we left, the dressing room was bare—both areas—living room and private dressing area.

I am telling you we laughed and laughed as we dragged each piece. I think we even sang. It was hilarious.

The next night at six p.m. when we entered her backstage dressing room, it was completely furnished with proper, acceptable furniture.

"Well, Cameron, you were right," said Debbie, her eyes wide.

By the way, we always called each other Cameron and Reynolds.

These touring adventures went from Las Vegas to Reno, Nevada, to Lake Tahoe, to Sparks, Nevada, Laughlin, Nevada (a real toilet), and New York for her musical, *Irene* (1973), to her touring show of *Annie Get Your Gun* (1977). Along the way were other shows in performing arts centers in different cities. We even went to Seaworld because she was booked to have a dolphin kiss her in their show! This "educational road trip" lasted from 1970 to 2014 when she retired. It lasted forty-four years!

I remember one time she was opening at the famous Coconut Grove nightclub in Los Angeles, and I was not at the rehearsal. The phone rang at my desk and it was Debbie.

"I'm having trouble with the stairs in the opening. The count isn't right or the dancers are coming in too early."

"Put them at the top of the stairs as soon as you are three steps down and the count will work," I answered, having seen the number zillions of times.

"Great! That's perfect," said Debbie, hanging up the phone.

I paused and was so pleased at how she trusted my opinion and respected that I had really learned from her. There was even one time in Las Vegas that the spotlight operator got sick and Debbie had me rush up to the booth and run it for her show! What a time I had.

The most surreal incident happened when she took me to go to *The Tonight Show* with her. I had been there many times with friends, and it was always like a party. All the stars who were on the show had dressing rooms lined up in one hall. It was a great place for me to do a column because so many interviews were at my disposal. On this particular night, Debbie was asked to come to the stage for a rehearsal, and she and I were walking down the

New Year's Eve.

hall. Debbie spotted Jack Benny standing in his dressing room door and she went over to him.

"Jack, this is Sue Cameron from *The Hollywood Reporter.* She's my friend and I have to go on stage now. Take her in your dressing room and entertain her."

Debbie walked away and Jack and I just looked at each other.

"I read your column," he said sweetly. "Please come in."

I sat on his couch and he went over to his dressing table, picked up his violin, and said, "Would you like me to play for you?"

"I certainly would."

Jack played for over 20 minutes. He was really good. All those violin jokes weren't true. He was an artist. What an incredible opportunity I was given.

Debbie knocked on the door and said, "I'm back!"

"Jack just gave me a private violin concert," I said, excitedly.

"That's what I was hoping for," said Debbie.

For many years Debbie and I spent New Year's Eve together because she was always working. We had so much fun staying up all night. As it always happens in show business, one's career has ups and downs. Debbie was in a down period this particular New Year's Eve. Her show was going to be at a terrible grade C hotel. I won't say where. She didn't even want to do a show on New Year's that year, but they paid her so much money, she couldn't turn it down.

It was in an area where most of the audience arrived by bus. They were very unsophisticated, "down-home folk." Of course they loved her show. We made the best of it, and after the second show we went up to her suite and started in "celebrating." Debbie liked wine; I had a limit of two vodkas. Regardless, it ended up to be around five or six a.m. Debbie still had on her full stage makeup and gown.

"Let's go!" said Debbie.

"Where?

"We're going to the casino," she answered.

Before I could ask why on earth we would want to do that, I was rushing down the hall after her.

We got down to the casino and she saw an older, overweight woman in blue jean overalls at the slot machine. Debbie walked right to her and started "coaching her." The woman was shushing Debbie without realizing who it was because she never turned around. Finally she turned around, saw Debbie, and screamed.

For the next hour Debbie "dive bombed" unsuspecting patrons of the casino. Truthfully, she was bored out of her mind and had decided this might be amusing. It was.

Let's talk about Debbie's husbands for a second or two. Her first one was Eddie Fisher. She really did love him and they were the "cute couple of the 50s." She was a virgin and very much believed in marriage. She had a horrible wedding night. She told me Eddie was very rough and uncaring. It was a very bad start. Almost immediately, she realized he'd rather be drinking and playing cards with

Connie Stevens, Tricia Leigh Fisher, Joely Fisher.

his male buddies than be home with her. She was miserable. And then daughter Carrie came along, and Debbie was ecstatic.

Elizabeth Taylor and Taylor's husband, Mike Todd, were Debbie and Eddie's best friends. Debbie and Elizabeth had known each other since school days at MGM. They all got along great and loved to travel together. Traveling was about to play a big part in Debbie's plan.

The public never knew this, but Debbie wanted to leave Eddie long before Eddie ever thought about Elizabeth. However, something else was more important to Debbie. She wanted Carrie to have a sibling. Debbie and Eddie's sex life had dissolved into nothing, but Debbie needed to figure out how to make it happen. When Elizabeth suggested a trip to Europe, Debbie immediately said yes. All she needed from Eddie was one time in a hotel room in Europe. She'd make sure it was romantic enough.

A few weeks after they returned from Europe, Debbie was pregnant. Mission accomplished. As far as she was concerned, Eddie was a sperm donor. All these things I'm telling you come from years of listening to Debbie tell me her story.

When she had Todd Fisher, named after Mike Todd, Debbie's plan was complete. Todd was her present to Carrie. She was so busy with Carrie and baby Todd that she wasn't thinking about divorce at that moment. All her focus was on the kids. She certainly did not expect to be dumped for Elizabeth, but when it happened she was filled with mixed feelings. She was so sad that her dream of what a marriage should be was ruined—but it was ruined by Eddie long before. She was humiliated by the public nature of it all. She was relieved she was rid of Eddie. She was angry at Elizabeth. Most importantly, she was worried about being a single mother.

A Note on Eddie Fisher:
I ended up getting to know him really well because he remained very friendly with Connie Stevens, his third wife. Connie only did that because she wanted him in their children's lives. Connie had two girls with Eddie, Joely and Tricia Leigh Fisher. I love them dearly. What was lovely is that Connie, one of the sweetest people in the world, also decided that she wanted to include me in her family. At times in my life, because of my closeness with both Debbie and Connie, I felt totally "Reynolds/Fisherized," and I loved it. I still am "Fisherized."

Eddie Fisher had extremely good taste in wives. Debbie, Connie, and Elizabeth all had tremendous senses of humor. They were all game for anything, and loved living life to the fullest. Debbie and Connie were particularly devoted to their children. I had the odd position of being in-between the ages of each set of mothers and daughters.

I first saw Connie at KHJ TV when I was dancing on *Hollywood a Go Go* while I was still in school. Connie was there to pre-tape a number, and I was so excited to see the "little songbird" from *Hawaiian Eye* (1959). Connie radiates light and is as vivacious as they come.

As usual, we met later on when I interviewed her for *The Hollywood Reporter.* She was a Las Vegas headliner the same time as Debbie, and I would frequently go up to see Connie's shows, too. Connie was very hip musically, singing songs that were done by black R&B artists, featuring her back-up singers who were part of a gospel choice.

"Kookie, Kookie, Lend Me Your Comb" it was NOT. She was sort of Aretha Franklin (light, very light) in a Bob Mackie gown.

Once you were in Connie's family, you were in for life. She never forgot you, whether your career was hot or not. I was invited to every party and family holiday/graduation/gathering at her house, and still go. Imagine a kid who loved everyone from Edd Byrnes to Sid Caesar, hanging out at Connie's on Christmas Eve, seeing all of them in line for the buffet. Troy Donahue, Poncie Ponce of *Hawaiian Eye* (1959), Suzanne Pleshette, Shecky Greene, George Burns, Buddy Hackett, and Milton Berle. It was an endless parade of the best comics and TV stars from my childhood. There was even a Christmas with Debbie and Esther Williams in attendance. There were tented-in dinner areas, big bands, Latin quartets; it was simply unbelievable, year after year.

Where Debbie lived in an ugly modern house Harry Karl forced on her, Connie lived in a classic Paul Williams-designed Georgian colonial that was built for the ice skater Sonia Heine. It had an Olympic-sized pool, sunken tennis court, and a third floor of the house that had Sonia's ice-skating rink in it. Later on, Connie added a recording studio and two townhouses to the property.

One of my very early Malibu/Hollywood parties at was at Connie's second home, on the beach at Malibu. I grew up in a wild combination of conservative doctor stepfather and wild entertainment lawyer "hang out-with gangsters

Tricia Leigh, me, Joely at Halloween.

and strippers" biological lawyer father. The party at Connie's kind of scared me. The women looked "too fast," and the men looked "too slick." I saw O.J. Simpson come in with his wife, Nicole, and she was wearing a see thru white, gauzy shift dress with no underwear. I was so uncomfortable, that I left and walked to the ocean in front of Connie's house and just sat on the sand.

Within minutes, a very precocious eight-year-old came and sat beside me. It was Connie and Eddie's daughter, Joely. I don't know why I did it, but I looked at this child and said, "I'm very uncomfortable in there. Those people scare me."

Little Joely Fisher said, "Me too. I don't like the woman in the white dress. You can see everything." I bonded with that kid in that second for life. Age didn't matter. We were kindred spirits. That kid saw through and "got everything." It's very odd, because I started out as Connie's friend, and evolved into Joely's "contemporary," even though I'm right in between their ages. Joely is a combination of Ethel Merman, Don Rickles, Nora Ephron, and Edith Piaf. Just go with me. Joely is the leader of my "Stevens world." I call her "Ms. Everything," and she calls me her "Sage." Every time each of us flies, we are that last call or text for each other. And, to Connie's credit, she accepted it. Thought it was odd, but accepted me always.

Joely's younger sister, Tricia, born fifteen months later, is the sassy brunette version of Connie and Eddie. Tricia is very sweet and kind, doesn't have a mean bone in her body, and tries to stay out of the drama as best she can. A singer, actress, and writer, she's carrying on the family tradition like a trooper. I love her. She also refers to herself as "The Family Ambulance Driver." It is a literal and metaphorical truth. She is a very talented writer, actress, and singer, and is filled with kindness for everyone.

Carrie Fisher was different. From the time we met when she was eleven, I was her mother's friend and treated as such. Like Connie and Joely, I was in between the ages of Debbie and Carrie. She was very focused on what she was doing, no matter what age she was. Carrie also went away to school at eighteen and there were the "lost years" when she didn't want to come home. After she returned, we really got a chance to know each other well. When Debbie moved to Carrie's property, the three of us spent a lot of time together.

Carrie was very sweet. She didn't show that side to most people. She was vulnerable, empathic, and very generous.

Years ago, if you can imagine this, with some kind of odd pact, Debbie and Connie never told their children they had half-sisters and brothers! The ex-wives of Eddie kept to themselves. If you can

One of Carrie's notorious birthday parties. A pregnant Joely and Sean Lennon also are October babies.

imagine this, Joely and Tricia Leigh Fisher did NOT know Carrie was their sister until they saw *Star Wars*!!! (1977).

This information only came out because Connie Stevens accidentally bought a beach house in Malibu that was next door to Debbie Reynolds. The day Connie saw the house and wanted to buy it, she noticed that the house next door had a pool.

"Who on earth would be so gauche as to have pool right next to the ocean?" asked Connie.

"Debbie Reynolds," answered the realtor.

That was it. It was time for the kids to meet. Carrie and Todd seemed to have only a mild interest in their father's other children at first. Joely and Tricia were thrilled to have half-siblings. As the years wore on, Joely and Carrie became very close. Tricia had less in common with Carrie, because she didn't have any alcohol or drug problems, but she and Carrie loved each other very much.

Todd was the only man in this harem, and he forged a life for himself as an accomplished electronics, sound, and design producer. He set up and organized the entire Debbie Reynolds Museum that was at her hotel. He was also in charge of costumes and memorabilia, and that was a huge commitment.

"I ended up having Connie's girls sleep at my house a lot," Debbie told me. Connie, rightfully so, didn't feel it was appropriate for them to be there when she had male company.

One Christmas Eddie Fisher was in Debbie's Thalians Mental Health Clinic (think about that one for a while), and Connie invited him over for Christmas Day. That was a tough moment. Carrie and Todd went to Connie's, and Debbie stayed home. Connie chose to have a "pleasant" relationship with Eddie for the sake of their children. Debbie's situation was totally different.

Eddie very rarely came around to see any of his children, whether they were by Debbie or Connie. When Joely or Tricia eventually had children of their own, (i.e. Eddie's grandchildren), he sometimes waited until the child was two or three before he even bothered to see them. But when he showed up, I have to tell you that I saw that boy-like Fisher charm and realized why all these women fell for him.

It wasn't easy for Eddie when he would come. There was still some hostility toward him at times. He frequently sat alone, or was relegated to the last seat at the end of the table (NOT the head) I began to feel sorry for him and I started to always sit next to him. He had a habit of just singing by himself. When he started to sing, I would join him. I loved singing, too. My mother was a professional singer and I'd inherited her voice. The first time I started to sing with him he said, "You can really sing!" Singing duets with him was magical. I'll never forget it. I had a really wonderful time with him.

I'll also never forget one time when Eddie showed up at Connie's for a birthday party for one of his grandchildren. It was a beautiful garden party, and Connie had rented round picnic tables with colorful umbrellas. Eddie walked in unnoticed and sat alone at a table. Naturally, I went over to sit with him.

"Hi, nice to see you," I said, kissing him on the cheek. "How are you?"

"I can't hear you," said Eddie. "I swallowed my hearing aids last night. They were on the nightstand with my pills."

Just as I started to attempt a response to that, Carrie Fisher started walking toward us with her daughter, Billie. Yes, both Connie and Debbie made sure that all the half-sisters and brother, Todd, knew each other and were family. It also wasn't unusual for Debbie to come to Connie's or Connie to come to Debbie's. It was quite a unique "clan."

Carrie got to the table, leaned over and kissed Eddie on the cheek and said, "Hi, Dad."

"He can't hear you," I said. "He swallowed his hearing aids."

Without missing a beat, Carrie bent down and started talking to his stomach!

That hearing aid story was one of the biggest laughs Carrie got in her *Wishful Drinking* show years later.

In 1983, Eddie came to me and asked me to write his book about his life. He told me he wanted to disclose all his secrets about Debbie and Connie and the women he'd slept with. I unhesitatingly told him no. There was no way I would help him hurt people I loved. It was a best-seller, and, to me, it was the best money I never took.

There was one more memorable uniting of all the "Fishers" when Debbie joined Connie and all of us at Connie's gorgeous house in Jackson Hole, Wyoming for a ski trip. Debbie didn't ski, and was just there to support Connie and do her charity show. She stayed in her room in her nightgown all day. Carrie absolutely refused to even go to Jackson Hole.

"We're leaving for skiing," I told Debbie, still in her bed.
"Have a nice time, dear."
"No one is here. What are you going to do about food?" I asked.
"Just leave a can of Campbell's Tomato or Chicken Noodle soup on the floor in front of my door, with a can opener and a spoon," said Debbie.
"But you have no way of heating it up."
"I'll be fine, dear, I'll just eat it out of the can."
Debbie had some very unique eating habits.

One night, after a big ski day, we all were sitting around after a late dinner, and the wine and champagne were flowing. A beautiful fire crackled, and conversation was flying. As the hours wore on into the middle of the night, the wine and champagne loosened the tongues of Debbie and Connie, and they really told no-holds-barred truths about Eddie. There were only about eight of us there for that jaw-dropping tete a' tete. Sorry. Reynolds-Fisher loyalty prevents me from repeating. Just know it was hilarious and hair-curling! (And, by the way, Joely videoed it! Location of tape undisclosed.)
Let's return to Debbie and life after Eddie.

Regardless of how wealthy Debbie was, she came from a very modest family in El Paso, Texas. Growing up, she never had any money. When you come from that kind of childhood, you always worry about security. Debbie made very good money making movies, but this big break-up was in the late 50s, long before the big Vegas money, the personal appearances, endorsements and TV shows weren't even a thought. Her movie career was going great, but she always worried about the future.

But way before *What's the Matter with Helen*, Debbie decided to look for a wealthy older man, preferably not someone in show business; someone who was stable. She found it, or so she thought, in shoe magnate Harry Karl. But, boy, did Harry come with baggage. He was married and divorced a few times to the same woman, a tacky almost-star named Marie MacDonald. Harry had kids, step-kids, and lots of issues. But he also had lots of shoe stores and lots of money.

They got married and Debbie didn't have a pre-nup. She gave Harry power of attorney, and they co-mingled their money. Good Lord what mistakes.

Debbie got pregnant twice by Harry and each time the baby died in the womb and Debbie had to keep the dead baby inside to let the pregnancy go full term and then deliver. Very few people know that. How awful, and what courage it took for her to go through it.

In the meantime, without Debbie's knowledge, Harry was spending every afternoon at the Friars Club, a private show business club, playing high-stakes poker. The game was rigged. There was a camera in the ceiling and Harry was being fleeced on a daily basis. He was losing hundreds of thousands of dollars.

Debbie soon realized she'd made a deal with the devil in thinking this was a stable, older man. She didn't care about his hookers, but one day, in 1982, Harry Karl died after open heart surgery. That's when Debbie found out that he'd lost all her money, too, AND, LEFT HER $6 MILLION IN DEBT because California is a community property state. She either had to declare bankruptcy or pay it back.

"I didn't want those people who were owed money to suffer, so I decided to pay it back," Debbie told me.

As a result, that's when Debbie went back on the road for years, frequently taking jobs that were beneath her, just because she was determined to pay the debt. She sold the big, ugly house and rented a beautiful house on Oakhurst in Beverly Hills. Mary was still with her. She owned a building in North Hollywood called the Debbie Reynolds Dance Studios that had rehearsal rooms. Dance classes were held there, and shows rented rooms to rehearse. It brought her some kind of income.

But the Oakhurst move couldn't last. It was too expensive and she needed to pay back that money.

Things were so bad that many, many nights, she would sleep in the studio. Some nights she'd stay over at her friend, Jerry Wunderlich's house. Jerry was an art director of most of her movies.

I remember once we were outside the dance studio standing next to her car and I saw a metal wardrobe bar across her back seat with clothes hanging on it.

"What's that?" I asked.

"I'm living in my car," said Debbie, matter-of-factly.

And she was.

Debbie Reynolds is an authentic person. She's honest and the same whether she has money or not. Any conversation we ever had was totally honest, no games. I'd never had that with any other person until we met.

Note: She truly knows the meaning of a mutual friendship. On the night of the book party for my very first novel, in 1993, she was in Las Vegas in the morning, having just finished a long engagement. She was exhausted and her usual course of action would be to stay in bed for a full day, and return to Los Angeles the next. Well, my dear friend, Debbie, got out of bed and was at my party that night. I'll never forget it. That's what friends do for each other.

A few months later from the day by the car, she'd made enough money to buy herself a small house in North Hollywood. It was a charming English cottage, on the wrong side of the tracks, but she didn't care. It was lovely and she owned it outright. She had fought her way back to having a roof over her head.

As an aside, as years went by and things got good again, Debbie bought two more houses in that neighborhood, one directly across the street from her for her brother, and one kiddy-corner from her for her mother. She paid all their bills, as she did from day one of being an actress. You can't imagine how many people she has supported since the day she became a star. I bet you didn't know that if you want to keep your band together, you have to pay them weekly whether you are working or not. Imagine how much that cost! Then there were assistants, a hairdresser, children, step-children and family members—all those bills to pay EVERY month, month and month, year after year. She also anonymously paid hospital bills for terminally ill friends and gave hundreds of thousands of dollars to our veterans. The public never knew any of this.

In 1974, the Academy Awards was produced by Jack Hayley, Jr., son of Jack Hayley, who was in the *Wizard of Oz* (1939) (and many others, for MGM). Jack, Jr. was raised among the stars of MGM, and he loved Hollywood and glamour. Jack decided that for this Academy Awards show he would bring back as many of the MGM leading lady contract players that he could get, to do a special dance number. It was the talk of the town.

"I have a special treat for you," said Debbie on the phone. "I want to take you to the Oscar rehearsal with all the MGM ladies. It will be a gathering that will never happen again. It's pure Hollywood history and you've got to see it with me."

The rehearsal was the day before the actual show, so it was going to be hectic. Each lady had received a letter explaining what they were to do, and arrived prepared.

The awards, at that time, were held in the Shrine Auditorium, a gigantic building in downtown Los Angeles. It had a huge stage and a very large audience capacity. What it didn't have was enough dressing room space to accommodate those ladies.

Debbie and I were shown to an area backstage that had been created to house all these women.

Picture one very large room, and along one sidewall were gray Army blankets hung over ropes to create privacy. There were

metal dress rods separating these blankets that were perpendicular to the outside blanket, creating little topless tents made out
of blankets. On each outside blanket, stars names were pinned
on white pieces of paper. They didn't have enough room for each
star to have her own tent, so they had to share in alphabetical
order. For instance, the first blanket said, "June Allyson and Lar-
raine Day." Another said, "Kathryn Grayson and someone." Then
it went to Janet Leigh and Ann Miller. I remember seeing Jane
Powell's name too.

But the minute Debbie and I started walking down the line of
blankets, she started to sniff very loudly and look around for an
odor. It was like a dog looking for its bone. Then I heard her say,
in an angry, suspicious growl, "Eddddieeee Fisshhhhherrrrrr." She
elongated the pronunciation. The more we walked along, the more
she sniffed. She kept repeating Eddie's name.

"What on earth are you doing?" I asked.

She held up her hand to shush me with a scowl on her face. I had
never seen her behave this way.

We proceeded down the blankets, and now she was actually
putting her nose close to each blanket. Clearly she was looking
for something.

"Edddddieeeee Fisssshhhhherrr. Eddddieeeee Fisssshherrr."

We were nearing the end of the line when we saw pinned on the
blanket, "Debbie Reynolds and Esther Williams." Debbie stopped
dead in front of the sign, sniffing louder than she ever had.

"Ah ha!" she yelled, pushing away the blanket to see what was
inside.

What we saw was Esther Williams injecting herself with a "Dr.
Feelgood" shot of vitamin B12, that also contained speed. Debbie
had recognized the smell because Eddie did it daily and it was all
over their house.

"I don't share dressing rooms!" yelled Esther, trying to hide the
syringe.

Esther picked up all her things and walked out, never saying
a word.

"I will never forget that smell for the rest of my life," said Debbie.
"It's one of the reasons my marriage was ruined."

Debbie would never forget that smell, and I will never forget the bloodhound hunt that ended in a mermaid shooting speed.

Note: Esther Williams was really cool. She was at Connie's Christmas parties and invited me to lunch at her house. I deeply regret never going.

In the mid-80s, the AIDS issue began to be known. No one in Hollywood would touch it. Before Elizabeth Taylor ever heard of AIDS or ever thought of founding AMFAR—where she takes credit as being the first star to "take on" AIDS, I sat in Debbie's living room in the North Hollywood house and watched her call every star she knew to do a benefit. Debbie had taken over the Hollywood Bowl to give the first ever benefit for AIDS, and she was turned down by 99% of the stars she asked.

Debbie gave the first big benefit, then Joan Rivers came next doing a benefit at the gay club, Studio One, in Los Angeles. Both Debbie and Joan were YEARS ahead of Elizabeth in working to prevent AIDS. I sound like I never liked Elizabeth. Not true. I always enjoyed her. I just want credit where credit is due. Debbie and Joan didn't wait for Rock Hudson to make it ok.

In 1984, I saw a sharp-looking silver-haired guy hanging around Debbie at a Thalians party. The Thalians was a mental health charity founded by Debbie in the 50s that has raised over $100 million for mental health. I didn't like this guy on sight. He was too slick and way too impressed with "Debbie Reynolds" and her lifestyle. I'm not going to mention his name.

Debbie told me that she was going to marry him. I reminded her of her promise to never sign over power of attorney. That was my only comment. She said she wouldn't.

She had wanted to buy a Las Vegas Hotel on the Strip as an investment. She'd paid back all the money and was now making a lot herself. She found a slightly run-down property on the Strip, but her new husband thought he'd found a better one on a side street just off the Strip. NEVER BUY A HOTEL THAT'S NOT ON THE STRIP. Debbie was right about the hotel she wanted to buy, but she cow-towed to her husband and bought the off-Strip property. It breaks my heart to say this, but it was a losing money-pit from the very beginning. I've never seen anyone put so much blood, sweat, and tears into something.

The renovations went way over budget. Debbie signed over power of attorney again. And this husband bankrupted her, too. He was so angry when she filed for divorce that he became violent. Debbie was afraid for her life. When she heard his key in the lock of the door of her Vegas condo, she somehow got up to a top shelf in a closet and covered herself with packages and shoes so he couldn't find her. She stayed there for hours just to be safe.

"I was sure if he found me he was going to throw me over the balcony," said Debbie.

The only funny thing that happened around this time was, when, on opening night, Debbie put me up in her penthouse apartment on top of her hotel. For many years, Debbie had been buying up original costumes from studios at auction, trying to save Hollywood history. No one would listen to her about building a Hollywood Museum or how valuable all these costumes were. Some of them were stored in that penthouse.

Many of the costumes were in the living room on actual dummies. Clark Gable was there in his *Mutiny on the Bounty* (1935) costume, Cary Grant was there in his *Bringing Up Baby* (1938) suit, Katharine Hepburn in her *Summertime* (1955) dress. There they all were.

All I can tell you is when I got up in the middle of the night to go to the kitchen to get water, those lifelike figures in the dark scared me to death.

This time, with the bankruptcy of the hotel, Debbie didn't have enough energy to fight anymore. She was sick and exhausted. She divorced that husband, declared bankruptcy, and returned to North Hollywood. She was down again, but so relieved.

"I'm never getting married again!"

"Please, don't!" I answered.

For over twenty or more years, Debbie begged important people in Hollywood to finance a Hollywood costume museum. Her collection of Hollywood costumes was the biggest in the world. It was so big, that it cost her a million dollars a year just to store them. She felt it was so important to preserve that history.

She asked David Geffen and Steven Spielberg for money and they said no. She put me on the board of directors and I set up a meeting for her with huge Los Angeles developers who owned, among other things, the entire corner and all the buildings at Hollywood and Highland/Chinese Theatre attractions, but it didn't work. She even had a negotiation going with Dolly Parton to put the museum in Pigeon Forge, next to Dollywood. It all fell through.

Most of all, she kept talking to Walter Mirisch and the people in charge of the Academy of Motion Pictures. They were the most logical partner. They turned her down for 20 years.

Let me tell you a story about Carrie and Debbie, as it is very apt, and will show you their relationship. It was the costumes that really showed me. Carrie was as terrified to live without Debbie as Debbie was to live without Carrie. No one realized what a childlike vulnerability Carrie had. It was all masked by her witty bravado.

The expenses Debbie incurred as well as the stress of trying to get a museum built were really causes of her beginning serious health problems. Debbie's health was really in danger. Carrie really was begging her to sell. They had a big fight over it. Debbie simply couldn't believe that no one shared her view of saving Hollywood history. Debbie was a star who really respected the business and its craft, and she wanted the business and its stars to always be honored. That was the driving force of her ferocity to make the museum happen. It really was her only dream for her whole life. I remember receiving a call from her once, right after she came back from Donald O'Connor's funeral.

"No one was there! No one!" she said in a combination of disbelief and disgust. "He was a BIG STAR! There wasn't even one press person there. I just can't understand the lack of respect," said Debbie.

Right after the fight with Carrie about the costumes, where Carrie wanted Debbie to sell because she was so afraid of losing her, they had to go to the Beverly Hilton Ballroom for some charity

Me, Lainie Kazan, Debbie, and Connie.

event. I was to meet Debbie there backstage. When I arrived, I saw Carrie and Debbie in a corner. Debbie was holding Carrie like a young child, and Carrie was sobbing into Debbie's chest. Carrie had tried everything she could to get Debbie to agree to sell and couldn't get a yes. I happened to walk in on Carrie's total breakdown out of fear of losing her mother. It was NO manipulation. It was completely real of a little girl not wanting to lose her mommy. Later on Debbie actually said to me, "She's terrified of losing me. I'd better sell the collection."

Debbie prayed many times a day. It was always, "Please, God, don't let me die before my daughter. She needs me to take care of her."

In later years she added, "Please, God, give Carrie as much time as you can here on earth." She was always aware of the danger.

Finally, Debbie's only smart financial move (as well as her concern about leaving Carrie alone) was to put the whole collection up for auction. It broke her heart. As soon as all the papers were signed and the auction dates were set, the Academy of Motion Pictures announced their plans for their own museum, one that would include costumes. It was a straight knife into Debbie's heart. What a cold, calculating, cruel thing for them to do.

Debbie sold Marilyn Monroe's *Seven Year Itch* (1955) dress for over a million dollars. Debbie grossed over 20 million dollars and was set for life. I know she would have given up all that money to have had her museum built.

There was an opening night party for the press and VIPs and possible bidders to look at all the clothes. I was there for Debbie, of course. Our eyes met and she rushed over to me.

"We can't look at each other any more tonight. If I see your eyes I'll start crying. I have to get through this," said Debbie, tears in her eyes.

It was an extraordinarily difficult evening.

The one bit of good news is that Debbie didn't sell everything. She kept back her own "personal stash" of things that meant something to her.

In my house I have incredible gifts from Debbie. I have a set of four dining table chairs that she bought for herself when she gave birth to Carrie. Eddie Fisher's mother needlepointed the seat covers. I have her precious, authentic Girl Scout pin. I have a pin given to her by James Cagney. I have extraordinary china she bought from that trip to Europe when Todd was conceived. I am very blessed, and I've only listed a few items of what she has given me. I could open my own museum.

Debbie still owns two houses in North Hollywood. A few years ago she moved to the gatekeeper's cottage on Carrie's property. The Oscar-winning designer Edith Head, as well as Bette Davis, originally lived in the huge ranch house where Carrie lives on the same property. Debbie's house is a gem of a cottage that looks like it's in the French countryside. Mother and daughter like to be near one another. It has worked out really well.

"I never really wanted to live in Beverly Hills again, but I had to do it because of Carrie," explained Debbie when she called me to tell me she was moving. "I get panicked calls from Carrie in the middle of the night, and it's killing me to keep driving from North Hollywood. I need to be near her twenty-four hours a day, if possible. You know that gatekeeper's cottage in the front?"

"Yes."

"Would you believe that that tiny section of land is not on Carrie's deed and I have to pay full price as if it's a large Beverly Hills house? It's incredible. It's all Carrie's land. I can't believe this has happened, but I'll pay anything to be there for her," said Debbie.

Debbie did a ton of adding additional rooms to the little house, building herself what she called a "Movie Star Bedroom"—seafoam-green padded moiré satin walls, a carved mahogany footboard for her king bed covered in satin spreads and throws; matching white porcelain urn lamps on either side with gathered cream shades; pictures of her parents and herself as a child on the nightstand with fresh flowers in a matching vase; and a painting directly above the bed of her, Carrie, and Todd. She also built a large bathroom with a Jacuzzi the size of a motel swimming pool. That whole area was her favorite place in the house.

On another subject, Debbie and I had a "thing" about Katharine Hepburn. We both thought she was the greatest woman around. Debbie, of course, saw her at MGM all the time, and had been asking her for years for an autographed picture. She never got it. As for me, I had never seen Katharine Hepburn in person. My awe was from a distance.

One day, during Oscar rehearsals, the director of the show for many years, Marty Pasetta, called me at my office. "I want you to come to the Oscar set at 11:30 a.m. today. I'll have a special pass for you. The set will be closed down for lunch, but Katharine Hepburn is coming in. No one knows she's doing the show. She's coming in to rehearse accepting an award for her friend Lawrence Weingarten. I know how much you love her."

Oh my God.

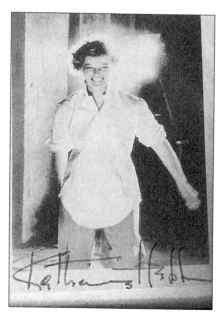

MY Hepburn picture.

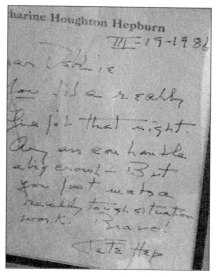

DEBBIE's Hepburn.

I drove to the Oscars and Marty told me to wait in the office area to the side of the stage. I was all alone. my heart was pounding. (This NEVER happened to me meeting famous people, EVER. My ego was just fine. My column was number one, I had my own radio show, and was on TV all the time. But this was different.)

I heard that famous Hepburn voice get closer and closer. Then Marty ushered her through the office on the way to the set. She was in her usual uniform of beige cargo pants, a black turtle neck sweater and beige jacket. She walked right over to me, extended her hand and very politely said, "Hello," as Marty introduced me. I saw those big, liquid-blue eyes staring right into mine and I opened my mouth to speak but no sound came out. All I could do was nod my head. I was mortified. I'm sure she never noticed. I followed her into the stage area and watched the rehearsal, and then I called Debbie as soon as I got back to the *Reporter*.

"Oh my God, you won't believe what happened," I screamed. And then I recounted what happened. I was beside myself.

Debbie very casually said, "I'm very happy for you, dear. Did you get her to sign anything?"

"No."

At another time Debbie and I went to see Hepburn in *Westside Waltz* (1981) in New York. We went backstage to greet her. I managed to say something complimentary about her performance. Debbie again asked her about an autographed picture, and Hepburn laughed.

In 1971, Hepburn was coming to Los Angeles when she was starring in the touring production of Coco, the musical based on the life of Coco Chanel. It had already played Broadway. Since I had moved to covering television for the *Reporter*, my days as theatre reviewer were over. Of course I was going to get my own tickets to see the show, but on opening night our theatre reviewer got sick and the editor asked me if I would go review Coco. I died on the spot.

Naturally, I called Debbie right away.

"You're not going to believe this! I get to review Coco! Isn't that incredible!"

"I'm going tonight, too," said Debbie very calmly. "You must call me before you write your review, dear."

"OK. See you tonight," I answered excitedly.

As luck would have it, Debbie was seated directly in front of me in the theatre. There we were, once again, with our idol.

The show started, and there she was, Katharine Hepburn in the flesh again for me to see. I settled in and watched the show. Twenty minutes into the show my heart was on the floor. It was so obvious that she show was terrible and Hepburn wasn't very good in it. My next thought was, *Oh my God, I have to review this!!!!* Then I remembered Debbie saying to me earlier in the day, "Call me before you write your review." She knew.

As soon as the lights went up for intermission, I tapped Debbie on the shoulder. She turned around and I whispered, "Oh my God, she's not very good."

"Shhhhh," replied Debbie in a scolding tone. "I told you to call me tomorrow, dear. Now say nothing more about this."

I was up all night. I knew that the reason people responded to my column and reviews is that I told the truth. If I didn't tell the truth about Hepburn and Coco, people would go see the show and think I was nuts. I would lose my credibility. I was in agony.

The next morning I went to the office and wrote a correct review. I was never vicious or cutting. I was as gentle as I could be, saying things like, "Miss Hepburn might be better served by doing Shakespeare." I called Debbie and read her the review.

"You cannot print that!" she ordered. "Don't you dare turn that in. I'm calling you in 30 minutes. Just wait."

In thirty minutes Debbie was on the phone to me.

"OK. I'm going to read to you and you just start typing," said Debbie.

Debbie dictated the review that she had written for Coco while I typed it in full. It was a glowing review and tribute to Hepburn.

"Now print that!" said Debbie.

And that's the review that ran in the *Reporter* with my byline on it. Now you know, too.

I was so traumatized, that I wrote a letter to Hepburn. I had her home address in Los Angeles. I wrote a slightly funny essay called, "Upon a Critic Reviewing Her Idol." I obviously never mentioned I didn't think she was very good in the show. It was a funny piece that was a kind of hour-by-hour description of a critic's process writing about someone she adores so much. I didn't tell Debbie I did it.

About two weeks later as I was opening my daily mail, I saw an envelope with the handwritten return address of Hepburn on it addressed to me! I opened it, and inside was a small black and white Polaroid snapshot of Hepburn with her name scrawled across the bottom!!!! I got THE autographed picture!!!!

Once again, I called Debbie immediately. She was genuinely happy for me—pretty much. A few months later when I was at Debbie's house I glanced up at her walls (as I usually did) with all the 8x10 signed glossies of almost every star who ever lived. There was Katharine Hepburn, her photo in a very large frame and a letter from her to Debbie right below the picture. The letter was signed, "Kate Hep." Wow.

"You got Katharine Hepburn! I'm so glad!" I shouted out.

"I knew I would, dear."

Debbie and I like to do dinner at each other's houses. She loved my spaghetti sauce more than anything. Sometimes I'd make chicken piccata to go with it. Debbie had very specific eating habits. She only liked Italian, Chinese, or Jewish Deli—and for some reason she was fascinated by canned Vienna sausages, and she only ate those grilled cheese sandwiches after performing.

We had spaghetti a lot when I lived in Malibu, as well as wherever my house happened to be. Debbie had to sell her house in Malibu because of Harry Karl.

Back to the spaghetti. I had so many favorite "spaghetti evenings," but I remember one particularly fondly. It was when Debbie had just moved into the converted gatehouse at Carrie's. Debbie had an antique wind-up RCA Victor record player from the 20s that played old records. When I arrived, I was treated to a private show of Debbie turning it on and singing Betty Grable songs to me. Let's call that the "appetizer."

The "entrée" was a little more active. Debbie was an incredible athlete. She originally was planning on being a gym teacher, as has been written about for years. Do you remember tetherball? It's a sport where a large metal pole is placed in the ground and a long cord is attached to the top and inserted into a volleyball. The object of the game is to, by hitting the ball, get the cord wrapped all the way around the pole. The two opponents face each other and one hits first, hoping the opponent misses so you can keep hitting as the ball goes around. I also was a very good athlete in school, by the way.

I challenged Debbie to a game.

I smugly said, "I'm going to serve." I wanted the first shot so I could keep hitting and just kill it.

"Go ahead," said Debbie.

I took my first shot and hit it as hard as I could, aiming right over her head. She jumped up, smashed it back, and whizzed it around the pole, hit after hit, so fast that I never could even get a crack at it.

"Oh my God. You really are an athlete!"

"Yes, dear. I TOLD you I was."

She was beaming.

"One more game!" I said, shocked that she had beaten me so easily.

"That's not necessary. You're just going to lose again, dear."

The "dessert course" of this evening was when I said, "Do you know that I know the whole jitterbug dance routine that you did with Tommy Noonan in *Bundle of Joy*? (1956)."

"Really?"

"Yes, I do. Put on a record and I'll show you," I said.

She went over to the stereo and put on an old Tommy Dorsey swing record.

"Ok," she said. "Show me."

I grabbed her hand, pulled her onto the living room floor, and we did the whole dance (Except for the lifts. I didn't want to hurt her or me).

Now THAT's how you spend an evening. I thank God I've been so blessed to have had countless evenings like that with her.

The only restaurant where we liked to eat was Trader Vic's. It was a fancy Polynesian restaurant at both the Hilton in Beverly Hills, as well as in the basement of the Plaza Hotel in New York.

Note: Carrie and Paul Simon had their wedding reception there.

"I am the first person to have been given a charge account at Trader's," said Debbie.

In Hollywood terms, it WAS a big deal. In Hollywood, if you were famous or had power and were a regular customer, Trader Vic's, Chasen's, and, I'm guessing, Romanoff's, La Rue, and The Bistro had private charge accounts where they would send you the bill. This was in the days before credit cards. It was a real badge of honor if you had that kind of account. I had one at Chasen's till the restaurant closed.

Debbie preferred to sit in her booth in the bar at Trader's. It had very high walls and was like a private room. She'd have her Scorpions, I had my Tahitians, and we'd gorge ourselves on pupu platters of crab rangoon, spare ribs, BBQ pork and egg roll. Debbie would always order a side of coconut shrimp. We'd stay for hours. It was very sad when a foreign developer named Beny Alagem infiltrated Beverly Hills, threw around his money and bought the Hilton. He closed Trader Vic's to make room for another hotel he was (over) building next door. That's just one of the things he's ruined in Beverly Hills, but that's another story.

An amazing afternoon at their houses on Coldwater Canyon. Carrie, Debbie, and I decided to "slide."

Debbie was so devastated that he closed "her restaurant," that the Hilton tried to appease her by turning part of their basement coffee shop into a tiny Trader's area. They invited her and gave her her pupus. She hated the food. It wasn't the same and she walked out mid-meal.

Another time I was going to cook a birthday dinner for Debbie and I asked what do you want for your birthday?"

"A vibrator," she answered.

"What kind do you like?" I asked, trying to be "cool."

"Oh, I know exactly what I want. It's called The Wand, and it's long and has the big round head on it," explained Debbie.

I hung up the phone and drove to The Pleasure Chest, a sex shop on Santa Monica Blvd. in West Hollywood, or "Boys Town." I bought the exact one she wanted, called a messenger service, and it was at her house within two hours.

She was thrilled.

One beautiful fall day I was sitting with Debbie and Carrie in Carrie's lower backyard patio. The property where Carrie and Debbie live looks like a gigantic park. There are guest houses, a tennis court, a pool, and parking for twenty cars. Trees are everywhere, and behind Carrie's house are at least four levels of terraced hillsides with the pool and her office/writing building and guest houses on each level. The lower patio was very large. It was brick with an outdoor fireplace with eating and sitting areas. It looked like a classic Mexican resort.

Debbie and Carrie and I were just having a casual conversation. Then Billie, Carrie's daughter, who was approximately twelve at the time, came home very exasperated.

"What's wrong? asked Carrie.

"My English class at school had a contest called the Crazy Family Contest where we each wrote an essay about our family. I came in second!" answered Billie, clearly frustrated.

"How could you possibly have lost?" said Debbie. "Your father's gay and married to a man, your mother is a bipolar alcoholic, your grandfather is mentally ill, and your grandmother is a tap dancing movie star who occasionally has too much to drink!"

* * *

September 11th, 2001: THE TERRORIST ATTACK AND EDDIE'S THREE WIVES

Debbie Reynolds, Elizabeth Taylor, and Michael Jackson were all asleep in their suites at the St. Regis Hotel in New York. They were tired after attending the ridiculous wedding of Liza Minnelli to a user named David Gest. Debbie had always felt like she was Liza's guardian after Liza's mother, Judy Garland, died. Debbie was always at their house.

"Judy's behavior was so erratic that I was afraid for her children. I went over to the house as much as I could, but I had to take care of my children too. I wish I could have done more."

When the planes hit the twin towers, phones rang in all the rooms. Elizabeth called Debbie first.

"This is horrible. We can't stay here. We have to get out," said Elizabeth.

"Terrible, just terrible," responded Debbie. "I'm not so much afraid, but I have a concert in Newport Beach, California in forty-eight hours and I don't want to go back on my word that I'll show up."

"I'll get us a plane," said Elizabeth.

"How can you do that? All the planes are grounded," said Debbie.

"I'll get a plane. Don't worry. I'll also ask Michael if he wants to fly home with us," continued Elizabeth.

A few hours went by as Debbie continued to watch the horror along with the rest of the world.

Debbie's phone rang.

"Hello?"

"Debbie, it's Connie (Stevens). I'm in my apartment in New York. I'm terrified. I'm on the forty-sixth floor and I saw the planes hit. How are you doing?"

"I'm sitting here waiting for Elizabeth to call me back to see about getting a plane to fly us out of here. What are you going to do?"

"I want out, too," said Connie, but I also have to take Lainie Kazan and Diane Ladd and her husband with me. I can't leave them behind."

"If Elizabeth gets a plane do you want to join us?"

"I'm having trouble getting Lainie and Diane to agree on when we should leave. I may need to stay a little longer," answered Connie.

"I'll let you know if Elizabeth gets a plane. I don't know how she can. It's impossible."

Twenty minutes passed.

"Hi Debbie. It's Elizabeth. I have a plane."

"How did you do that?"

"Remember I was married to Senator Warner? He owes me a lot of favors. I called one in. We'll be leaving tomorrow morning at eight a.m. I've made arrangements to have a helicopter waiting for you when we land in Los Angeles to take you to Newport Beach so you can do your concert on time. Michael's decided he's not going to go with us."

"Well, you've still really got it!" said Debbie.

NOTE: *Debbie made her show on time. Connie, Lainie, Diane, and her husband, Robert Hunter, waited too long. They ended up having to rent the only car left in New York, some used economy car, and they drove across the country to get home. Connie is not the best driver, and she insisted on driving the whole way. The fighting became so loud, that the journey fell apart in Arizona. Connie gave them the car to go the rest of the way. She bought a $250,000 motorhome, hired a driver, and arrived in Beverly Hills forty-eight hours later.*

* * *

Debbie and I also liked to surprise people when they least expected it. When she had her own Las Vegas Hotel, after she did her two shows in the big show room, she'd go to the lounge. She hired various comics and musicians to play there—very often it was her piano, bass, and drums group (rhythm section) that she took with her everywhere. Occasionally, she'd get up and sing a couple of numbers. It attracted people to stay in the hotel longer and she'd make more money from the bar bills. She worked practically twenty-four hours a day.

One night, I was entertaining some friends from Los Angeles. We had seen her in the main showroom, which Todd had built and designed to look as much like the Desert Inn's Crystal Room as possible, and then I took them into the lounge. These friends were hilarious and loved a good time. But there was one thing they didn't know about me.

Debbie knew that I was a drummer. I'd been playing since I was eleven. Often, when Debbie came to my house for dinner, I'd play for her.

She got up to sing, walked by my table on the way to the stage and whispered in my ear, "Do you want to play the drums while I sing?"

I nodded.

She got on stage and took the mic.

"Ladies and gentlemen, we have a special guest with us tonight. Miss Sue Cameron is going to play the drums for me while I sing."

I got up from the table. My friends were screaming, "No!" "What?"

I just smiled and ambled to the stage, trying to not laugh, and sat down at the drums.

I knew Debbie's songs by heart and she turned back to me and said, "Shall we start with 'Time After Time'?"

"Sure," I said.

"Hit it, boys, " said Debbie.

My God, you can't make this stuff up.

When Eddie Fisher started getting sick, his daughters, Carrie, Tricia, and Joely rallied around him. Through the years they all had been pushing for closer relationships with him, both as a group and separately. He was open to that, and in his later years it gave both father and daughters much happiness. Eddie had been living in San Francisco with his last wife, Betty, and was enjoying life. Unfortunately, she died and he started to go downhill slowly. When he died, he was quietly buried in a Chinese cemetery just south of San Francisco. You heard that right.

Carrie, Tricia, Joely, and Connie wanted to organize a memorial for Eddie in Los Angeles, so they had a Sunday brunch at Factor's Deli in the Beverly Hills area. The bagels and lox were plentiful, and so were the tears—of laughter and grief. All three girls got up and spoke. It was really a very sweet send-off.

* * *

"Little Miss Girl Scout" was always full of surprises, even as she got older. About two years ago I got this phone call from Debbie:

"I need some marijuana. Can you get any?"

I wanted to say, "You live with Carrie Fisher. I think she can get you some!"

I did not say that.

Instead I said, "I don't use it because it makes me choke, and I hate drugs." But my answer was, "Of course I'll get it for you. I'll bring it this afternoon."

Debbie had been in tremendous pain from an, as of yet, undiagnosed cyst or benign tumor that was pressing on the nerves of her back.

I called my only friend I knew who had "marijuana cigarettes." That's what I called them. We made the "drop" in Beverly Hills and I drove right to Debbie's.

When I walked into her bedroom, Carrie was on the bed lying next to her. Carrie did that every day when she was home. I was uncomfortable because I didn't expect to be making a "drug" delivery in front of Carrie.

I took out the cigarette and showed it to Carrie.

"Your mother asked me to bring this to her. Is it ok that she has it?"

I wish I could describe the look on Carrie's face. It was somewhere between resigned, accepting of the absurdity, and a "whatever."

She nodded yes.

"Ok," said Carrie, getting up. "I can go back to my house now."

She was relieved she could have some time to herself. She took care of Debbie every day that she could.

"Where do you want to do this?" I asked.

"In the living room. Can you get me there?" asked Debbie, having trouble walking from the pain.

"I will even if I have to carry you," I replied.

We got to the couch and sat down.

"Do you see those andirons by the fireplace? They belonged to Eva Gabor. That chair over there was Ann Miller's, and, of course, you remember Harold Lloyd's piano."

I knew all that information. Debbie had begun to repeat herself, but I didn't care at all. I could stay around her for days, listening to her stories and watching her brain work.

"Carrie got all her brains from me, you know. Eddie didn't have any," she said on more than one occasion.

I took out the cigarette and found matches. Me trying to teach anyone how to do this was a joke, but here I was.

"Have you ever done this before?"

"No, dear."

"OK. Here's what's important. When I light it for you, you take a drag by trying to not touch it with your lips. You want air and smoke. Then, once you inhale, you hold your breath as long as you can."

"Alright, dear."

She took a good long drag and held it.

"Excellent," I said. "Now do another."

She did two more.

We waited about ten minutes.

"Do you feel anything?" I asked.

"Nothing. This stuff doesn't work."

"Are you really holding it in?"

"Well, dear, I'm a singer, and even though I use my chest to breathe, I'm blowing out of my nose. It's a technique."

"No. No. Try it again and I'll hold your nose!"

That worked. We did it a couple of times more and I saw her relax.

"Oh...I LIKE this," said Debbie. "I'm floating and I don't care about my back anymore."

"This is great. I'm so happy for you," I said.

"I need more of this right away. I'm having a houseguest coming tomorrow who's in her early 90s. I think she'd like this. Can you get some more?"

Just as I was wrapping my head around that request, I was startled to see a large, African-American man, standing in the dining room holding bags of food from La Scala, an Italian restaurant in Beverly Hills, and Nate 'n' Al's, a deli in Beverly Hills.

"Carrie thought you might be hungry, and from what I'm smelling in here, I bet you are."

I was totally freaked. How did this deliveryman get in? Was he going to rat us out to the cops?

Debbie didn't seem concerned at all.

"We were talking about getting more of these cigarettes," said Debbie.

Oh, God, I thought.

"I can help you. I also own a dispensary," said the deliveryman. "What do you want? Cookies? Brownies? I can get anything."

"My goodness," said Debbie. "You mean you can eat it? I have all these choices! I'll take six cookies and six brownies."

"I'll have it to you by six p.m. Enjoy the food."

He left and I turned to Debbie. "What just happened? Who is that man?"

"Oh, he's Carrie's chef. I guess he's a dealer, too."

Through the years I have heard hundreds of stories from Debbie. Here are some of the best in her words:

"I was doing *Singin' in the Rain* and Gene Kelly hated me. He didn't want me for the part at all. I don't blame him. I was a kid with no experience. He rehearsed me until my feet were bleeding and then made me dance some more. It was really hard, but it was the best training I could have ever gotten. When we were shooting the number with the two of us on the ladder, I was on the top of the ladder and he was going to twirl in and sing a line and then twirl out. I always chewed gum on the set and it made people crazy. I couldn't help it; I just did it. The music cued up for the song and I remembered I still had the gum in my mouth. I quickly took it out and stuck it on the ladder. Just then Gene twirled through and stepped on the ladder to look lovingly at me, and when he went to twirl out, his toupee got stuck to the gum and he twirled away and his hair stayed on the ladder. I've never seen anyone so mad."

"The last scene we shot for *Singin' in the Rain* was the last scene of the movie—the kissing scene. Well, I had just turned 18 and had no experience in kissing. I was just terrified. I didn't know how to kiss. I didn't know what to do. The cameras started rolling and I leaned in to kiss Gene. Our lips touched and I got so nauseated that I threw up on him."

Debbie and Carrie's last appearance together. It was for a costume auction at her dance studio. I was on the stairs, out of camera range, waiting for them.

"When I first was in the business, I ended up at a cocktail party at the comedian Milton Berle's house. I hardly knew anyone there and was a little uncomfortable. Then I saw Milton and he was coming toward me carrying a tray of hors d'oeuvres. In the center, surrounded by crackers, looked like some kind of sausage/pate. I picked up a knife to cut into it and Milton screamed. It was his penis on the tray! Everyone was laughing at me for falling for the gag. It was then that I found out that Milton's personal claim to fame was that he thought he had the biggest penis in Hollywood. All I wanted to do was get out of there."

"I was so crazy about Mary Pickford as a child, that when I became famous I tried to meet her. She was a recluse at that point and she didn't want to see anyone. At her home at Pickfair, they had an old-fashioned thing on the front door. It wasn't a phone; it looked like some sort of horn-shaped thing on a chord. If you picked it up, Mary would pick it up. I would sit for hours at her front door and talk to her that way."

"Elizabeth Taylor and I made up when we ended up on a cruise on the Queen Mary. She was with Richard Burton and I was married to someone. I found out they were on board just after we left the dock, and I sent word to their suite to join us for cocktails. They came, and we just started laughing. We both were schmucks for marrying Eddie. I remember looking at her and saying, 'He was such a schmuck.' Elizabeth screamed with laughter and hit me on the leg."

"He sure was," she chimed in. "We both were idiots. What on earth were we thinking?"

Debbie went on to explain, "In later years, as Elizabeth became sicker, I would go to her house a lot. I'd literally climb in bed with her and we'd eat chocolate sundaes and watch old movies on TV. We became the kids again that we were in the schoolroom at MGM. I really liked her. She never meant to hurt anyone. She was a good broad. You know she just never understood that she could sleep with a man without having to marry him. That's why she had so many husbands. I married my husbands and didn't WANT to sleep with them!" said Debbie, chuckling.

Continuing, Debbie said, "Toward the end Elizabeth was suffering so. She couldn't get out of bed even to go to the bathroom. I was very sad when she died, but I'm glad her suffering was over."

Note: I was privileged to have met and spent many, many hours with Lillian Sidney. Here's the story of Debbie's other mother.

"One of the most important people in the world to me was Lillian Burns Sidney. She really was like my mother. Louis B. Mayer appointed her as head of talent for MGM. She was an acting coach to everyone from Katharine Hepburn to me, but she was so much more than that. She would advise you on everything from what to wear to what to say on interviews. She wielded tremendous power and Mr. Mayer took all her suggestions and opinions very seriously. She was a very imposing person who sat upright in perfect posture, and she had classic diction. She actually scared a lot of the actors with her presence. She was married to the director, George Sidney, who was a major director. Just some of his movies were *Show Boat* (1951), *Annie Get Your Gun* (1950), *Anchors Aweigh* (1945), *Pal Joey* (1957), *Eddy Duchin* (1956), *Bye Bye Birdie* (1963), and *The Harvey Girls* (1946).

"He was the love of Lillian's life," continued Debbie. "And then one day, as she got older, he started having an affair with much younger Corinne Entratter, the wife of the man who booked all the performers for The Desert Inn. George left Lillian for young

Corinne, and it darn near killed Lillian. It was horrible. Lillian became a hermit and just stayed in her apartment until she died. I visited her almost every day. When she died, I got the call because I was her executor, and I remembered that George Sidney bought two places in a mausoleum at Hillside Cemetery. Even though he had another wife, I was determined to get Lillian what she wanted. I called Hillside Cemetery and said, 'Hello. This is Debbie Reynolds. You must pick up Mrs. Sidney at her apartment and cremate her right away and place her with her husband. The plaque should say Mrs. Lillian Sidney.' Well, of course, because I was a movie star, they did exactly as I asked. For years and years Lillian stayed next to George. Then, one day, Corinne showed up to visit George and she saw Lillian there."

"I got a call from Hillside Cemetery saying there must be some mistake, and Mrs. Lillian Sidney needed to be removed. I told them I'd come pick her up. I took her urn home with me, and it's in my bedroom right now. But I was fuming. I was still determined that Lillian be somewhere with George. I called Janet Leigh and asked her to come over to my house right away. I told her what had happened, and that I had a plan.

Janet came over and we drove to Benedict Canyon, the beautiful street where George and Lillian had their home during their happiest years. Janet and I had part of Lillian's ashes with us. We approached the house where they used to live, and I just rang the bell. I had no idea who even lived there. The door opened and this man just stood there looking at Debbie Reynolds and Janet Leigh in shock.

'Hello. I'm sorry to bother you. I'm Debbie Reynolds and this is Janet Leigh. Our friend Lillian and her husband used to live in this house. Would you mind if we went into your backyard and spread her ashes? He said ok...still in shock."

Note: Although Debbie has left Lillian's remaining ashes to me, it was better that they went to another, more appropriate person, Channing Mitchell, who also felt like Lillian was his mother figure.

God Bless You, Mary Frances Reynolds. I love you more than life itself.

Amen.

* * *

Resting between takes of Bright Lights that night.

Today, as I write this, it is December 21st, 2016. Debbie Reynolds is 84 1/2 years old. She reveres her privacy, so I will only say here that she has had several small strokes, she only has one kidney working at 20%, and her eyesight is significantly impaired. I personally witnessed one of her strokes. It was a TIA, meaning she would go

I was invited by Carrie and Todd to sit at their table the night Debbie was given the Honorary Oscar. Here you see Meryl Streep leaning in to talk to Carrie and Todd. It was a very difficult evening because the Academy waited too long to give it to Debbie. She was too sick to receive it in person. Our hearts were breaking. Debbie's beautiful, talented granddaughter, Billie Lourd, graciously accepted.

"out" for twenty minutes and then wake up. It was very scary. They would only get worse.

Because of her failing eyesight, Carrie has bought her at least four electric colored ball lights and put them up everywhere because it gives Debbie something to look at. Debbie can walk, but she needs people on either side of her. She rarely leaves her house, and mostly stays in her bedroom. Fortunately, I am one of the few people she lets visit her.

It is not easy for me to see Dynamo Debbie physically diminished. But when I look into her eyes I still see strength, wisdom, and that twinkle that always gets the joke. She has a beautiful white fluffy Corton dog, given to her by Carrie. Carrie named him Dwight, after President Dwight Eisenhower. Dwight will not leave Debbie's side.

It is Christmas time and I just gave Debbie a child's accordion as a gift. I thought she might have fun playing with it in bed.

"I play the French Horn, you know," says Debbie.

"Of course I know. I'll never forget your explanation of the 'Triple Tonguing Technique' it takes to play it."

We both start to laugh, and it was 1970 again at least for a minute and a half.

"You know," says Debbie, very seriously, "I had the weirdest feeling a couple of days ago. I was surrounded by death. It was everywhere. I felt it. I just sort of laid here feeling it, and then I knew it wasn't for me this time. I know I'm old. A lot of people say, 'I'm never going to be old,' but they're stupid. You get old. It's just a fact. I know that death is what I'm facing. If I go, I go. I don't want to travel anymore or do anything. I have created the perfect world for myself in this house. I have a Christmas tree up all year just because it makes me happy. Go look. Even the Christmas Eve table is set already. Carrie's presents are at her place and Todd's are in his. I'm so glad Carrie's is coming home tomorrow from Europe. She just goes and goes. I never know what she's planning next. I know I just have to let her go do what she wants because she's going to do it anyway. I was very concerned about this trip. She had pneumonia and shouldn't have gone, but she had to shoot *Star Wars*. She shot that whole movie with pneumonia. Now she's in Brussels, still with pneumonia. I just wanted her to come straight home, but she just HAD to go to Brussels. What can I do? She won't listen. At least she'll be here tomorrow."

And, Debbie continued.

" I've been quietly spending time letting go of resentments I've had toward certain people. It's an important thing to do. Those things don't matter anymore. I think I'm going to be here for a while longer, although a couple of days ago I thought I was going to go, but it wasn't my time. I'll be here in the New Year and we'll see each other in a couple of weeks. I just want peace in my life now, and I have it."

Debbie was getting tired and I knew it was time to go.

"I'm going to go now," I said. "But I'll be back really soon."

"I know, dear. I love you," said Debbie.

"I love you too."

I stood up to leave, took a few steps and had an odd, strong sensation that I'd never see her again. I stopped and turned around, seeing this magnificent woman, this gift from God, wearing a cream satin peignoir set, ever the movie star, even though she had on no makeup and was the color of her nightgown. I memorized her beautiful blue eyes staring at me, and her sweet smile, taking a picture for my mind that I thought would be the final shot.

Note: Two weeks prior to Carrie getting on that plane from London, Debbie told Margie Duncan, her dear friend and stand-in from the MGM days who still runs the Debbie Reynolds Dance Studios, that she'd changed her mind and wanted to be cremated. Debbie was very insistent that this be done and written down immediately. She told the same thing to Donald Light, the wonderful gentleman who was her assistant, caretaker, and live-in companion.

December 23rd, 2016

It has been forty-eight hours since Debbie told me about her death premonition that she knew wasn't for her. And then, over the Internet I read that Carrie had a massive heart attack. I called Debbie's house right away, and her devoted assistant, Donald, told me that they were waiting for more information and that Debbie was not going to be told yet.

I was freaking. If Debbie said it to me once over the years, she said it a hundred times—"I just don't want to outlive Carrie." She didn't want that pain for herself, but more importantly, she knew Carrie would be lost without her and not able to handle it.

I then called Carrie's sisters, Joely and Tricia Leigh. I got Tricia first as she was driving to the hospital. She was crying and I was trying to calm her as best I could. We didn't need a car accident. She told me she'd call with any news. Tricia, as usual, was in her "ambulance driver" position.

Joely was on stage doing a Christmas musical for the *American Idol* and *So You Think You Can Dance* producer, Nigel Lythgoe. She was in Laguna, California—two hours away from the hospital. I got her by text in between scenes. She told me the producers were calling her understudy to come in and take over. In the meantime, she had to go back on stage and deliver a happy performance, not knowing whether Carrie was alive or not. Now, THAT's a show business pro. She comes from good stock.

Later on that day Debbie was told by Donald, "Carrie's had a heart attack. She's at UCLA." And then he started to cry.

"Don't cry, dear," said Debbie very calmly. "I'm the one who's supposed to be upset."

I can tell you now that this was a moment that Debbie had been expecting for years, but it was even less surprising because of her vision a few days before. Now it made sense to her.

"Debbie told me the day Carrie got on the plane that it was going down. She just knew Carrie wasn't coming home. She knew," said Donald.

Debbie visited Carrie at the hospital twice. She was weak from her own illnesses that were being kept from the public. It was very difficult physically for her to do, let alone what her emotions were. What happened in that room will remain confidential. I will only tell you that Debbie was very religious and it all revolved around prayer.

I also know now, at the time of this writing, that Debbie knew Carrie had been back on drugs for months. That was why she didn't want her to go to Europe. There'd be no supervision as if that would have made any difference I'm so sorry to say. It was heartbreaking.

December 26th, 2016

Just got a call from Joely saying that Carrie was extremely critical. She had been in an induced coma, which is proper procedure for what doctors believe is any kind of brain damage. Carrie's brain didn't receive oxygen for fifteen to twenty minutes. The brain usually dies at six. We all knew from the moment we heard that number of minutes that Carrie was going to leave this earth. She was brain dead when she was taken off the plane.

"Things are really bad," said Joely. "I'll call you from the hospital."

December 27th, 2016

The doctors had begun the process of weaning Carrie off the coma meds to see if they could wake her. At some point her heart just stopped beating. No one, especially Carrie, would want to live with any diminished capacity. God saved her from that and she is now safe and free.

Debbie is not safe and free. Her worst nightmare has come true. I wish I could wave a wand (NOT the vibrator) over her, bring a healthy Carrie back, and make everything ok. My heart is breaking for her.

Todd called from the hospital. "I have bad news," he said. "I'm coming home to talk to mother."

Todd arrived soon after and went into Debbie's room. Todd sat by the bed and said, "She's gone." What happened next is private. At that point there was total acceptance from Debbie and no surprise at the outcome at all. She only had two small moments of crying in the next twenty-four hours. What had happened was expected for years.

Shortly after Debbie got the news, I found out that that my beloved, "unsinkable" Debbie, had risen again. Even though she was stricken to her core by losing Carrie, she had found renewed energy. She told Todd that she must be around to help to guide her granddaughter. She's doing it for Carrie. Her purpose continues. I can breathe. Debbie isn't going to give up, and I'm not going to lose her, because my biggest fear was losing her if Carrie ever died first.

God bless Debbie and Carrie. Debbie Reynolds, is, by far, the strongest and most unique person I've ever known. To have her in my life is an immeasurable blessing. We are still going strong after forty-six years.

December 28th, 2016

The next day, Todd was sitting beside Debbie's bed. She was talking very calmly about estate procedure and Carrie's funeral arrangements that she wanted. All of a sudden her head fell back to her pillow.

"You're having a stroke," said Todd, seeing her drooping lip.

"I am not," said Debbie defiantly. "Look! I'm smiling. Can't you see it? I'm fine."

Todd saw that her smile was crooked.

"We need to call the doctor and an ambulance," said Todd.

"I am not going to the hospital! Don't you call anyone. I don't want to go to the hospital!" said Debbie.

And then she went unconscious.

It was a nice story for the public to think that she said, "I want to be with Carrie" and then closed her eyes, but that's not what really happened at that moment.

The truth is that she'd said zillions of times that if anything happened to Carrie she didn't want to live, so truthfully, she didn't have to say it one more time. We all knew.

The doctor and the ambulance came. She was already almost gone.

Thank God I was in my therapist's office when I found out she'd had the stroke and was on her way to the hospital. My friend, Elizabeth Keener, texted it to me because she wasn't sure I was near any media to find out.

"That's it. I know she's gone," I said to my doctor as I was slowly going into shock. I could feel my body being erased. "She told me this is what would happen, and here it is. Oh, God, Oh, God. I know it's what she wants—I'm happy for her, but so sad for me."

Truth is truth.

I was so antsy and deranged, that I had to leave the appointment. I knew not to turn on any radio, TV, or Internet. I called my dear friend, producer Jill Phelps, told her what was happening, and that I needed to come to her house. Jill and her house were "safe places" for me.

"I heard about it on the news. There's no more new news yet. Turn off your car radio and just drive here," said Jill.

I did exactly that.

I pulled in Jill's driveway, in my own silent world. My car had become a sealed capsule from what was happening. She was standing at the front door looking a little ashen.

"Come in," she said, quietly.

"Uh oh. I don't like how you're looking."

"Just sit on the couch. There's some water in front of you. If you have a xanax you might want to take it," she continued.

I knew. She didn't have to tell me. I sat on the couch, took the pill, took a deep breath and said, "OK. You can tell me now."

"She's gone."

I nodded my head and I remember just sitting there, feeling my body start to tingle. It was almost like the way a heating pad must feel as it increases in temperature. I was not getting hotter; I could feel my muscles getting hysterical. I started to shake.

Jill came over and I put my head in her lap and just lost it. God bless Jill for taking good care of me.

I don't remember much of anything after that except for some dazed phone calls I made to Joely Fisher and Lucie Arnaz (I think).

Debbie was gone.

A part of me wanted to go with her.

When I left Jill's and went home, I went to my jewelry drawer and took out Debbie's original Girl Scout pin that she gave me many years ago. It was something she treasured, and she wanted me to have it. I pinned it to my pajamas and tried to sleep. It was unbearable. And, it still is. Several times a day I just start to cry. I know it will get better, and I know Debbie would want me to stop. She'd already told me during that last visit that she was ready and that she loved me.

Debbie now is beautifully ensconced in a silver/champagne-colored casket with embossed flowers on each corner. The casket is lined in cream satin, and she is wearing her favorite red suit and shoes. Carrie's ashes are inside her casket in a giant Prozac capsule that was on Carrie's desk. Inside a tiny hidden drawer in the casket are some of Lillian's ashes. It's perfect.

I just bought the plot next to her crypt. My head will literally be next to hers. She didn't want to be without Carrie, and I don't want to be without her. And, that's a perfect ending (or beginning) for both of us.

Postscript: As soon as Debbie died, "suddenly" the Motion Picture Academy Museum called to schedule an appointment to see if they could acquire all the memorabilia/costumes she kept for herself. Here's what I would like to say on behalf of Debbie Dear: Academy "F--K YOU!"

I know Debbie. If she were here to mentor me (yet again) she would not want me to say it. Part of her would be thinking it, I know, but she was so grateful to the Academy for getting an honorary Oscar, she'd be focused on that. I was so honored to have been invited by Carrie and Todd to sit at their table with Billie, Meryl Streep, and Jane Fonda the night that Debbie received her Oscar. It was horribly painful to know that the Academy waited so long that Debbie was too sick to receive it in person, but she was still so happy about it.

I remember when I visited shortly after it was taken home to her. She was sitting up in bed, with her Oscar on the nightstand next to her. I walked in and she grinned and said, "Wanna see my Oscar?"

She picked it up and held it as if she were at a podium. I will always remember her smile as she held it so proudly, being recognized by the industry she loved so much. I'm going to keep that image in my head every time I start to cry.

To end this chapter and book, I am showing you the saddest photo I have ever taken. I went into Debbie's closet just to be "closer to her" on that same visit right after she died. Here is what I saw. I ended up destroyed on her living room couch.

*I went to Debbie's house right after she
died. It was horrifically painful. I tried to
manage a smile as I held something so
precious to her. My face is very swollen
from sobbing.*

Inside Debbie's closet.

Chapter Thirty-Two

DELICIOUS TID-BITS

I've had some pretty wild or impactful incidents in my Hollywood journey. I couldn't write this book without including them somewhere.

There is a world-wide organization called Women in Film, with 25,000 members. It would never have existed without Tichi Wilkerson, the publisher of *The Hollywood Reporter*, and me. At the beginning of the women's movement, Hollywood guilds, like the Writers Guild, began forming women's committees. The heads of the guilds didn't like it, but there was nothing they could do about it.

A woman from the Writer's Guild, Joyce Perry, snuck me a study that their committee did showing how many TV series scripts were written by men and women in the entire season. It was a time when each series did 22 episodes. The study showed that ninety-eight percent of shows had no women writers. Only *All in the Family* and *The Mary Tyler Moore* show had a few women writers. However, the stats still looked like 20-2 or 19-3 in favor of men.

I printed their entire study in my column in *The Reporter* with a very strong plea to the industry to notice the injustice and fix it.

All Hell broke loose. My phones were ringing off the hook from women who were hungry to shine a light on the issue.

I went to Tichi's office and we both discussed how our phones were ringing.

"Let's form an organization," we said, at exactly the same time.

"You call a few of your friends and I'll call some of mine and we'll have a brown bag lunch in my office in two days," said Tichi.

That's the true story of the founding of Women in Film. Only two people were in the room when it happened. The people who came to the lunch were invited to be founders because we invited them. Two women never came back, and the others continued to serve for years.

I am now the only founding member alive. That's terrifying. The only thing I can say is that, in that one moment of "let's start a group," I ended up doing something that has had an impact all over the world for over 44 years and counting. We had no idea how significant it was at the time. Now it is the most important thing I have ever done.

Women in Film Awards with Geena Davis, me, Meryl Streep, and Carrie. Carrie insisted she stand on a ladder so I would be the short one.

* * *

At one time I ended up going on the road with the rock group LaBelle at the height of their fame. "Voulez-Vous Couchez Avec Moi Ce Soir" was the number one record in the country. I was invited to go along with Dusty Springfield to the Oakland/San Francisco leg of their tour. Dusty was going to be a surprise guest in their concert, coming on stage during the finale when they sang "Voulez Vous."

We flew to San Francisco, and then met them at a hotel in Strawberry, California, a tiny town across the bridge from San Francisco. It looked like Mayberry.

As soon as we checked in, we had to leave and go to Oakland for the sound check. There was no time for lunch. The Paramount Theatre in Oakland is one of those grand theatre palaces, and it was gorgeous. We were all shown to the coldest, dirtiest dressing rooms I've ever seen. There was no food for us there either.

By the time the sound check was over, we only had time to go back to the hotel and change clothes for the show. No time to eat. They all had one hour to get ready for the show.

"Don't you ever get time to eat?" I asked Nona Hendryx, whom I really liked.

"After the show," she answered.

"Gee, these conditions are hard. You have no food and bad dressing rooms," I said.

"It's always like this," said Nona.

"How awful!"

"I think there's something you need to experience,' said Nona. "Tonight, just before we go on and the curtain is down, I'm going to place you behind one of our giant amps. It's so tall you'll have to look over it, and only your eyes will be seen. Trust me on this."

I waited in the dank, dirty, airless dressing room until it was showtime. The lights went out and their road manager walked me on stage and put me behind the giant amp. I looked over it, but could see nothing.

Then the lights went on and the band started to play the intro music. I saw a sea of smiling, cheering people filled by the light of their hearts as well as the stage. The noise kept soaring higher and higher, and LaBelle took the stage. When those three ladies walked out the sound was deafening. The floor even started moving with the beat. It was like being swallowed up in the most glorious and strongest love that I'd ever seen. It was simply mindboggling, and I learned then and there why they don't mind always eating bad room service cheeseburgers at four a.m. That wave of love is instantly addicting, and when and if it ever leaves, I can now understand why so many rock stars take to drugs and die young.

The morning after the concert, Dusty, Nona, and I decided we were going to play tennis on the hotel's court. Dusty was running late, so Nona and I went to the court first. For those who don't know, Nona Hendryx, and all members of LaBelle, are black.

I'd made a reservation for the court, and Nona and I walked up to the manager to say we were here and ready to play. He looked at Nona and said, "You can't play here. You're going to have to leave right now."

"What?!!!!" I said. I had never, ever seen any racial preju-
dice. "That's ridiculous! We're
going to play here right now!"

I'll never forget the pained
look on Nona's face. This
treatment was not new to
her. For me, what I was seeing
was stunning, and the most
horrible thing I'd ever seen.

"Stop," said Nona, putting
her hand on my arm. "Let's
just leave." Her eyes were
looking down at the ground.

"No. This isn't right," I
shouted.

Dusty and me on the court. It does not
show how upset I was.

At this point, Dusty walked up and surmised what was happening. I was wildly angry.

"We need to go," said Dusty. "Just do what I say."

Nona, Dusty, and I left, and they had to calm me down. I had
no experience about how to handle things like that—when to fight,
when not to. Dusty was thrown out of South Africa when she
refused to play for all-white audiences. She'd had experience.

We went into the hotel and went to Patti's room. She took the
news in resigned stride and then brought out two electric skillets.
You weren't allowed to cook in the room. So Patti made greens
with ham hocks and black-eyed peas. While all that was simmer-
ing on the stove, I was treated to a private concert of Dusty and
LaBelle. Music can sometimes cure everything.

* * *

Among the zillions of interviews I've done with rock groups, two
incidents really stand out. The British rock group Freddie and the
Dreamers were in Los Angeles to promote their new album. They
were staying at what is now the Luxe Hotel on Rodeo Drive in Beverly Hills. It was not unusual for me to do interviews in hotel suites, but

these boys were particularly rowdy. As I look back on it, they were practically still teenagers and they were just having an immature, good time, but that's not what I felt at the time. At one point, I needed to use the ladies room and Freddie said he'd show me where it was. As I walked in the door, Freddie pushed me through and locked it behind him. He suddenly jumped on me and was trying to kiss me all over. I started screaming, and his fellow band mates pounded on the door, threatening to kick it in. He finally let go of me. To be very accurate, I don't think he was ever trying to rape me. He was just a kid with a hit album who was out of control.

Another British rock group was Herman's Hermits. They were led by pretty-boy Peter Noone, and were very nice. Their record company invited me to do a story on what their day of a concert performance was like from beginning to end. Their concert was a huge one in Dodger Stadium in Los Angeles. About 56,000 people were coming make that 56,000 young girls.

I went in a back entrance to the stadium, and Herman's Hermits representative took me to their dressing room. It was a large one, with a hospitality suite/living room in addition to the dressing area. All the boys were in the living room, which is the area closest to the door. We were having a really good time talking about music and their lives, when all of a sudden we heard a rumbling like there was an earthquake.

I jumped out of my seat and one of the boys said, "Look out, the girls are loose!"

Within seconds, masses of girls had started to break the door down to get to the boys. It was terrifying because they were out of control and the guards couldn't handle it. We all were sitting ducks, and I knew I'd be trampled. In the mess, just as hands were coming in through the broken door and it was about to give way, Derek Leckenby, one of the Hermits, lifted me up and threw me, along with himself, in an armoire and shut the door.

"Don't worry," he said. "This happens all the time."

"Not to me!"

"Shhh. Don't make a sound," cautioned Derek.

I could hear furniture being tossed about, screams, people running, and then the voices of male guards. The armoire rocked a bit, but stayed steady.

"It'll be over very soon now," said Derek sweetly.

He was right. After about five minutes it was very quiet and he opened the door to the armoire. We exited and saw overturned furniture, food, and drinks. The rest of the band eventually ended up in their dressing area, although their clothes were torn. Someone had also taken a watch right off one of them.

* * *

The beauty Raquel Welch has rendered men speechless for years. I first met her when she was just beginning to make a name for herself. I watched her as she walked up the stairs to KFWB Radio to have one of her first interviews. She looked anxious. I remember she was wearing an emerald green sleeveless dress. Truly, hardly anyone had heard of her. I was there to take her picture and just listen to the on-air interview to do my story.

She walked into the interview booth and took a three-by-five index card out of her purse. She folded it in half like a place card and wrote "ROCK-ELLE" on it to face the interviewer so her name would be pronounced correctly. This is how early it was in her career. I have never forgotten that, and I marveled at the time how bright and detail-oriented she was, as well as ambitious.

We became "socially friendly" through the years, and I ended up doing some more interviews with her. At one point, much later in her career, we were sitting in a very high office building in Century City. The office had ceiling to floor windows and was beautiful. We started the interview and were having a great time. Suddenly, an earthquake hit and the building started to sway from side to side. We looked at each other and both ducked under the table, where we sat for about a half an hour waiting for it to be safe. End of interview.

* * *

Helen and I celebrating her birthday on the beach at Malibu.

My friend Helen Reddy is an extraordinary person. She is very humble, non-materialistic, and her song that she wrote, "I Am Woman," is the most important song written for women's rights in the history of the world.

We met in the parking lot of Capitol Records, just as her first hit, "I Don't Know How to Love Him" became number one on the charts. The parking lot was full of press, and Helen was very calm and collected. As we got to know each other, I saw her through the highs of huge houses and servants, headlining in Vegas, and the lows of divorce, and because of joint bank accounts she ended up with practically nothing.

Her attitude never changed. Life was always what it was. She moved to a smaller place, became her own booking agent, booking her own concerts. She also became her own travel agent. Through hard work and gumption, she built up her assets. She also chose never to live a Hollywood lifestyle again.

At one point, she went to school to get a license as a hypnotherapist because that had always interested her. If you go to her for that service, she never charges you. Money means very little to her.

She has put her arms around me and comforted me many times through the years when I've lost a loved one. We even did a session at one of my lowest points, and both Phoebe Snow and Dusty Springfield came to me and said, "Stop crying. We're right by your side. Laugh. Go live. We're never leaving you."

Helen is someone who is always smiling and loving the world.

* * *

I'm sorry to say, but years ago I would sometimes be home alone on a Saturday night and I'd watch *The Love Boat*. It's true that many of my friends were on it, either as regulars or guest stars, but I actually enjoyed it. It was escapist mind-candy. At some point, to freshen the series up, the producers added "The Love Boat Mermaids" as a dance troupe to do one number per show. The night I was watching, one "mermaid" was dressed only in a towel, and I noticed they had

Teri and me in odd wedding outfits.

given her lots of lines. She was being singled out. I immediately noticed a sparkle that shot right through the screen. She was a young brunette, with masses of curly hair and a smile that wouldn't quit. She also had a kitten-like sexuality and innocence about her that told me she was going to be a star.

On Monday morning I called the producer and said, "Who's the mermaid in the towel?"

He said, "She just came to town. Her name is Teri Hatcher."

I said, "Please set up a meeting with her for me right away."

There you have it. We met and really clicked. Teri was a math and econ major from Northern California, who was also a San Francisco 49ers cheerleader. She's one smart cookie. She auditioned for the producers in a cattle call when they came to San Francisco. I got her an agent and we went to work. Her first job was in one episode of *MacGyver*, and when the producers saw her performance on film, they hired her right away in a recurring role. She did the movies *Tango and Cash* (1989) with Stallone, and *Soapdish* (1991) with Whoopi Goldberg and Sally Field. Producer Norman Lear gave Teri her first regular weekly series role, and then it was on to *Lois and Clark* and then *Desperate Housewives*.

It was really fun discovering her, working with her, and seeing all the success. Teri has always been gracious and acknowledged me repeatedly.

* * *

The Academy Awards show is a very special night in Hollywood. People kill to get tickets. I have gone many times, and, in the case of two different years, was backstage throughout the entire show. That's a whole different world from what you see on TV.

Stars are usually very nervous at this event, no matter how big they are. They do feel like grown-up kids dressed for the prom who have to be on good behavior. A green room, or lounge with bar and food and comfy seats with TV monitors is provided for them, and that's usually where they stay before and after they go on. Sometimes they choose to return to their seats in the audience, but others frequently prefer the lounge where they can drink and hang with their buddies. Again, let me mention high school. The girls sit with the girls dishing and drinking and giggling, and the boys are with the boys doing shots and smoking. It's very clicky. You have to be "invited" to sit with the girls, and they boys welcome you with open arms. I much prefer being in a private back smoking area (although I hate smoke) with Zac Efron, Michael Fassbender, and Jared Leto.

My favorite part about being backstage happens before the show starts. The backstage area where they enter the stage is very small. They have two bathrooms between the lounge and the stage. Before the show, everyone wants to use the bathrooms because they don't want to have to relieve themselves while being trapped in the audience.

In 2014, there were two bathroom lines. Sally Field, Cate Blanchett, Jennifer Lawrence, and Amy Adams were lined up on the left. Robert De Niro, Matthew McConnaughy, John Travolta, and Kevin Spacey were on the right. The clock was ticking and people needed to keep moving. I was in line after John Travolta.

Finally, it was my turn. John came out of the bathroom and I said (like a "schoolmarm"), "Did you wash your hands?

"Oh, yes I did," he replied with a smile. "I even wiped down the sink."

"Good boy," I replied.

I finished using the bathroom and came out quickly. I noticed that the other line had moved up where Jennifer Lawrence was going to go in next. For some reason, I waited to see what would happen. It was worth it.

"I've gotta pee, everybody," she announced as she opened the door. Within seconds the door opened.

That morning at the Chinese Theatre. Kim's husband, Bob, is seated on the right.

"Help! I can't get out of my dress and I've gotta go!"

Just as Sally Field went in to help her, she was swept aside by Jennifer's boyfriend at that time, and he rescued her.

Fun times.

* * *

In 2011, Kim Novak was given the honor of putting her hand and footprints in the Chinese Theatre courtyard on Hollywood Blvd. It is extremely prestigious, and all of the major movie stars have done so. I was also very excited because I was picked to emcee the ceremony. As Kim's best friend, I couldn't think of anything I'd rather do.

One of the most important portions of this ceremony is to have an equally important star come to the stage and introduce Kim. Well, Frank Sinatra, Jimmy Stewart, Rita Hayworth, Jack Lemmon, and William Holden were "not available."

I picked up the phone and called Debbie Reynolds.

"Hello, dear," said Debbie.

"I really hate to ask you this because it requires you getting all dressed up with full hair and makeup at nine a.m., but I would really love it if you would introduce Kim Novak at the hand and footprint ceremony at the Chinese Theatre."

"You're calling me because everybody's dead, right?"

"Yes," I answered.

"I always liked Kim," said Debbie. "She was a good girl. And you know I love you. I'll do it."

The morning of the event was really sunny and there were hundreds of people lined up to see the ceremony. I got up on stage, welcomed the crowd and talked about Kim and how wonderful this was. The last thing I heard from Debbie before I went on stage was, "Don't go on too long about me, dear. They know who I am."

It was time to introduce Debbie, and I was so happy that I publically could tell everyone how much she meant to me. From behind the curtain her voice rang out,

Connie Stevens, Kim Novak, myself, and Lainie Kazan celebrate Kim's Hollywood footprint ceremony at Musso & Frank's.

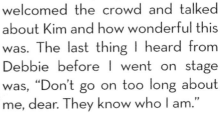

Candy Darling.

Florence.

"That's enough, Cameron. I knew you'd go on too long." At that point she came from behind the curtain, still admonishing me, waving me off center stage. The audience loved it, and so did I. I will cherish those moments on that day with Kim and Debbie forever.

* * *

For no reason at all, other than to show the wild extremes of my life, the first photo is of the famed, tragic, luminous drag queen of the 60s, Candy Darling, and me at Ciro's nightclub, juxtaposed with the most wonderful Florence Henderson, hugging (for about two minutes long) me about two months before she died.

P.S. I love you, Jessica Walter, Rona Barrett, the "Saturday Girls," Naushaba, and Robert LaFontaine.

Epilogue

AN ESSAY ON PUBLIC MOURNING

We all lose people we love. It's just awful. We all know what it's like to look at their clothes in the closet, to cry over pictures and be devastated by loss. But, when you lose someone who is famous, it's just different. I'm not being elitist in any way by saying that. It just presents a different set of problems that the public doesn't know about.

When you lose someone who is not famous, the emotions and sadness are the same, and, yes, as you are driving along a song may come on the radio that reminds you of that person. I get that.

But when someone famous dies and they are one of your closest friends, and/or you were in the room with them when it happened, it's a different kettle of fish.

You can't mourn in peace or in private. You have to be sharp and take care of business. Believe me, when a celebrity dies, it is BIG business. People try to get family members to be interviewed on their shows; camera trucks are pulled up in front of their homes and also at the funeral. You have to hire twenty-four hour a day security. Press passes have to be issued and statements need to be written.

All media platforms are commenting about your loved one, and the comments and stories are being said or written by people who never knew them. If you watch a news broadcast, a talking head might appear with a "nice comment" about your friend, but that person is "pretending to be close" just to get on TV. I assure you, it is very rare that a blood relative or best friend will go on TV right after a death to talk about it.

What is worse, is that you must watch all of this to keep track to see if you need to take any action. Your fondest wish is to NOT have to watch anything because it's too painful.

After the initial onslaught, things begin to die down a little bit. But you haven't been able to mourn yet. You had to stuff all those feelings down. Even if some time goes by, you aren't ever safe if you turn on the TV or go on the Internet. You switch channels on your set, and there's Debbie Reynolds on Turner Classic Movies. You have no defense. You can't prepare. She's right in your face, and you break down. If you go to the market, someone or something will hit you from the newsstands. It could even be years later, and you'll be shopping in a store and a Cass Elliot song comes on. You are never free from the loss.

Next come the greedy people trying to make movies about your dead friend without permission. Dead stars are in "public domain." Any movie or TV show can be done. Let's also not forget about book deals that authors and publishers fight over. Who can get out the fastest book on a star? What is so horrendous is that most of these books are written by people who never met them.

We, who were really there, have to protect ourselves twenty-four hours a day from an assault of incorrect information, sleazy hangers-on, and, what I call stray bullets.

A stray bullet is something that comes out of the air and attacks your heart just when you are feeling safe. There are really no words that can accurately depict this special kind of pain. It is emotionally incalculable. It takes years to finally get through the mourning, but you never get through it 100%. You just have to live with less light around you, trying to concentrate on the gratitude that you were so privileged to be part of their lives in an intimate way.

Beloved Kim and Debbie.

About the Author

Sue Cameron has been a daily columnist and TV editor for *The Hollywood Reporter*, columnist for *TV Guide, Hamptons,* and a *COSMO* contributor. She was also director of daytime program development for ABC Network, and is an original founder of Women in Film, an organization with 25,000 members worldwide. She has written over 2500 columns and interviews reporting on Hollywood celebrities and social and political events. She was a columnist for *Beverly Hills 213* for eleven years. She is a consultant for various entertainment individuals. Among her past and present clients are Teri Hatcher, Joely Fisher, Suzanne Somers, Valerie Harper, Kim Novak, Debbie Reynolds, and many others who don't want their names revealed.

Cameron has appeared as a Hollywood commentator on *Dateline NBC*, the *E! Channel, Maury Povich, Entertainment Tonight,* CNN's *Show Biz Today, Inside Edition,* A&E's *Biography,* and *Lifetime's Intimate Portrait,* as well as hosting her own show on KABC Radio. In addition, Cameron was a regular Hollywood TV news reporter on various local and network shows. Cameron also travels all over the world lecturing about Hollywood on luxury cruise ships.

Her first novel for Warner Books, *Honey Dust,* was sold to Lifetime Movies. Her second novel, *Love, Sex and Murder,* was sold to NBC. Her first cookbook, *The New Bible Cookbook,* was published in Oct. 2010, and she is currently hard at work on her third novel.

Printed in Great Britain
by Amazon

78690598R00214